Shifra Stein's

Day Trips®

from Houston

Help Us Keep This Guide Up to Date

Every effort has been made by the author and editors to make this guide as accurate and useful as possible. However, many things can change after a guide is published—establishments close, phone numbers change, facilities come under new management, etc.

We would love to hear from you concerning your experiences with this guide and how you feel it could be made better and be kept up to date. While we may not be able to respond to all comments and suggestions, we'll take them to heart and we'll make certain to share them with the author. Please send your comments and suggestions to the following address:

The Globe Pequot Press
Reader Response/Editorial Department
P.O. Box 833
Old Saybrook, CT 06475

Or you may e-mail us at:
editorial@globe-pequot.com

Thanks for your input, and happy travels!

GETAWAYS LESS THAN TWO HOURS AWAY

Shifra Stein's

Day Trips®

from **Houston**

Seventh Edition

by

Carol Barrington

A Voyager Book

The Globe Pequot Press

OLD SAYBROOK, CONNECTICUT

Contents

SOUTHWEST

EAST

NORTHEAST

SOUTHEAST

PREFACE

After coping with the race-pace of Houston, a getaway trip can be a lifesaver. But where to go with little time and even less money? The answer is to explore what lies just beyond that last subdivision and skyscraper on the city's ever expanding horizon.

For the past three decades Texas and its largest city have been El Dorados for those willing to trust and test their own abilities and take chances—it must be something in the air. The seeds of today's Houston were sown more than 150 years ago by risk-takers like Austin and Crockett, Houston and Travis—and chapters of their life stories can be found just beyond the city's doorstep.

But history isn't all. Within a two-hour drive, you can canoe in a primeval swamp, angle for a free crab dinner, and learn to sail. There are ferries to ride, beaches to comb, and quiet country roads to mosey along on bikes. Ever been to a horse farm or country race-track? How about a cotton gin or rodeo? With this book in hand, you'll find hundreds of things to do within a comfortable drive of home.

Take along a good Texas map. Using it with the "Wandering The Backroads" sections of this book will let you mix and match portions of adjacent trips to suit your personal interests and available time. Do call ahead if you are planning an important stop; Barrington's First Law says that facts often change the instant they appear in print. Also, many of the restaurants and special activities listed are individual enterprises and sometimes economically fragile. Check to make sure hard times haven't claimed yet another victim.

One hint: In nearly three decades of exploring the backroads around Houston, I've learned to travel Lone Star-style, stopping to chat as I go—and so should you. Texans are among the world's most friendly folk. They have taken me to see wild ducks wing in at sunrise and have taught me to seine shrimp from the surf and then cook them in salt water on the beach. Even the restaurants mentioned are either personal or local recommendations.

There are fresh adventures popping up all the time. If you find something new and enjoyable, please share it with me by writing to my publisher. Together, we can make future editions of this book even more fun.

Happy Day-Tripping!

Carol Barrington

USING THIS BOOK

In most cases hours of operation are omitted because they are subject to frequent changes. Instead, telephone numbers are listed so you can call for specifics. Also, be aware that many of the restaurants and activity options are closed on major holidays, although that may not be noted in the text.

Restaurant prices are designated as $$$ (expensive, $17 or over), $$ (moderate, $7–$17), or $ (inexpensive, under $7).

Listings in the "What to Do" and "Where to Eat" sections generally are in alphabetical order.

The symbol (CC) denotes that at least one credit card is accepted.

Please note: No payment of any kind is either solicited or accepted to gain mention in this book.

ADDITIONAL RESOURCES

For a Texas map and travel guide, contact the Texas Department of Transportation, Travel and Information Division, P.O. Box 5064, Austin 78763-5064, (800) 452-9292. The travel counselors at that number also can advise on events, lodging, attractions, and trip routings throughout the state.

For information on state parks, wildlife, or fisheries, contact the Texas Parks and Wildlife Department, 4200 Smith School Road, Austin 78744, (800) 792-1112. To reserve campsites, group facilities, and cabins in state parks, call (512) 389-8900. To cancel a reservation, call (512) 389-8910.

The East Texas Tourism Association puts out a free fun map. Contact the association at P.O. Box 1592, Longview 75606, (903) 757-4444.

For information on the Sam Houston National Forest, contact the Sam Houston Ranger District, P.O. Box 1000, New Waverly 77358, (409) 344-6205.

For information on the Davy Crockett National Forest, contact the Davy Crockett Ranger District, East Loop 304, Crockett 75835, (409) 544-2046.

The Texas Forestry Association puts out a booklet on woodland hiking trails; P.O. Box 1488, Lufkin 75902, (409) 632-8733.

For lists of Christmas tree farms, wineries, and pick-your-own fruit farms statewide, contact the Texas Department of Agriculture, P.O. Box 12847, Austin 78711, (512) 463-7624, or the Texas Agricultural Extension Service, 2 Abercrombie Dr., Houston 77084, (281) 855-5600.

For a listing of Texas herb growers, contact THGMA, Route 8, Box 567, Brownsville 78520.

The Houston Audubon Society maintains a "Texas Rare Bird Alert" tape: (713) 992-2757.

TOMBALL

One of the most scenic drives from Houston into the Brazos Valley or Lake Conroe area begins by following T-249 (Tomball Parkway) north through rural woodlands. Although none of the towns included in this day trip is of major interest in and of itself, together they have enough interesting stops to make a great drive.

First up is the farming community of Tomball, named for turn-of-the-century congressman Thomas H. Ball. Turn east on Main Street at the T-249/FM-2920 intersection to find the heart of town. For advance information and an excellent map of the Tomball/North Harris County region, contact the Tomball Area Chamber of Commerce, P.O. Box 516, Tomball 77377-0516, (281) 351-7222. If you're traveling on a weekday, you'll find that office at 13011 Park Drive, Suite 111.

WHAT TO DO

Burroughs Park. 9738 Hufsmith Road, 1.3 miles east of FM-2978. So new it hasn't yet been discovered, this beautiful, 330-acre park offers a large lake with floating piers for catch-and-release fishing (large-mouth bass and catfish), 2 miles of nature trails, a playground accessible to handicapped children, an elevated boardwalk, a shrub maze, baseball and soccer fields, and extensive picnic facilities; for pavilion rentals call (281) 353-4196. A wildlife rehabilitation center is currently under construction in the old Tomball Railroad Depot that's been relocated here. Developed at a cost of more than $3.2 mil

1

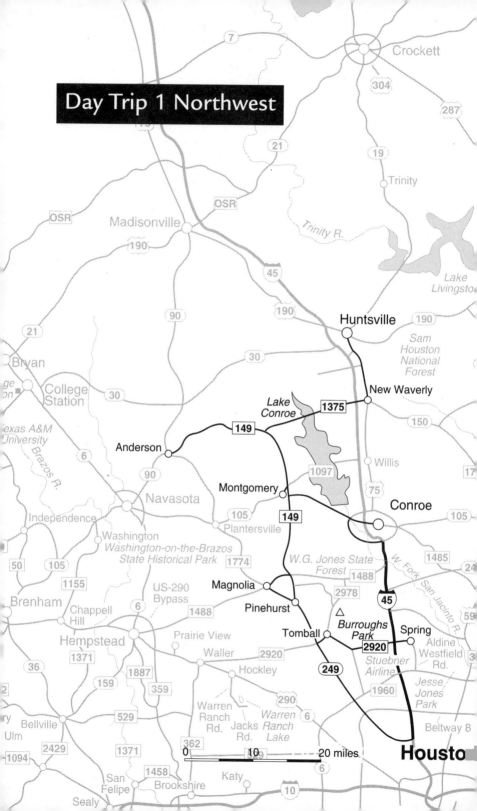

lion, this rural park preserves classic Big Thicket growth, including blackjack oak, bogs and water elm ponds, canebreaks along creeks, short-leaf pines, stands of hickory, and holly and farkleberry bushes. Open daily, dawn to dark.

Camelot Horse Center. 18010 Burkhardt, 1 block south of FM-2920 and 7 miles north of US-290 via Cypress-Rosehill Road. This full-service horse training facility is devoted to classic English riding, including dressage. The public is welcome to visit, observe, and attend horse shows and demonstrations; no rental horses or trail rides are available. Appointments required; closed Monday. (281) 351-8368.

Christmas Tree Farms. Although tree cutting officially begins Thanksgiving weekend, many tree farms offer great family activities such as barnyard animals, educational tours, hayrides, hot dog roasts and so on during other times of the year. Call the following for information and directions: Merry Christmas Tree Farm, (281) 351-5850 or 351-0818; Old Time Christmas Tree Farm, (281) 370-9141; or Spring Creek Growers, (281) 356-4141 or 259-8114.

Flying High at David Wayne Hooks Airport. 20803 Stuebner Airline at FM-2920, Tomball/Spring, (281) 376-5436. The largest privately owned airport in Texas, this sprawling place offers numerous ways to get a bird's-eye view of Houston. Looking for an unusual birthday or anniversary present? Helicopter Services (look for sign on large hangar) offers demonstration rides in a Robinson R-22 (thirty-minute introductory flight, $60; one hour, $200) or a pictorial look at Houston, including the Ship Channel and River Oaks, from 800 feet up in a Bell Jet Ranger (minimum one hour, $650). This is a federally licensed facility; all aircraft are maintained to federal standards, (281) 370-4354.

Hooks is home to numerous flight schools that offer sightseeing tours as well as discovery flights (in which you actually can put hands on the controls). National Aviation at the seaplane basin offers discovery flights (thirty minutes, $20; one hour, $60) and pleasure flights for up to three people ($70 per hour); its staff welcomes families and small groups for ground tours as well, (281) 370-5235.

In the corporate center hangar, ProAir has a twenty-minute introductory flight ($20-$25) and sightseeing tours ($60-$115), (281) 376-2932. United Flight Systems offers thirty-minute discovery flights ($20), (281) 376-0357. All are open sunrise to sunset daily. (CC).

For $695 Texas Air Aces will strap you into the front cockpit of a T-34 Mentor aircraft for air combat, aerobatics, and formation training in the skies over northwest Houston. *Not to worry:* A qualified pilot can override your moves from the second seat. These high-performance airplanes have laser gun systems, gunsights, threat detection/warning systems, and integrated, four-camera video recording equipment. Your five-hour adventure begins with an extensive preflight suit-up and briefing session that instructs you in offensive tactics, defensive maneuvers, use of the weapons system, and safety. After flying you review your air battles via videotape, which you then take home. Reservations are required, at least one month in advance for weekend flights. *FYI:* More than 80 percent of these novice "aces" have never flown before, and anyone over 4 feet 8 inches tall is welcome, regardless of age; clients have ranged from nine to ninety-three. Observers are welcome at no charge. Look for Hanger A-5 at the south end of Hooks; (281) 379-ACES or (800) 544-ACES; ask for "Phantom" Don Wylie.

The Kleb Farm Museum. 19027 Stuebner-Airline Road (west side of road, north of Louetta), Klein. Descended from early German and French settlers in the Spring/Klein/Rosehill region, Thornwell Kleb (pronounced Clayb) has collected farm memorabilia and equipment nearly all his life, a hobby he now enjoys sharing with school groups and the general public. Almost all items came from local sources, including articles used by one of his ancestors at the Confederate powder mill on Spring Creek. Kleb's farm alone qualifies as a museum in this rapidly developing area. Visitors welcome by appointment, at no charge. (281) 376-5960.

Kleb Nature Preserve. 20605 FM-2920 (Waller-Tomball Road), on south side, seven miles west of Tomball. In addition to picnic tables, pavilion, and toilet facilities, there's a mile-long trail through dense, second-growth forest, ideal for birding or a walk in the woods. This mini-Big Thicket is what much of north Harris County looked like before the subdivision era. Open daily, dawn to dusk.

Old South Gardens. 23330 Bailey Drive (east of Tomball; call for directions). More than 500,000 daylily plants blossoming over ten carefully cultivated acres make this place a vision of color from late May through mid-July. For the lowdown on growing daylilies, attend their festival, held annually around the Memorial Day weekend. Call for specifics and daily hours of operation. (281) 351-7971.

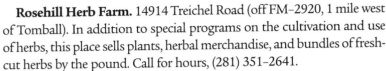

Rosehill Herb Farm. 14914 Treichel Road (off FM-2920, 1 mile west of Tomball). In addition to special programs on the cultivation and use of herbs, this place sells plants, herbal merchandise, and bundles of fresh-cut herbs by the pound. Call for hours, (281) 351-2641.

The Roy C. Hohl Nature Trail. (Temporarily closed as of press time, owing to highway construction.) On east side of T-249 (Tomball Parkway) at the Cypress Creek Bridge, approximately 1 mile north of the FM-1960/T-249 intersection. This pocket of woods is a roadside mix of botanical life zones worth exploring when the weather is nice. For an update on access and facilities, call (281) 353-4196.

Spring Creek Park. On Brown Road, one mile north of Tomball via T-249; watch for sign. On weekdays this oak-shaded park is a delightful place for a picnic. There's a large children's play area, and an asphalt-banked ramp for skateboarders. Unfortunately, this park often is spoiled on weekends by rowdy crowds. (281) 353-4196.

Tomball Community Museum Center. North of Main Street at the end of Pine Street. Clustered on this cul-de-sac are some bits of the past collected by the Spring Creek County Historical Society. The Trinity Evangelical Lutheran Church was a volunteer construction project of local German families in 1905, and all furnishings and appointments today are original to this white clapboard structure. Now often used for weddings and christenings, it also glows with public services on Thanksgiving morning.

The Griffin Memorial House is next door. Built in 1860 by one of Houston's earliest pioneers, Eugene Pillot, it stood at the intersection of Willow Creek and an early stage route known as the Atascosita Trail. Sam Houston frequently spent the night in this house, waiting for the morning stage, and it also was a local gathering place. The antique furnishings are of the later Victorian period and in themselves constitute the Magdalene Charlton Memorial Museum. The complex's other transplanted buildings include the pioneer country doctor's office where Dr. William Ehrhardt practiced for more than fifty years; a museum containing early farm machinery, tools, and a hundred-year-old gin moved in from nearby Spring; a log house and corn crib built in 1857 in Serbin; and the Henry Theis House, built locally prior to 1866. Free, but donations are greatly appreciated. Open Thursday midday and on Sunday afternoon; hours vary. Tours also by appointment. (281) 255-2148.

WHERE TO EAT

The Bake Shoppe. 22516 T-249 (Tomball Parkway) in the Spring Cypress Village Shopping Center. This tidy, family-run place has lunches and pastries like you wish Mom did make. The sandwiches come on homemade bread, and the cranberry chicken lunch entree is popular. Expect a line if you come between noon and 1:00 P.M.; the good food here draws executives from nearby Compaq. Open Monday–Friday until 4:00 P.M., Saturday until 2:00 P.M. $. (281) 320-2253.

Goodson's Cafe. 27931 T-249 (Tomball Parkway). Mrs. Goodson hung up her potholders and closed down her ramshackle but famous cafe on the outskirts of Tomball several years ago, and now she has gone to her reward. But her recipe for hang-off-the-plate chicken-fried steak lives on at this second-generation eatery. The menu also offers chicken, burgers, salads, and fish for lunch and dinner daily. $-$$; (CC). (281) 351-1749.

My Favorite Place. 15731 FM-2920 West (immediately east of Telge Road; watch for a toque-topped chef hailing motorists from the south shoulder of the road). Inventive and tasty food in a Victorian tearoom setting, this spot offers a welcome alternative to conventional Texas menus. Lunches feature sandwiches, quiches, soups, and salads; dinner offerings range from steaks and emu filet mignon to chicken breast with Boursin cheese filling and orange roughy in a lemon wine sauce. Open for lunch Monday–Saturday; dinner Friday and Saturday. $-$$. (281) 255-9960.

Rancho Grande. 30134 T-249 (Tomball Parkway). This family favorite serves Tex-Mex with creative twists; the "No-Name Enchiladas" are tasty enough to start a trend. Open daily for lunch and dinner. $-$$; (CC). (281) 351-1244. The Carillo brothers also operate a second Rancho Grande at 2207 North Frazier Road in Conroe; (409) 441-0440.

The Rib Tickler. 28930 T-249 (Tomball Parkway). Half-pounder hamburgers and hickory-smoked barbecue are the house specialties. Open for lunch and dinner, Tuesday–Sunday. $-$$; (CC). (281) 255-9431.

Scott and Sherry's Cafe. 1231 Alma, Suite S, behind Academy on FM-2920. This pleasant place draws budget watchers with tasty all-you-can-eat specials that include meat, veggies, potatoes, and a trip to a bountiful salad bar. The prices are so low that you can't afford to eat at home. Open daily for lunch until 3:00 P.M. $-$$; (CC). (281) 351-9045.

The Whistle Stop. 107 Commerce. Whether you're a devout "foodie" or diligent budget-watcher, this very affordable spot makes Tomball a repeat destination. Trained at the New England Culinary School with post-graduate work in Hawaii and New Orleans, chef Tad Krueger puts some delicious twists on Texas favorites at this small cafe. Dropping in for lunch? Try his chicken salad sandwiches or chicken tortilla soup and then indulge in homemade dessert. Italian buffet dinners feature such entrees as white seafood lasagne or chicken in lobster cream sauce. Open for lunch Monday–Saturday 11:00 A.M. to 3:00 P.M.; dinner Thursday–Saturday. $; (CC).

MAGNOLIA AND MONTGOMERY

From Tomball drive north on T-249 to Pinehurst. Those brambles along the railroad tracks on your right are dewberry bushes, loaded in May and ripe for picking. Come prepared with a bucket, gloves, a long-sleeved shirt, stout shoes, and a stick for scaring away snakes before you reach into the bushes.

At Pinehurst you must make a choice: either to continue straight north on FM-1774 to Magnolia and Plantersville or to swing to the right, cross the railroad tracks, and follow FM-149 north to Montgomery. The first option, FM-1774, leads to a pick-your-own orchard during the summer months and to the sixteenth century in the fall; watch for longhorn cattle in the fields on the right and for beautiful horse farms such on the left.

WHAT TO DO

Antiquing in Magnolia and Montgomery. Both towns have a growing number of antiques shops, the majority of which are open Tuesday through Saturday. The third Saturday of every month is Market Day in Magnolia, with specials located outside each shop.

Hoffart's General Store. One mile south of T-105 on FM-1486 in Dobbin. The country equivalent of a 7-Eleven, this is the kind of place that has homemade sausage in the meat case and free puppies and kittens in pens on the front porch. Open Monday–Saturday. (409) 597-5460.

The King's Orchard. Seven miles north of Magnolia on FM-1774 (1 mile north of the Renaissance Festival grounds—see entry). At various times during the summer you can pick your plea-sure of strawberries, blueberries, blackberries, raspberries, apples, plums, peaches, figs, and Asian pears at this thirty-two-acre farm. Open from the third Saturday in March through the third Sunday in September. Call for fruit availability. (409) 894-2766.

Silverado Farms. 30337 Dobbin Huffsmith Road, Magnolia. Hidden deep in the woods northeast of Tomball and best accessed via FM-2920 East, FM-2978 North, and Hardin Store Road, this unusual, twenty-seven-acre facility includes an extensive petting zoo behind the Outback Western World Feed & Supply. Animal lovers get up close to deer, miniature horses, potbellied pigs, pygmy goats, peacocks, dwarf bulls, llamas, ostriches, and so on. Weekend visitors also often find rodeo-style competition going on in the farm's arena. Picnickers welcome. Free. Open Monday–Saturday. (281) 259-WEST.

Texas Opry House. 32243 Old Hempstead Road, Magnolia. Country music in a country setting, this tidy, family-run operation puts on a lively two-hour music show featuring local entertainers every Saturday night, year-round. Expect singers, dancers, actors, and comedians at this mini–Grand Ole Opry, all backed by the house band. Have you always had a hankering to be in show biz? Give them a call; they hold tryouts on a regular schedule. No alcohol is allowed or served, but the concession stand does a land-office business in homemade cakes and brownies. Bring the kids. $. (281) 356-6779.

The Texas Renaissance Festival. Six miles north of Magnolia on FM-1774, 6 miles south of T-105 in Plantersville. For seven week-ends starting around October 1, the sights and sounds of Merrie Olde England brighten up this 247-acre woodland park. Visitors are encouraged to dress to the sixteenth-century theme and cavort with the jugglers, sword swallowers, harpists, belly dancers, and jesters to their heart's content. Swordsmen fence, Shakespeare enlivens the Globe Theatre stage, and King George and his royal court parade around the grounds at high noon. Grand fun for the entire family, with full-contact jousts and chariot races, assorted craftspeople, stout food, and more. Fee, but ask in advance about Houston-area sources for discount tickets. Children 4 and under are free. Also, plan some alternate routes home; the departing traffic south via FM-1774 and SH-249 is always bumper-to-bumper from 3:00 P.M. on. Route 2, Box 650, Plantersville 77363. (800) 458-3435.

WHERE TO EAT

Cajun Connection Cafe. 910 Magnolia Blvd., Magnolia. This tiny family-run spot serves authentic jambalayas, étouffées, and shrimp/sausage po'boys that will have you thinking you're on the other side of the Sabine. Open for lunch and dinner daily (closes at 4:00 P.M. on Sunday). $-$$; (CC). (281) 259-8836.

Henry's Hideout. Four miles north of Magnolia on FM-1774 (approximately 2 miles south of the Renaissance Festival grounds). Billing itself as the "Horniest Place in Texas" and the "Museum of 5,000 Horns," this surprisingly spiffy saloon is one of a kind. The walls are studded with hunting trophies, and the ceiling is a mass of deer horns. It seems that Henry started collecting horns in 1950 and can't stop; his place gets "horn-ier" by a hundred or more sets of antlers every year. In addition to the friendly bar outlined with a world-class collection of neon beer signs, numerous pool tables are scattered around, and you'll find live music and dancing in the adjacent dance hall on Friday and Saturday nights. The menu runs from barbecue to pizza, tamales, and sausage-on-a-stick. Open daily from lunch to 2:00 A.M. $; (CC). (218) 356-8002.

Honey's Hometown Cafe. 18904 FM-1488, Magnolia. Expect basic standards here—salads; fish, chicken, and burger baskets; sandwiches; CFS; catfish multitudinous ways; and charbroiled steaks—at family friendly prices. Save room for the homemade cobbler. Open for breakfast and lunch daily until 3:00 P.M.; inquire about later dinner hours. $-$$. (281) 259-8900.

CONTINUING ON

Turning right from T-249 at Pinehurst and continuing north on FM-149 (The Montgomery Trace) takes you through rolling woodlands to Montgomery. An Indian trading post later settled in 1837 by Stephen F. Austin's fourth and last colony, Montgomery prospered for half a century as a major center for mercantile activity in this farming region. Today it is a tiny village with a 6-block collection of old homes, most of them just north of T-105. Home tours in April and December give peeks behind some of those doors. There are several low-key antiques shops in this hamlet and an interesting graveyard at the old Methodist church. Fifteen other sites have historical markers, and guided tours can be arranged for groups. For local information stop at the Country Store on FM-149, just north of the traffic light, or contact the Lake Conroe Area Chamber of Commerce, P.O. Box 1, Montgomery 77356, (409) 597-4155. The Honeysuckle Rose Bed & Breakfast now welcomes overnight guests in Montgomery, (409) 597-7707.

WHAT TO DO

Christmas Tree Farms. There are numerous cut-your-own places in the Montgomery-Plantersville area. Call for directions: Buena Vista Christmas Tree Farm, (409) 597-6060 or (800) 299-TREE; El Kay Christmas Tree Farm (blueberries also, in summer), (409) 597-6107 or (713) 899-2341; Red Caboose Christmas Tree Farm, (281) 259-9776; Texas Real Trees, (281) 367-5745; and Underwood Farms, (409) 856-6465.

Fernland. Tucked away in the woods off FM-2854 (Old Montgomery Road), midway between Montgomery and Conroe, this collection of three restored and furnished log houses, a Greek Revival farmhouse, and a fully operational blacksmith shop recalls pioneer life in East Texas between 1830 and the Civil War. The site also is enjoyed by botanists and garden clubs because of its abundance of native plants. The ferns are particularly lovely in spring, but watch out for water moccasins. Open only to groups by advance appointment. (409) 588-3669.

WHERE TO EAT

Old Montgomery Steak House. One block west of the FM-149/T-105 intersection, Montgomery. Somewhat obscurely housed in a vintage building complex on the north side of the highway, this local gathering place serves made-from-scratch hamburgers, home-style meals, and hand-cut steaks, all at yesterday's prices. The home-baked breads are delicious. Open Monday-Saturday for breakfast, lunch, and dinner; Sunday for dinner only. $-$$; (CC). (409) 597-5155.

The Depot. On FM-149, just south of T-105. Popular with families heading home after a day on Lake Conroe, this place is known for its old-fashioned hamburgers. Lunch and dinner daily. $-$$. (409) 597-6733.

Heritage House. One mile west of FM-149 on T-105. A favorite stop on the Houston-to-College-Station run, this spot is known for its country cooking, chicken-fried steak, and homemade pies and rolls. Open for lunch and dinner, Tuesday–Sunday. $-$$; (CC). (409) 597-6100.

The Melon Patch Tea Room. 605 Eva (T-105), Montgomery. This spot serves sandwiches, soups, salads, and desserts inside a vintage clapboard schoolhouse. Open for lunch, Tuesday–Sunday. $. (409) 597-7700 or 448-6214.

Polo Inn. 508 Liberty (FM-149), immediately south of the T-105 signal in Montgomery. Although nondescript in appearance, this small eatery dishes up some excellent Italian standards prepared with homemade sauces and fresh herbs. Other choices include gourmet hamburgers, fish or steak sandwiches, and subs. This is as close as Montgomery currently comes to having a sports bar; TV, pool, darts, and other games are part of the scene. Open for lunch daily; dinner Tuesday–Sunday (closed from 2:00–5:00 P.M.). $-$$; (CC). (409) 597-5588.

Texana Mexican Food. 305 Eva, on south side of T-105, one block east of the FM-149 signal in Montgomery. Bright, clean, and under the same ownership as Bennett's Steak House across the street, this spot serves some of the better Tex-Mex around. Open for breakfast, lunch, and dinner daily. $-$$; (CC). (409) 597-4300.

Other restaurant choices in the T-105/Lake Conroe area are listed in the Conroe section.

WANDERING THE BACKROADS

To continue this day trip from Montgomery to Conroe and Spring, travel east on T-105. A turn west on T-105 will connect you with Trips 3 through 6 in this sector.

Or you can continue north on FM-149 through Montgomery to Anderson (Trip 5, this sector). From Anderson you can return to Houston via Navasota and Hempstead on T-90 and T-6.

How about heading east to New Waverly and Huntsville (Trip 2, this sector)? From FM-149 on the northern outskirts of Montgomery, turn northeast on FM-1097; this enjoyable road arcs east to Willis, crossing Lake Conroe in the process.

CONROE

In 1880 the Central and Montgomery Railroad had a line running from Navasota to Montgomery. With the extension of the track in 1885 to a small sawmill run by Isaac Conroe some 15 miles to the east, the town of Conroe came into being. Within five years Conroe was thriving with 300 citizens and aced Montgomery out of the county seat honor by some sixty-two votes. Always the center of a prosperous lumber industry, it hit the financial big time with George Strake's discovery of oil southeast of town in 1931.

Conroe today needs no introduction to Houstonians, as it is a prosperous business and bedroom satellite 39 miles north on I-45. Although little history has been preserved here, it's fun to visit the Crighton Theater (circa 1930) near the courthouse on North Main. Restored in vaudevillian style, it again hosts the performing arts upon occasion; (409) 756-1226 or 760-ARTS. To day-trippers, however, Conroe primarily is attractive as the gateway to an extensive forest and water playground and as a locale for great factory discount shopping, courtesy of the eighty-five-store Conroe Outlet Center north of town on I-45. For those who want to stay over to play another day, Heather's Glen Bed & Breakfast offers Victorian-style lodgings in the former Wahrenberger Mansion in downtown Conroe, (409) 441-6611 (reservations required).

WHAT TO DO

Moorhead's Blueberry Farm. Who says you can't grow plump, luscious blueberries in Texas? Albert Moorhead has fifteen acres planted with thirty-five different varieties that ripen from early June through late July. Cost is $1.25 per pound, and the best picking times are in the early morning and late afternoon. Mr. Moorhead also grows the new, nonastringent Fumu persimmons, known as the apple of the Orient, which ripen in November. What do you do with persimmons? He has great recipes—and this new fruit is good to eat out of hand or use in pies. Other pickin' crops include figs in late August through mid-September and blackberries in early summer. His farm is deep in the woods between Conroe and Porter. From US-59 North take the Porter exit, go west on FM-1314 for 10 miles, turn left into Bennette Estates, and then follow signs. From I-45 take exit 83, go east on Crighton

Road 2.5 miles, turn right on FM-1314 for 7.4 miles, and turn right into Bennette Estates. Open daily, dawn to dusk. (281) 572-1265.

Heritage Museum of Montgomery County. 1506 North I-45. Take the T-105 exit from I-45 North and stay on the frontage road to Candy Cane Park. The Grogan and Cochran families jointly owned and operated twenty-five sawmills in Montgomery County, the first of which was on the 55,000 acres later developed as The Woodlands. This makes their 1924 frame home a fitting matrix for local history. One gallery features "Glimpses of Montgomery County," including Dr. Charles Stewart's original drawings of the Lone Star flag and state seal of the Texas Republic (still in use). A second gallery focuses on people and events that influenced the area. Free, but donations gratefully accepted. Open Thursday–Saturday. (409) 539-6873.

J-Mar Farms and Bed & Breakfast. Take the League Line exit from I-45, go west approximately 2 miles, turn right at Longmire, and follow signs. This sixteen-acre spread delights children with its petting zoo (potbellied pigs, goats, sheep, donkeys, and one talented horse), numerous other farm animals, pony rides, Indian Village, hayrides, and fishing lake—cane poles provided. The facility specializes in parties, but individual families are welcome. Fee. Open Tuesday–Sunday. (409) 856-8595 or (800) 636-8595.

Lake Conroe. Numerous points of access from I-45, T-105, and FM-149. The dam, an excellent county park on the lakefront, several of the larger marinas, and the entrances to three major resorts lie 10 to 12 miles west of I-45 in Conroe via T-105. The upper west side of the lake can be reached from FM-149 in Montgomery via FM-1097; the east side can be reached by both FM-1097 and FM-1375 from I-45 north of Conroe.

One of the most beautiful lakes in the state, Lake Conroe is 15 miles long and covers 22,000 acres. A complete list of marinas, campgrounds, and public services is available from the Greater Conroe Chamber of Commerce, P.O. Drawer 2347, Conroe 77305, (409) 756-6644 or (800) 283-6645.

Want an affordable weekend escape or just a great round of golf? Several resorts on Lake Conroe welcome guests with advance reservations. One is Walden, (409) 582-6105 (for lodging information and reservations), (409) 582-1060 (for marina), or (409) 448-4668 (for golf course); another is April Sound, (409) 588-1101 or (800) 41-ROOMS.

Del Lago Resort Hotel & Conference Center has numerous package vacations, a golf course, a long sand beach and lagoon, and a full-service marina offering watercraft rentals and guided fishing via pontoon boat, (409) 582-6100 or (800) 335-5246.

Located 7 miles west of I-45 via T-105, Lake Conroe Park & Pavilion offers swimming, two fishing piers, playground and picnic facilities, but no boat ramp. Admission ($1.00 for those over five) is charged from March through Labor Day; thereafter the park is free. (409) 788-8302.

The *Southern Empress*, an authentic replica of an old-time paddle-wheeler, offers a variety of extended lake cruises. Reservations are required for the dinner cruises and advised for the Moonlight Memories and weekend afternoon departures. $$-$$$; (CC). (409) 588-3000, (409) 447-3002 (Houston metro line), or (800) 324-2229.

Rudy's Peach Orchard. 1737 Sawdust Road, 1.7 miles west of I-45. This four-acre farm grows nine varieties of peaches, thus stretching the picking season from May 1 through July 4. It also sells plums, nectarines, watermelons, and blackberries at various times of the year, as well as jams, jellies, and picante sauce made from the farm's own produce. Open 9:00 A.M. to 7:00 P.M. Monday-Saturday; Sunday from noon. Tours available for groups. Call the Fruit hotline, (281) 298-5464, for an update on what's available.

Three Circle Ranch. 531 Koenig Road, 10 miles west of I-45 via FM-1488 and Peoples Road. This sixteen-acre horse boarding and training facility welcomes the public to frequent shows; call for current schedule, (409) 321-2373.

W. Goodrich Jones State Forest. Five miles southwest via I-45 and FM-1488 west. Logged in 1892 and burned in 1923, these 1,725 acres again are a verdant wildlife refuge, now under the watchful eye of the Texas Forest Service and part of the Texas A&M system. The Sweet Leaf Nature Trail is self-guided, and a small lake offers picnicking, fishing, and swimming. (409) 273-2261.

The Woodlands. North of downtown Houston 27 miles via I-45. Although its lakes and neighborhood parks are for residents only, this giant development offers several recreations to the general public. More than 50 miles of trails thread beautiful woods, just right for hiking, jogging, in-line skating, or biking (bring your own wheels and park by the Visitor Center). Visiting golfers are welcome on the Tournament Players Course (fee) of the Woodlands Country Club, (281) 367-7285; don't miss the new Texas Golf Hall of Fame directly behind the eighteenth green, (281) 364-7270. With a current YMCA membership plus a small guest fee, visitors also can enjoy the South Montgomery County YMCA's huge all-sport facility in the Village of Cochran's Crossing, (281) 367-9622.

Consider planning a trip around a performance in the Cynthia Woods Mitchell Pavilion, the Woodlands's beautiful outdoor performing arts center. April-to-October playbill offerings range from bluegrass to ballet and Broadway shows, rock to Rachmaninoff, Gershwin to Willie Nelson, and the setting recalls Tanglewood and Interlochen. Advance tickets are available from Ticketmaster, Sears, Fiesta, Sound Warehouse, and Foley's; day-of-performance tickets can be bought at the box office; or you can charge by phone, (281) 629-3700 or (800) 284-5780. Do inquire about parking fees, use of paging devices, and restrictions on lawn chairs, coolers, picnics, and so on. No photography of any sort is allowed. (281) 363-3300.

If you want to make a weekend of it, check out the tennis, golf, and pampering packages at The Woodlands Executive Conference Center and Resort. (CC). (281) 367-1100.

WHERE TO EAT

Although numerous franchises offer good eats along I-45 in the vicinity of The Woodlands Mall, the following are worth the search.

Amerigo's Grille, 25050 Grogans Park Drive, The Woodlands. When it's time to eat "Italian," come here. The atmosphere equals the high quality of the food; save room for the tiramisu. Open for lunch and dinner weekdays, dinner only on Saturday. $-$$; (CC). (281) 362-0808.

Cafe Aquarius. On FM-1097, five miles west of I-45. This combination sports bar and grill near the upper east side of Lake Conroe offers tasty food in a clean atmosphere, with outdoor dining when weather permits. This spot also swings most Friday and Saturday evenings with live music, name bands, themed parties, and special events. Open for lunch and dinner daily; try the beach volleyball and outdoor billiards while waiting for your prime rib sandwich. $-$$; (CC). (409) 856-6705.

Captain Jack's on the Lake. #1 Marina Drive at Inland Marina (at the Lake Conroe dam). All the S's—salads, soups, sandwiches, steaks, and seafood—are good here, along with hamburgers, homemade desserts, and the daily specials. Open for lunch and dinner Tuesday–Sunday, breakfast on weekends. $–$$; (CC). (409) 588-3902.

Continental Grill. 9989 Highway 105 West. Chef Giovanni creates exceedingly good (and often unusual) beef, veal, fish, and chicken entrees at prices substantially under similar quality fare in Houston. Local favorites include Chicken Artichoke, Mussels Garlic, Lobster Capellini, and rack of lamb. Open for dinner daily. $$; (CC). (409) 588-4666.

Hooks Seafood Restaurant. 820 North Loop 336. The heady scents of tasty Cajun cooking tickle your appetite the instant you walk in the door of this family-owned place. An immaculate re-conception of a former fast-food building, Hooks serves all the favorites, from fried catfish and shrimp to assorted broiled dinners. The crawfish étouffée comes steaming and perfectly seasoned, and the seafood po'boys arrive on warm sourdough bread. Open for lunch and dinner daily. $–$$; (CC). (409) 539-4665.

Marisabel's. 25120 Glen Loch Drive, adjacent to the Woodlands (take Sawdust Road west approximately 2.5 miles from I-45). Hard to find and tiny when you do, this local favorite serves good "Texican." Open for lunch and dinner Monday–Friday; dinner only on Saturday. $–$$; (CC). (281) 292-7718.

Papa's on the Lake. 9400 Highway 105 West, seven miles west on I-45. One of the hot spots on Lake Conroe, this bar and grill serves pizzas, salads, sandwiches (including muffulettas), and a variety of snacks as well as beer and wine. There's a large deck overlooking the lake and live music on summer weekends. Open daily for lunch and dinner. $–$$; (CC). (409) 447-2500.

Pepperoni's Sub & Pizza Cafe (formerly D'Angelo). 4747 Research Forest Drive, The Woodlands (in Cochran's Crossing shopping center). Great sandwiches are the draw here, along with pizzas and tasty light fare. Open daily for lunch and dinner. $–$$; (CC). (281) 292-9488.

Santa Fe Cafe and General Store. 1111 League Line Road in the Conroe Outlet Center. This fragrant bakery and restaurant specializes in soups, salads, sandwiches, pasta platters, and yummy desserts, a great stop when you need a rest from shopping. Open daily for breakfast, lunch, and dinner (until midafternoon on Sunday). $; (CC). (409) 856-0742.

Vernon's Kuntry Barbecue. On the north side of Highway 105,

3.5 miles west of I–45. This beer garden serves delicious brisket, ribs, links, hamburgers, and chicken. Open daily for lunch and dinner. $–$$; (CC). (409) 539-3000.

Vernon's Kuntry Katfish. 5901 Highway 105, 6.5 miles west of I–45. Even if you don't like catfish, come here. Tasty choices run from frog legs to chicken-fried steak and burgers, and the home-made desserts and breads are terrific. Open for lunch and dinner daily. $–$$; (CC). (409) 760-3386.

Villa Italia. 203 Simonton in downtown Conroe; 6035 Highway 105 West. This "Italian Ristorante" specializes in rack of lamb, Dover sole, and assorted veal entrees, along with California and French wines. The menu also offers assorted pasta, seafood, chicken, and steak. Open daily for lunch and dinner. $–$$; (CC). (409) 539-1915 in Conroe; (409) 539-5599 on T-105.

CONTINUING ON

From Conroe Day Trip 1 swings south on I–45 to the Spring-Cypress Road exit. Turn left (east) under the freeway and follow Spring-Cypress to the railroad tracks.

SPRING

Back in the late 1800s, a community called Spring sprang up to serve the International and Great Northern Railroad as a switching station north of Houston. As the railroads prospered through the turn of the century, so did the town, and in 1902 the Wunche Brothers' Saloon was built within a toot of the roundhouse. It had eight rooms upstairs to house railroad personnel.

But we all know what happened to the railroads of America and to the many small towns that depended on them. By the 1920s the roundhouse had relocated to Houston, and the Texas Rangers had enforced the Prohibition laws by shooting every bottle in the saloon. Then came the depression of the 1930s, and when I–45 bypassed Spring in the 1960s, it was the final blow. The old town area lapsed into civic limbo as businesses began to thrive around the new freeway interchange a mile west.

So much for yesterday. Today Old Town Spring is in its second bloom and is a great day-trip destination. Specialty shops, eateries, a few antiques stores, flea markets, art galleries—all are right at home in the quaint old houses. If you are particularly interested in traditional ironworking and blacksmithing, you might want to call Wayne Meadows, (713) 462-1586, in advance to make sure he will be working in his shop across from the Wunsche Brothers Cafe and Saloon when you visit. In general, the shops are open Tuesday-Saturday and on Sunday afternoon. If you are coming north from Houston, take the 70A exit from I-45 and swing east (right) at the signal on Spring-Cypress Road. When you see the OLD TOWN SPRING sign, you're there; (281) 353-9310.

B&B also is a possibility here. McLachlan Farm, a 1911 home on thirty-five acres 1 mile south of Old Town Spring, welcomes overnight guests, (281) 350-2400.

WHAT TO DO

Carter's Country. 6231 Treaschwig Road. From I-45 take the FM-1960 exit east; turn north on Aldine-Westfield Road to Treaschwig. Tucked away in the woods, this well-designed place offers pistol, rifle, trap, skeet, and country clay shooting at a variety of distances. Children can shoot BB guns here if they have adult supervision. Open daily. Fee; (CC). (281) 443-8393.

Mercer Arboretum. 22306 Aldine-Westfield Road, north of FM-1960. This 214-acre county park is a sleeper, often overlooked by day-trippers. What they miss is an outstanding collection of native Texas plants, a series of self-guided nature trails, a bird sanctuary, special gardens (ferns, ginger, water lilies, azaleas, and so on), picnic areas, and educational programs, all along a wooded stretch of Cypress Creek. There's also a canoe launch site here. Free and open daily. (281) 443-8731.

Splashtown USA. 21300 I-45 North (exit 70A). When summer's heat hits, there's no better cooler than the thrill slides, tube rides, and wave pool at this forty-six-acre water park. You're not allowed to bring your own food and beverages inside the gates, but you are welcome to bring lunches and coolers for a family picnic on the outside grounds. Food also can be purchased inside the park. Open daily from June to mid-August; weekends only in May and from mid-August to October 1. Live entertainment and special events often highlight those off-season weekends. Fee; (CC). (281) 355-3300.

WHERE TO EAT

British Trading Post. 26303 Hardy Road, Old Town Spring. Have a hankering for meat pies, mushy peas, or a shandy? This is the place. Lunch only, Tuesday–Sunday. $. (281) 350-5854.

Hyde's Cafe. 26608 Keith, Old Town Spring. Formerly the Spring Cafe, this local institution still brags that it has the best food and slowest service anywhere. The old Spring Cafe was widely known for its marvelous hamburgers, and the tradition continues, including the time-honored thirty- to sixty-minute wait. If that's too long, try the fried veggie tray, buzzards' chili, BBQ, or sausage-on-a-stick. Open for lunch and dinner Tuesday–Sunday; lunch only on Monday. $. (281) 350-8530.

Wunche Brothers' Cafe and Saloon, 103 Midway, Old Town Spring. This historic landmark, circa 1902, offers some nifty live music (everything from progressive country to rock and roll) Tuesday–Saturday evenings, along with loads of down-home food. Lunch ranges from burgers to sandwiches and salads, and the sideboard holds free samples of Texas-grown jellies (fig, dewberry, mayhaw, tomato, muscadine, and elderberry). Save room for dessert—the chocolate whiskey cake is a house specialty. Open for lunch on Monday; lunch and dinner Tuesday–Saturday. $–$$; (CC). (281) 350-CAFE.

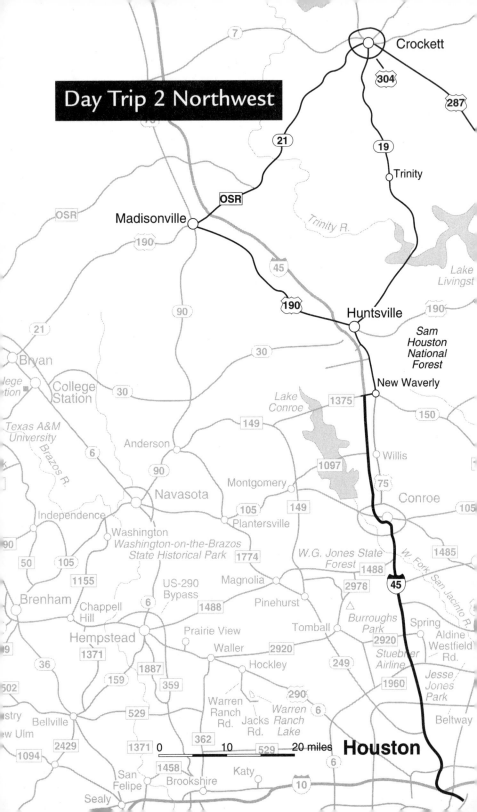

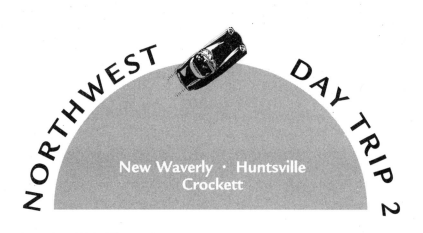
NEW WAVERLY

Begin this day trip by driving north on I-45 from Houston approximately 60 miles and turning east at the New Waverly exit. Settled in the 1850s, the community of Waverly thrived for a time on a pioneer cotton and cattle economy. Fearing damage to their cattle and the town's economy, residents turned down the International and Great Northern Railroad Company's request in 1870 for a right-of-way through town, a fatal mistake. The tracks were laid 10 miles west, people began relocating around the station of "New" Waverly, and the original Waverly was doomed. Visitors to the latter now find only an old cemetery with interesting headstones and the visually charming Waverly Presbyterian Church, built around 1904 and still filled every Sunday. "Old" Waverly is 6.8 miles east of I-45 on T-150.

New Waverly had a heavy Polish immigration from 1870 to 1902. After working in the fields to pay back the area's landowners who had advanced their passage money, the Poles began their own businesses and left a strong ethnic stamp on this community. Stately, Gothic-style St. Joseph's Catholic Church in the heart of town is one of their legacies. Built between 1905 and 1908, it is well worth a visit.

WHAT TO DO

Christmas Tree Farms. Call Iron Creek Farms for directions, (409) 767-4541. This is also good birding territory, so bring binoculars.

Old Danville Auction. 292 Old Danville Road, Willis. Take the Shepherd Hill Road exit from I-45, go west one-half mile, then turn right on Old Danville Road. A decorator's delight, this spot auctions major lots of American antiques (furniture, china, linens, and so on) every four weeks. Call for current schedule. (800) 439-7615.

The Sam Houston National Forest. Although not fully developed, this extensive woodland offers fishing, hunting, camping, hiking, photo opportunities, berry picking, birdwatching, picnicking, and boating access to Lake Conroe. For additional information on locations listed, contact the U.S. Department of Agriculture, Forest Service, Sam Houston Ranger District, P.O. Drawer 1000, New Waverly 77358, (409) 344-6205. *Note:* The ranger station, 3 miles west of New Waverly on FM-1375, is open on weekdays. Unless otherwise noted, all of the following are free-use facilities.

Cagle Recreation Area. From I-45 at New Waverly, take FM-1375 west 4.2 miles; then turn southwest on FSR-234 for 3 miles. Facilities restricted to parking lot ($3.00) and boat ramp into Lake Conroe. No restrooms, electricity, or potable water.

Kelly's Pond Campground. From I-45 at New Waverly, take FM-1375 west 11 miles, turn south 1 mile on FSR-204, and then drive west 1 mile on FSR-271. This scenic spot offers limited primitive tent camping (fire grates and picnic tables but no restroom facilities or water) and fishing in three small ponds. Nice for a picnic, but no boating or swimming.

Off-Road Vehicle Trails. Two ORVT loops totaling 55 miles, with an additional 100 or more miles of unmarked trails within an "open country" area, are provided for four-wheel vehicles, motorcycles, horses, and bikes. No vehicles more than 40 inches in width are allowed, however; check ORVT regulations posted at the Sam Houston Ranger Station. East trailhead access: From New Waverly take FM-1375 approximately 4 miles west to FSR-233; turn north and follow signs. West trailhead access: From New Waverly take FM-1375 approximately 11 miles west to FSR-215; go north and bear left on FSR-208; trailhead is on immediate left. *Note:* Hikers may be happier on the quieter Lone Star Hiking Trail, accessed from Stubblefield Recreation Area (see below).

Little Lake Creek Wilderness Area. From I-45 at New Waverly, take FM-1375 west 14 miles; turn south on FM-149 for 4 miles. Good for hiking.

Scott's Ridge. From Willis exit of I-45, take FM-1097 west 8 miles, then FSR-212 north for 1 mile. No facilities aside from boat ramp accessing Lake Conroe. Parking fee $2.00.

Stubblefield Lake Recreation Area and Campground. From I-45 at New Waverly, take FM-1375 west 11 miles to FSR-215; turn north and follow pavement to signs. That latter road passes a seventy-acre wood-pecker colony with more than forty cavity trees, a National Forest Service effort to save the endangered red-cockaded woodpecker. The birds are active primarily at sunrise and sunset. Situated on the wide and shallow west fork of the San Jacinto River, this park offers twenty-eight campsites for either tents or RVs (up to 20 feet in length). Fee. You'll find tables, fire rings, and hot showers. Swimming not recommended (broken glass, possible alligator problem), but shallow-draft boating, canoeing, and bass fishing are pleasures in these beautiful headwaters of Lake Conroe. The park also accesses the Lone Star Hiking Trail. Interested in joining the Lone Star Hiking Trail Club, Inc.? Call the National Forest Service, (409) 344-6205.

WHERE TO EAT

Waverly House. At the intersection of FM-1375 and T-75 on the western edge of New Waverly. When a Houston newspaper asked its readers to vote for the Best Country Cafes in Texas in 1989, this friendly place was in the top ten. Known for its homemade cream pies, it also dishes out freshly baked cobbler almost year-round. Order the chicken-fried steak only if you're starving or sharing; it laps over both sides of the plate. If you are in New Waverly on a weekday, don't pass up the workingman's steam-table lunch. Open for lunch and dinner daily; closes at 2:00 P.M. on Sunday. $-$$; (CC). (409) 344-2185.

CONTINUING ON

From New Waverly continue this day trip by driving north on I-45 to Huntsville.

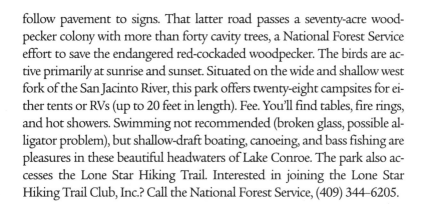

HUNTSVILLE

In the early 1830s an adventurous frontiersman named Pleasant Gray thought this rolling, wooded wilderness looked like his former home in Huntsville, Alabama. Because there were good springs nearby, he settled in and established an Indian trading post. By 1836 the tiny settlement of Huntsville was thriving, and in 1848 Sam Houston built his family home and plantation, Woodland, at the southern edge of the city.

Sam's home now is right downtown, across from the Sam Houston State University campus, and those old Indian trails long since have been formalized into highways. Today's visitors can "stand with Sam," however: A somewhat startling sixty-six-foot-high statue of this Texas legend now borders I–45, the centerpiece of a visitor center and park. This is the world's tallest statue of an American hero. Open Tuesday–Sunday, this new Sam Houston Statue Visitor Center also distributes Texas state maps and official travel information, the only such resource in the north-from-Houston region. Access is exit 109 from I–45 north, exit 112 from I–45 south.

To reach downtown Huntsville from either direction on I–45, take the T–30 exit and head east. You'll soon find a main square retrogressing visually to the 1860s, courtesy of an ongoing trompe l'oeil program designed to bring back the style and architecture of the city's past.

Driving-tour booklets are available weekdays from the Sam Houston Statue Visitor Information Center or the Huntsville Chamber of Commerce, 1327 Eleventh Street, P.O. Box 538, Huntsville 77342-0538, (409) 295-8113 or (800) 289-0389. Weekend explorers will find area information available outside that office. Expect numerous antiques stores around the square and a motorized trolley, circa the 1890s, that runs a regular route through downtown on weekdays and during special weekend events.

Want to overnight? B&B is offered at several vintage homes. In town The Whistler is an 1859 Victorian that has been in the same family for six generations; (409) 295-2834 or (800) 432-1288 or (800) 404-2834. Bluebonnet Bed and Breakfast is a 1912 beauty, recently moved from town to seven acres on FM-1374, (409) 295-2072. Longhorn House is a restored 1892 farmhouse 17 miles north of Huntsville on FM-1696, (409) 295-1844; a stay at this working longhorn cattle ranch includes a tour, fishing, and hiking.

WHAT TO DO

The Blue Lagoon. North of Huntsville on Pinedale Road, off FM-247. Also known as Cozumel in the Pines, this old rock quarry offers some exciting scuba territory to certified divers. There are two large lakes, both with 40-foot visibility underwater and sunken shipwrecks to explore. You must have your C-card with you to be admitted, and no children under fourteen, pets, or glass containers are allowed. Open Friday–Sunday in winter, daily in summer. Call for directions and further information. $$. (409) 291-6111.

Christmas Tree Farms. This is prime tree-cutting territory. Call any of the following for directions: A-C Black Angus, (713) 941-3332 or (409) 295-9523; Big Bill's Christmas Trees, (409) 295-4824; Mill Hollow Christmas Tree Farm, (281) 469-2981 or (409) 377-4044; Killian's Christmas Tree Farm, (409) 874-2293; and Roman's Tree Farm, (281) 554-7329 or (409) 295-4655.

Gibb Bros. Building. On the corner of Eleventh Street and Sam Houston Avenue. Started in 1841 as a store, this business evolved into the town's first bank because Thomas and Sanford Gibbs owned the only safe. The third structure on this site, the current building dates from 1890 and was recently restored to its early appearance after being disguised for decades by a modern brick front. The Gibb Brothers banking offices continue on the second floor, making this the oldest business in Texas still on its original site and under the same family ownership.

The Gibbs-Powell Home. Eleventh Street and Avenue M. This excellent example of Greek Revival architecture was built in 1862 and can be toured on weekend afternoons and by appointment. Donation. For group tour information contact the Huntsville Chamber of Commerce, (800) 289-0389 or (409) 295-2914.

Henry Opera House. Twelfth Street and Avenue K. Such elegance as this must have represented in the 1880s is hard to visualize. Only the tall windows on the upper floor give a hint of the building's cultural past. Built as a Masonic investment in 1883, it soon became the property of Major John Henry, who installed Huntsville's first department store on the ground floor and used the second floor as an opera house.

Huntsville State Park. Eight miles south of Huntsville via I-45, then west on Park Road 40. Here 2,000-plus acres center on Lake Raven and offer swimming, canoeing, and limited sailing and motorboating. Hiking and birding are excellent and Lake Raven Stables offers trail horseback riding year-round, (409) 295-1985. The forest is dominated by loblolly and shortleaf pine, dogwood, sweet gum, sassafras, and assorted oaks. Good camping and picnicking. Fee. Open daily. (409) 295-5644 or (800) 792-1112.

Oakwood Cemetery. Two blocks north of Eleventh Street on Avenue I. (Those 2 blocks of Avenue I are T-1, the shortest official highway in the state.) Sam Houston sleeps with good company in this historic cemetery. Deeded as a free burial place in 1847 by Huntsville's founder, Pleasant Gray, Oakwood has several tombstones carrying burial dates as early as 1842. Self-guided tour information is available at the Sam Houston Statue Visitor Center.

Sam Houston Memorial Park and Museum. 1836 Sam Houston Avenue (between Seventeenth and Nineteenth streets). During a turbulent life that saw him the governor of Tennessee, a general in the Texas Army, the victor at the battle of San Jacinto, and the first president of the Republic of Texas, Sam Houston had many homes. None was as lovely or as beloved by him as Woodland Home, built on this site in 1847. Restored in 1981, this square log house with its white clapboard siding is just one of the pleasures in this shady park/museum complex.

Start at the museum, touring the right wing first to keep the chronology straight, and then visit Woodland, its separate kitchen, Houston's law office, and a blacksmith shop. Close by are the War and Peace House and the unusual Steamboat House, where Houston died in 1863. The docents in both homes speak of Sam and his wife, Margaret, as if they might return at any moment. The park's small lake was a fresh, bubbling spring during Houston's residency here; today it is reshaped to resemble the state of Texas and is a pleasant spot for a picnic lunch. Spring visits get a bonus of flowering dogwood and azaleas. Sam Houston's grave also is interesting, across town in Oakwood Cemetery. Part of the Sam Houston State University complex, the park and museum are open Tuesday–Sunday. (409) 294–1832.

Sam Houston State University. Five blocks south of the town square on Sam Houston Avenue (US-75). Founded in 1879 as a normal institute, SHSU's campus had three buildings worth exploring until a disastrous fire in early 1982 destroyed the Gothic wonder known as Old Main (1889). Now only historic Austin Hall (1853) and the restored Peabody Memorial Library (1902) recall the school's early days.

The public is welcome on campus; to find out what's going on when you'll be in town, call the SHSU Public Relations Office, (409) 294–1836. Guests also can attend slide/lecture programs given by the school's planetarium staff several times a month. Some outings include viewing through the university's 16-inch telescope. (409) 294–3664.

SHSU's Agricultural Center also is open to visitors by appointment. In addition to the plant science greenhouse, you can see the beef cattle, swine, poultry, horse, and sheep facilities. (409) 294–1215.

Texas Prison Museum. 1113 Twelfth Street, on the south side of the city square. Want to keep your kids on the straight and narrow?

Bring them here for a look at a 9-by-6-foot cell. Guides also explain other exhibits that include Bonnie and Clyde's rifles and some blood-chilling photos from their area escapades; "Old Sparkie," the actual electric chair used through 1964; rare balls and chains; and assorted contraband confiscated within the nearby prison. Housed in an old bank building, this interesting museum can special-order any type of prisoner-made leather goods, from "Bubba" belts to snuffcan holders, dolls to artwork. Prices are reasonable, and both quality and craftswork are excellent. Open Sunday and Tuesday–Friday from noon to 5:00 P.M.; Saturday from 9:00 A.M. to 5:00 P.M. Closed on Monday. (Fee for those over twelve). (409) 295-2155.

The Walls. Three short blocks east of the town square. This is the original main unit of the Huntsville State Prison. *Of interest:* The "prisoner count" whistle that blows daily at 7:00 A.M. and again in the late afternoon assures Huntsville residents that all's well—every felon is accounted for. Self-guided tour information for the prison is available at the Sam Houston Statue Visitor Center.

WHERE TO EAT

The Cafe Texan. 1120 Sam Houston, near Twelfth Street. Chickenfried steak and pepper steak are "home-cooked" here. Open for breakfast, lunch, and dinner daily (specials at lunch). $-$$; (CC). (409) 295-2381.

Fiesta Taqueria. On the south side of US-190, 0.9 mile past the T-19 bridge. Locals love this simple place for its outstanding fajita burritos, fajita enchiladas, and homemade tamales; the latter can be ordered to go. Open daily for lunch and dinner. $. (409) 294-0568.

The Homestead on 19th. 1215 Nineteenth Street. Considered by many locals to be the best eatery in town, this chef-owned (John Eschenfelder) restaurant serves creative American cuisine in a nineteenth century courtyard setting. Open Monday–Friday for lunch, Thursday–Saturday for dinner. $$-$$$; (CC). (409) 291-7366.

The Junction Restaurant. 2641 Eleventh Street. Just look for an 1849 plantation house with an old-fashioned buggy on the front porch. Inside, the house specialties are catfish, fresh seafood, steaks, and chicken; there also are some light entrees for dieters. Open daily for lunch and dinner. $-$$; (CC). (409) 291-2183.

King's Candies & Ice Cream. 1112 Eleventh Street on the square. First cousin to King's Confectionery on The Strand in Galveston, this old-fashioned sweet shop makes traditional shakes, malts, and banana splits at its soda fountain; squeezes lemons for the lemonade; makes its own candy; and serves Blue Bell ice cream. Good place for a lunch sandwich also. Open Monday–Saturday. $; (CC). (409) 291-6988.

The New Zion Missionary Baptist Church. 2601 Montgomery Road (FM-1374), 2 miles east of I-45. A few years back a Houston housepainter named D. C. Ward volunteered to paint this country church, and when his wife, Annie Mae, began fixing some barbecue ribs for his workday lunch, the wonderful aroma stopped traffic. The congregation took the hint and began selling the Wards' barbecue on weekends from a shady spot near the church.

Next came a "real" kitchen and dining room, serving up some of the best barbecue in East Texas, the profits from which built a new brick church with stained glass windows. In a hurry? Just ask for the $7.58 family-style special—four meats, beans, potato salad, iced tea, and tax—that arrives as fast as the staff can dish it up. Open 8:00 A.M. to 7:00 P.M. Tuesday–Saturday, till 8:00 P.M. on summer weekends. $–$$. (409) 295-7394.

WANDERING THE BACKROADS

The OSR turnoff, 40 miles north of Huntsville on I-45, is a meandering country drive with more than a touch of history. The initials stand for Old San Antonio Road, but it also is known as El Camino Real, because it was created by the order of the king of Spain in 1691. The Spaniards, through their control of Mexico, claimed Texas from 1519 to 1821, but the French also coveted this rich, wild land, sending explorers into Texas in the late 1600s. To reinforce its claim, Spain created a series of missions in East Texas and blazed this road to bolster and serve those primitive outposts. Today T-21 follows, after a fashion, that historic route from San Marcos northeast to the Louisiana border, one portion linking the Madisonville area to Crockett. If you love vistas of rolling fields edged by ancient oaks, don't miss this drive.

Turning west on OSR from I-45 takes you through the tiny but historic community of Normangee en route to Bryan–College Station (Trip 3, this sector).

CONTINUING ON

From Huntsville, two routes take you to Crockett, the final stop on this day trip. The shortest follows T-19 for 49 miles and passes through the communities of Trinity and Lovelady. Several emu ranches along the way welcome visitors with advance appointments (see "What to Do" section for Crockett), and you'll also find Victorian-style bed and breakfast accommodation at The Parker House in Trinity, (409) 594-3260 or (800) 593-2373; and at Log Cabin Bed and Breakfast in Lovelady, (409) 636-2002.

A longer but very scenic alternative travels 30 miles north to Madisonville via either US-75 or I-45, then swings northeast 36 miles to Crockett via T-21, part of the previously mentioned Old San Antonio Road.

CROCKETT

Davy Crockett and two companions had to do some fast talking here. Local folks found Crockett's campsite near this area in 1836 (the trio were en route to their destinies at the Alamo) and nearly hanged them as horse thieves. The fifth oldest town in Texas and loaded with vintage buildings, Crockett has a history that is easy to trace.

Visitors should start at the traditional square in the heart of town—good gift-shopping territory—and then go exploring. For advance information contact either the Houston County Chamber of Commerce, 700 East Houston, P.O. Box 307, Crockett 75835, (409) 544-2359, or the Houston County Historical Commission, Third Floor, Houston County Courthouse, Crockett 75835, (409) 544-3256.

Consider turning this day trip into an overnight with accommodations at Warfield House, built in the 1890s and now elegantly restored as a B&B lodging in the heart of town, (409) 544-4037.

WHERE TO GO

Davy Crockett Spring. West Goliad at the railroad underpass, west of the town square. Though not much to see, the spring still flows and serves as a public drinking fountain at what is thought to be Crockett's campsite.

Discover Houston County Visitor's Center–Museum. 303 South First Street. Although its historical displays are still being developed, this former railroad depot (circa 1909) is the starting point for brochure-guided tours of Indian massacre sites, early burial grounds and churches, Caddoan burial mounds, and the Mission Tejas Park. If you'd like a personal escort into the surrounding countryside, call ahead. Current museum exhibits include a 1929 fire truck, assorted farming tools, and a miniature train. Open on Wednesday afternoon or by appointment for groups. Donation welcome. (409) 544–9520 or 544–3255, ext. 27.

Downes-Aldrich Historical Home. 207 North Seventh Street. Listed in the National Register of Historic Places, this Victorian survivor now is the historical and cultural activities center for the town. Open Wednesday, Saturday, and Sunday afternoons, March–December. Fee. (409) 544–4804.

Emu Ranches. The following welcome visitors with advance appointments; ask about restrictions on children: Emu Plantation, (409) 636–2500; Gallant Emu Enterprises, (409) 655–2761; Hayco Emu Ranch, (800) 745–7343; and Morning Star Ranch, (409) 636–7277.

Monroe-Crook Home. 709 East Houston Avenue. Built in 1854 and listed in the National Register of Historic Places, this Greek Revival home is open for public tours on Wednesday morning and weekend afternoons, March–December. Fee. (409) 544–5820.

WHERE TO EAT

Fowler's Steak and Seafood. T-7 east and Loop 304. Check out the daily specials at lunch and dinner at this long-established local favorite. Open Tuesday–Sunday. $-$$; (CC). (409) 544–9690.

Thomas Corners. See the "Wandering the Backroads" section.

The Wooden Nickel. Loop 304 East. A jillion junk-tiques decorate the porch and walls of this zany restaurant, and there's a very miniature golf course out back. The blackboard menu of down-home food ranges from Mexican to burgers to BBQ and back again, and there are steam-table specials as well. Open for lunch and dinner Tuesday–Saturday, until 3:00 P.M. on Sunday. $-$$; (CC). (409) 544–8011.

WANDERING THE BACKROADS

There are numerous possibilities if you feel like extending your drive well beyond the two-hour limit of this book. First option is to continue north on OSR (T-21) from Crockett through the Davy Crockett National Forest to the Mission Tejas State Historical Park, (409) 687-2394. The Rice family log home is special here, built between 1828 and 1838 and used as a stage stop. Nearby is a commemorative log structure similar to the old Spanish mission established here in 1690 to serve the Tejas Indians, the first of its kind in Texas.

Continuing northeast another 7 miles on OSR brings you to Caddoan Mounds State Historic Site, 6 miles southwest of Alto. In addition to two large ceremonial mounds, archaeological digs have led to a full-size replica of a Caddoan house built with Stone Age–type tools. A visitor center explains all. (409) 858-3218.

A second option from Crockett follows T-7 approximately 18 miles east to the Ratcliff Lake Recreation Area in the Davy Crockett National Forest. A picturesque 45-acre swimming and fishing lake surrounded by extensive picnic areas and campgrounds, this facility also sports canoe rentals and countless deer amid a hardwood forest that's particularly beautiful in spring and fall; (fee), (409) 544-2046. The 20-mile-long Four C Hiking Trail begins here and continues northeast to the Neches Bluff Overlook on the Neches River, just south of T-21 northeast of Weches. For further trail information, contact the Texas Forestry Association, P.O. Box 1488, Lufkin 75902, (409) 632-TREE.

If hunger strikes as you drive on a weekday between Crockett and Ratcliff Lake, take a break at Thomas Corners in the tiny community of Kennard. This combination service station, cafe, and general store is run by Houston expatriates Bill and Linda Thomas—he's now the town's mayor and she's the city secretary—and both the food and hospitality typify East Texas. Open from 5:00 A.M. to 5:30 P.M. Monday–Friday; 'til 12 noon on Saturday. $; (CC). (409) 655-2360. Also, you'll find an area information booth at the T-7/FM-357 "Y".

A third long-drive alternative is FM-229 northwest from Crockett to Houston County Lake. Locally, this is considered the best bass fishing in the state.

Following US-287 southeast from Crockett takes you through the Kickapoo Recreation Area near Groveton and hits the northern limit of the Livingston-Woodville day trip in the northeast sector of this book.

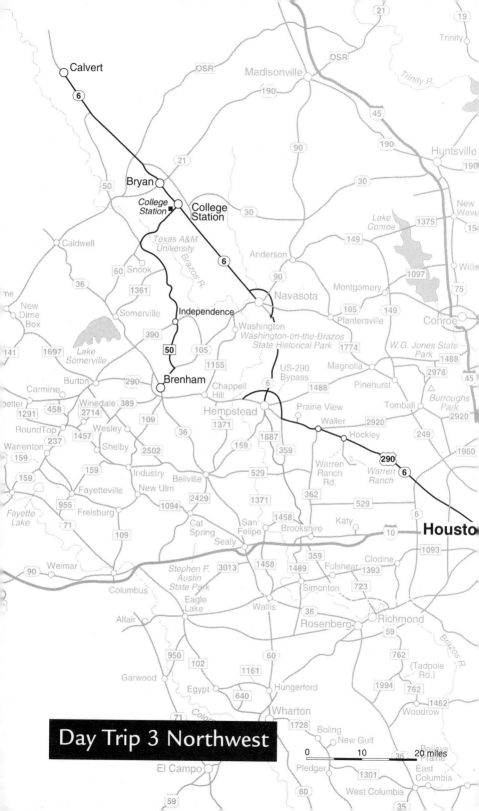

Day Trip 3 Northwest

BRYAN–COLLEGE STATION

From Houston follow T-6 and US-290 north to Hempstead and continue north on T-6 through Navasota into Bryan and College Station.

These joint communities tend to have a single connotation to Houstonians—Texas A&M University. While visitors to that sprawling campus will find much of interest, there are several other things to do near Aggieland.

Bryan and College Station today flow into a combined metropolitan area that ranked first in growth in the state and sixth in the entire country in the 1980 census. Not bad for a slow starter. This rich sliver of agricultural land bounded by the Brazos River on the west and the Navasota River on the east was sparsely settled until the advent of the Houston & Texas Central Railroad in 1866. The Reconstruction years after the Civil War were rough on the young town of Bryan, and it wasn't until the formal opening of Texas A&M College in 1876 that the area settled down to some semblance of respectability.

Some footnotes on Bryan's past are interesting. The original street grid inadvertently provided for today's traffic by making Main Street wide enough to turn a five-yoke oxen team, and the college was deliberately sited on the open prairie 5 miles south of town so as to be well removed from the influence of demon rum flowing freely in Bryan's saloons.

An information-loaded historic guide and map covers Bryan's old commercial and residential districts, as well as the remains of several small pre–Civil War settlements outside town. This and other area guides are found at the Bryan–College Station Chamber of Commerce Convention & Visitor Bureau, 715 University Drive East, College Station 77840, (409) 260-9898 or (800) 777-8292. (Monday–Friday only; contact in advance for maps and brochures if you intend to explore on a weekend.)

Leaving Texas A&M to its own section following, here are some suggestions of what to see in Bryan and College Station.

WHAT TO DO

Birding. The Brazos Valley hosts an enormous variety of bird life. A self-guided tour covering five areas and a list of birds common to the Brazos County Arboretum are available from the Convention & Visitor Bureau.

Brazos Center. 3232 Briarcrest, Bryan. Take the Briarcrest exit east from T-6 bypass. This is the special events place for the area, holding giant weekend antiques shows in February, July, and October. Year-round visitors can enjoy the Brazos Valley Museum of Natural Science and a small nature trail on the grounds. Free. Open Tuesday–Saturday, September through May; Monday–Saturday, June through August. (409) 776-8338 (center); (409) 776-2195 (museum).

Canoeing on the Brazos River. First, so you'll sound like a native, it's pronounced Braa-zas, not Bray-zos, as you might expect from the spelling. Although its water is muddy with sediment, the Brazos generally is quiet and otherwise scenic, a good one- or two-day float if you have your own canoe. As of this writing there are no canoe rentals available in the Bryan–College Station area. You'll find float information in several river books available at major bookstores.

Christmas Tree Farms. Call either of the following for directions: Evergreen Farms, (409) 775-1717, or J. P. Seven Christmas Trees, (409) 846-7916.

Lake Bryan. From T-6 north of Bryan, take the FM-2818 exit south for approximately five miles. At Sandy Point Road (blinking yellow light) turn right and go 3.4 miles; lake will be on your right.

Operated by the City of Bryan Parks and Recreation Department, this 886-acre lake is surrounded by 1700 acres of oak-shaded land, of which 150 acres are developed for both primitive and RV camping, picnicking, and other recreational uses. There's lots of water access, including a sand beach and special restricted area for jet ski operation, as well as walking trails and a challenging mountain bike trail around the lake. Patrolled by park police, this family area is open daily March–November. Primitive camping is $10 per night, RV sites with water and electricity are $15. Hot showers are on the 1997 construction schedule. Admission is $5.00 per car. For information or to reserve an RV site, call (409) 361-3656.

Local Color Art Gallery & Store. 310 University Drive East, College Station. Exhibits, juried shows featuring regional artists, and outstanding handcrafts make this a place to stop and shop. Open Monday–Friday. (409) 268-ARTS.

Messina Hof Wine Cellar and Vineyard. 4545 Old Reliance Road, Bryan. Exit T-6 at Boonville Road; stay on access road going north; turn right on Old Reliance Road; winery is 3 miles east on the left. Paul and Merrill Bonarrigo began planting grapes in 1977; their successful vineyard now covers forty-six acres and produces about 90,000 gallons (500,000 bottles) annually. Using the classic European grape Vinifera grafted onto Texas root stock, they bottle sixteen varieties of wine, including chardonnay, cabernet, port, red and white zinfandels, and champagne. Harvest time is July and August, and you can pick and stomp grapes yourself by signing up in advance for their Pickers' Club (free). The turn-of-the-century Howell manor house has been restored as the winery's retail sales and tasting room; it is open daily, and there are winery tours at specific times. The Bonarrigos also invite the public for Springfest in April and a premiere party for new wines and vintages in November. Other special events occur monthly throughout the year (get on their mailing list), and there's a Vintner's Loft hideaway for couples seeking an overnight retreat (nonsmoking adults only) and a Sicilian-style restaurant (see "Where to Eat"). (409) 778-9463 or (800) 736-9463.

EXPLORING TEXAS A&M UNIVERSITY

Even if you haven't a prospective student in tow, this handsome 5,250-acre campus has much to offer. Located in the heart of College Station and hard to miss on the west side of T-6, Texas A&M was the first public institution of higher education in the state. Originally an all-male military college, it now has a co-ed enrollment in excess of 42,500 and is in the top ten schools nationally in funding for scientific research.

Aggie traditions are stories in themselves. Ask about the Elephant Walk, the Twelfth Man, and Silver Taps at the Visitor Information Center in Rudder Tower for an insight into what makes Aggies so loyal to their alma mater.

A book of suggested walking tours on campus can be bought in the student bookstore, (409) 845-8681, in the Memorial Student Center or in advance from the Texas A&M University Press , (409) 845-1436. First-time visitors should begin at The Visitor Center in the lobby of Rudder Tower, (409) 845-5851; see Rudder Tower information below.

WHAT TO DO

The Clayton W. Williams Jr. Alumni Center. Corner of George Bush Drive and Houston Street. Displays include an Aggie ring collection. (409) 845-7514.

Floral Test Gardens. On Houston Street across from Moore Communications Center. Some 1,000 varieties of seeds and bulbs are grown here annually, part of the all-American seed-testing program across the country. You are welcome to look around on your own. Picnic areas and the floriculture greenhouses are nearby. Tours of the latter are easily arranged, (409) 845-8553. Questions about growing vegetables? Call Dr. Sam Cotner, (409) 845-5341. Want to know what's wrong with your flowers? Call Dr. William Welch at the same number.

The George Bush Presidential Library Center. Take the University Drive exit from T-6 in College Station, turn west, and follow signs. Scheduled to open in the fall of 1997, this $42 million project sits amid 90 acres of oaks and greenbelt on the western edge of the A&M campus. As the nation's tenth (and most computerized) presidential library, it houses all of George Bush's vice-presidential and presidential records as well as memorabilia and personal documents from his public service career as congressman, ambassador to the United Nations, chairman of the Republic National Committee, liaison to China, and director of the Central Intelligence Agency. Unique museum exhibits include a replica of President Bush's Laurel Library at Camp David, precise down to the books on the shelves and paper clips on the desk; a section of the Berlin Wall; a mock-up of the cabin of Air Force One; and a replica of the cockpit of a Navy Avenger, the plane Bush flew as a fighter pilot in World War II.

Museum archives also hold extensive memorabilia from the Gulf War, including a Humvee, an Iraqi missile launcher, and an old wooden door from Kuwait listing in gold the names of all the American service men and women who perished during that conflict. Gifts from heads of state dazzle, yet the human side of George Bush's rich personal life comes via exhibits of his favorite fly rods and a baseball glove worn with he played first base on Yale University's College World Series team. There's also a restored 1947 Studebaker, the same make and model Bush drove to Midland after his graduation from Yale. Fee. Open daily; call for hours and information on changing exhibits. (409) 260-9552.

Horticulture/Forest Sciences Building. On the west campus. Don't miss the art and decorative exhibits at the Benz Gallery of Floral Art, open during weekday business hours. (409) 845-5341.

Memorial Student Center (MSC). Part of the University Center complex. Ask at the Visitor Center in Rudder Tower as to the current locations of the Buck Schiwetz paintings and the Texan Campaign Staffordshire China (circa 1850). Also of interest are the Centennial Wood Carvings in the corridor between the student lounge and the cafeteria (six walnut panels that trace the history of the school from 1876) and assorted art exhibits in the University Center Galleries. For a current schedule of what's showing and where, call (409) 845-8501. Also, don't miss shopping in the student bookstore.

Memorial Student Center Opera and Performing Arts Society. This campus group presents a full professional program every year, ranging from jazz bands to ballet. For current production information call (409) 845-1234.

Nuclear Science Center. Off campus, near the Easterwood Airport. This multimillion-dollar facility houses the largest nuclear reactor on any campus in the Southwest and produces radioactive isotopes for scientific research. Tours Monday–Friday. (409) 845-7553, 845-7551, or 845-7552.

Rudder Tower. At University Center on Joe Routt Boulevard. The Visitor Center in the lobby introduces you to the university with maps, an excellent movie and booklet about the school, and campus guides. Visitor parking (fee) is adjacent to the building. Open Monday–Friday and on football weekends; call for hours, (409) 845-5851.

Sam Houston Sanders Corps of Cadets Center. Built with private funds in 1992 and dedicated to the past, present, and future of the university's famous corps, this outstanding facility exhibits several one-of-a-kind artworks, as well as the Metzger-Sanders Gun Collection (antique and historic firearms). Open Monday–Friday and on football weekends. (409) 862-2862.

Tours also can be arranged through the Cyclotron Institute, (409) 845-1411; the Computing Services Center, (409) 845-4211; and the Veterinary Medicine College, (409) 845-5051.

WHERE TO EAT ON THE A&M CAMPUS

The Creamery. In the Meat Science and Technology Center, adjacent to the Kleberg Building. The best chocolate ice cream in the world is sold here, along with milk, butter, cheese, eggs, and meats produced on the university's farms. Open weekdays. $. (409) 845-5652.

Memorial Student Center. Two choices here: the cafeteria (409-845-1118) and Hullabaloo, a food court on the lower level (409-847-9464). $.

WHERE TO EAT IN THE AREA

Black Forest Inn. On the north side of T-30, 20 miles east of Bryan-College Station toward Huntsville. Robert and Diane Johnson's skill with the classic Continental food of Europe as well as our own fresh Gulf seafood brings devotees from as far away as Austin and Dallas, just for a meal. Everything is fresh and made from scratch with no additives or preservatives, including Diane's own mayonnaise and salad dressings. Reservations are a necessity, particularly weekends or if your party numbers four or more. Open for dinner Wednesday–Saturday. $$–$$$; (CC). (409) 874-2407.

Cafe Eccell. 101 Church Ave., College Station. Housed in what was the old city hall, this classy bistro features California-style food so fresh even the fish have never been frozen. Barbecued chicken pizza is a best seller, along with award-winning desserts such as the fresh strawberry tart. In addition to daily specials, the basic menu changes seasonally, and the wine list is considered one of the best in town. Open for lunch and dinner daily, brunch on Sunday. $-$$; (CC). (409) 846-7908.

Chicken Oil Company. 3600 South College, Bryan. This giant wooden building is filled with antiques and memorabilia, and its hamburgers have been voted the best in town in local polls. Open for lunch and dinner daily. $. (409) 846-3306.

Czech-Tex Barbeque Steakhouse and Bakery. In Snook, ten miles west of College Station via FM-60. No address is necessary for this popular eatery; just look for the biggest building in Snook. Kolache in the bakery and an assortment of Czech food on the menu echo the area's strong ethnic heritage, but the big draws are the generous, handcut steaks. Open Tuesday–Saturday for lunch and dinner. $-$$$; (CC). (409) 272-8501.

Fajita Rita's. 4501 Texas Avenue South, Bryan. Great Tex-Mex and margaritas, served in a bright cantina atmosphere. Open for lunch and dinner daily. $-$$; (CC). (409) 846-3696.

The Grapevine. 201 Live Oak (behind La Quinta Motel on Texas Avenue), College Station. The emphasis of this quiet bistro is on light foods that are tasty and good for you. Chef-owner Patsy Perry does special things with fish and chicken, and she has quite a following for her homemade soups, quiche, cheesecake, and mousse. Cheese and wines also are important here; there's a large selection of the latter by the bottle, and five house and two special-selection wines are available by the glass. Open for lunch and dinner Monday–Saturday. $-$$; (CC). (409) 696-3411.

Panabella's Grand Cafe. 202 S. Bryan, Bryan. Located amid the antiques of Old Bryan Marketplace, this delightful spot adds Continental flair to tearoom standbys such as quiche, sandwiches, and salads. Romantics should reserve for a candlelight Saturday night dinner. Open for lunch Monday–Friday, lunch and dinner Saturday. $-$$$; (CC). (409) 779-2558.

Royers' Cafe. 2500 S. Texas Avenue, College Station. In a major departure drom the hay-bale ambiance of Bud and Karen Royer's first eatery in Round Top, this second venture's cream/black/red interior with its red stars crisply recalls an early Texas store. The food, however, is Round Top squared. Expect the creative Royer touch on numerous versions of pasta as well as a variety of seafood, Black Angus beef, and poultry offerings. Grilled stuffed snapper heads the popularity list, and if you haven't room for a slice of pie, choose one of the ten daily offerings to take home; the Royers mail-order the latter all over the country. Open for lunch and dinner Tuesday–Sunday. $–$$; (CC). (409) 694-8826.

Tom's Bar-B-Que & Steak House. 3610 College Avenue South, Bryan, and 2001 Texas Avenue South, College Station. No question what to order in this longtime local favorite, but the fact that your food comes on butcher paper accompanied by a slab of cheese and a butcher knife (no forks or spoons) may come as a surprise. Open daily for lunch and dinner. $–$$; (CC). (409) 846-4275 in Bryan; (409) 696-2076 in College Station.

Vintage House Trattoria. 4545 Old Reliance Road, Bryan (Messina Hof Wine Cellars). Ever had Spiedini di Manzo? Cotoletta? Involtini di Pollo Gorgonzola? Experience a Sicilian-style meal here, and then top it off with some sips of the winery's gold medal winner, Papa Paulo Port. Also unique here: Port 'n cream ice cream and port wine fudge. Open Wednesday–Sunday for lunch, Friday and Saturday night by reservation for dinner. $–$$; (CC). (409) 778-9463 or (800) 736-9463.

WANDERING THE BACKROADS

From College Station turn west on FM-60 at the University Drive signal and follow the local folks some 15 miles to Snook. The big attractions include fresh sausage from Slovacek's (409) 272-8625, and a chance to chow down at Czech-Tex Barbecue Steakhouse and Bakery (see "Where to Eat" listings for Bryan–College Station).

As an alternative to returning home from Snook through College Station, backtrack only as far as FM-50 and swing south to Independence and Brenham (Trip 6, this sector). Those fine fields you pass north of Independence are part of the Texas A&M Experimental Farms.

If wanderlust really takes over and you want to stretch the two-hour driving limit of this book, continue north on T-6 from Bryan some 45 miles to Calvert. Established in 1868, this nice old town is the unofficial antiques center of Texas. There's a flea market the first Saturday of every month, and you can tour some outstanding vintage homes during the Robertson County Pilgrimage in spring and the Christmas celebration in early December. Calvert's Main Street is a 4-block collection of old brick and iron-front buildings, most of which now house antiques shops that are open Wednesday–Sunday. For information on B&B accommodations in the area, call (800) 290-1213. For information on Calvert call the chamber of commerce, (409) 364-2559, on Tuesday or Friday.

You can return to Houston from Bryan–College Station one of three ways. The first is the simplest—just reverse the route you followed coming up.

The second is more scenic. Follow T-6 south to Navasota and swing east on T-105 toward Conroe. Turn south on FM-1774 for a forest drive through Plantersville and Magnolia before connecting with T-249 south at Pinehurst. *Note:* This route is to be avoided on weekends from October 1 to November 15 because of Renaissance Festival traffic. T-249 South from Pinehurst ultimately intersects I-45 North inside the Houston city limits.

If you feel like exploring further, go east on T-30 to Huntsville (Trip 2, this sector) and then scoot south on I-45 to home.

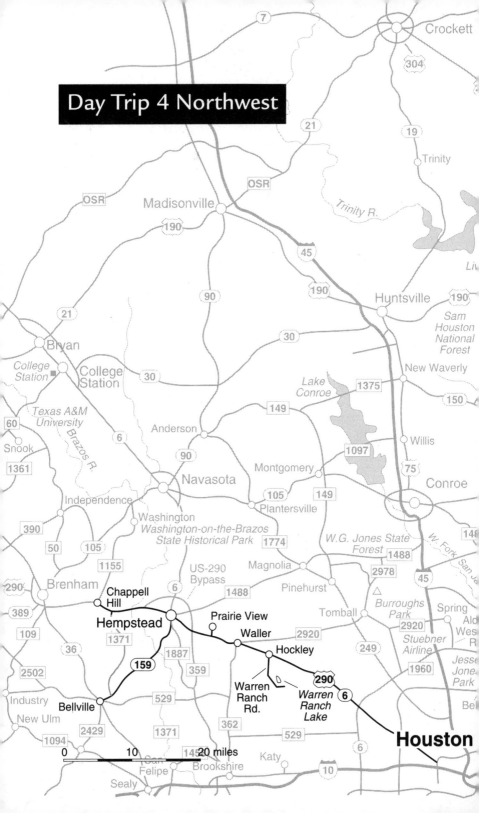

HOCKLEY AND PRAIRIE VIEW

The primary path from Houston into this northwest sector is US-290, rambling its way through Cypress and a lot of interesting country en route to Austin and points west. Hockley is pure country—ranches, the remains of an old general store, and a great fishing hole. Prairie View today is home to Prairie View State University, but just over a century ago it was the site of the Kirby Plantation, known as Alta Vista. Deeded to the state in 1876 for use as a college for black youths, the old mansion was the school's first educational building. It is gone now, along with de facto segregation, but look for St. Francis Episcopal Church, a small frame building (1870) moved to the campus from Hempstead in 1958. The first Episcopal church north of Houston, it still has the original pews, handmade by its first congregation.

WHAT TO DO

Birdwatching at Warren Ranch Lake. In Hockley turn west at the tallest rice dryer and follow Warren Ranch Road 3.4 miles. The lake will be on your left. It is private and a protected refuge, but the viewing (with binoculars) is excellent from the shoulder of the road. The largest winter concentration of ducks and geese in North America is found in the rice fields of this area, and the fifty wild acres of this lake have been known to host as many as 20,000 ducks and geese at one time. With luck you may spot a bald eagle, America's national bird and an endangered species. For information call the Houston Audubon Society at (713) 932-1392.

43

Boys and Girls Country. Thirty miles northwest of Houston on US-290, then right on Roberts Road. This working ranch provides stable, homelike environments for ninety-six youths. During the spring and summer, this facility has a small but neat nursery that sells hanging baskets, herbs, and perennials at excellent prices on weekdays; call ahead if you want to shop at the nursery on a weekend. (281) 351-4976.

Christmas Tree Farms. When it's cutting time, call the following for directions: Christmas Tree Land, (409) 372-2737; H. Foster Christmas Tree Farm, (409) 826-3645; Oil Ranch (see below); Smith Tree Farm, (281) 528-3787; Saint Nicholas Christmas Tree & Fish Farm, (409) 931-3850; and Spitzenberger Farm, (281) 466-9409. Most of the above are south of Hempstead, in the Hockley-Waller area.

Cook's Blueberry Farm. From the signal on US-290 in Hockley, go north approximately 6 miles on Hegar Road (look for sign), then right 1.75 miles on Magnolia Road and left on Murrell Road to the farm. Both blues (June) and blacks (May) are yours for summer picking here. (409) 372-5338.

The Fishin' Hole. 14120 Cypress-Rosehill Road, just north of old US-290. These two fishing lakes are stocked with farm-raised catfish, and the motto is "Catch all you want—Keep all you catch." No license is required, and bait is available. Your catch is weighed and charged at $2.00 per pound live, $2.40 per pound filleted. If it's hot and sunny, bring your own shade. Open Wednesday–Sunday in summer, Friday–Sunday in winter. (CC). (281) 373-0123.

Hockley Sale Barn. On the east side of old US-290 in the heart of Hockley. In spite of "progress" threatening the very rural life-pace of the area, this slice of time-honored Texana just keeps on auctioning horses and tack every Saturday night throughout the year. Much like the Huffman Horse Auction (Day Trip 3, Northeast section), sales of used tack (bridles, blankets, and so on) start at 7:30 P.M., followed by new "equine essentials" and horses every month. Thinking about buying a store bidding. There's no admission fee to the auction—even those who know zip about horses at all are welcome—you'll find a full-service restaurant on site, serving sandwiches, chicken-fried steak, as well as homemade ice cream and cobblers. $; (CC). (281) 379-6503 or (409) 372-9125 (evenings).

MVP (Most Valuable Pilot) Aero Academy. 21904 US-290, Cypress (Weiser Air Park, between Huffmeister and Telge roads). Want to role play or loop-the-loop, Red Baron Style? Wrap a white silk scarf around your neck, put on your leather helmet and goggles, and buy some passenger time in this firm's open cockpit biplane. Available when weather permits (clear skies and above 70 degrees F.), these flights cost $75.00 for a half-hour, $150 for an hour with no extra charge for aerobatics (your option). MVP also offers half-hour discovery flights ($25) in a two-seater Cessna 150, great for anyone thinking of taking up flying. (CC). (281) 469-3009.

Oil Ranch. Twenty miles northwest of Houston via US-290, then turn right on Hegar Road and right on Magnolia Road. Families are welcome to play "cowboy for a day" at this pleasant spread. Activities include pony rides in the corral, swinging on ropes in the hay barn, hayrides through the pastures, paddleboating on a small lake, and exploring a large maze inside Fort George Bush. There are also an Indian village, petting zoo, swimming pools, Christmas Tree Farm, and miniature golf course, and kids can hand-feed the cattle and learn about the cattle industry. Special events include barn dances and free pumpkins around Halloween. Reservations required; groups welcome. Fee. Open all year. (CC). Call for a free brochure and/or reservations. (281) 859-1616.

Skydive Houston. From US-290, turn left on FM-362 (three miles south of Waller) and follow signs. Care to float above the countryside? When weather permits, this company welcomes both neophyte and experienced skydivers. First timers can choose between a tandem dive, static line dive (military style), or accelerated free fall, and more advanced lessons are available. Cost ranges from $149-$270, depending on style of jump. Open Wednesday-Sunday. (CC). (409) 931-1600, (800) JUMP OUT.

Steam trains at Zube Park. From the intersection of US-290 and the Sam Houston Tollway, go north on US-290 for 17 miles, then north on Roberts Road for 1.2 miles; watch for a large gazebo and park on your right. Thanks to a $1 per year annual lease between Harris County and the Houston Area Live Steamers Inc. club, rideable model steam trains now chug along 1250 feet of 7.5 gauge track at this county park. Want to ride? The public is welcome aboard (free) from 10:00 A.M. to 4:00 P.M. on the third Saturday of every month, weather permitting. Each of the coal or oil-fired steam engines pulls three to five cars capable of holding up to three adults. All are scale models of past or existing trains. Club members also operate model steam boats on the park's pond. For information on the steamers club or to confirm that the trains will be operating, call (281) 578-8688.

WHERE TO EAT

The Pecan Tree. 2206 US-290, Waller. Locals love the chicken-fried steak here, with Pecos chili running a close second. These folks pecan-smoke all their own barbecue and whip up their own cobblers from scratch—the pecan cobbler is certainly unusual, possibly unique. Open Monday for breakfast and lunch, Tuesday–Sunday for breakfast, lunch, and dinner. $–$$; (CC). (409) 372-2000.

    Stockman's Restaurant. 2014 US-290, Waller. Where else can you get all-you-can-eat charbroiled steak, this place's Tuesday night special? In addition to a full menu, Thursday's special is charbroiled or deep-fried quail, and Friday's is all the catfish and popcorn shrimp you can handle. There's also a hot-plate lunch daily. Open Monday–Saturday for breakfast, lunch, and dinner, Sunday for breakfast and lunch. $–$$; (CC). (409) 372-2060.

HEMPSTEAD

Resist the opportunity to zip past Hempstead via the US-290 bypass. You'll find a lot of history, some discount shopping, and good eating in this quiet town.

    Given its somewhat sleepy air today, it's hard to believe that Hempstead once was known as Six-Shooter Junction, and that for several decades after the Civil War, it was a wild and woolly place. The rolling land south of town was settled as early as 1821, although only scattered historical markers tell the stories now.

    The town was platted in 1856–57 as the terminus for the Houston and Texas Central Railroad, an early line that tooted over much of Waller County before expanding north to Bryan-College Station. During the Civil War the railroad made Hempstead a major supply and troop depot for Confederate forces, and when the war ended, the defeated men began their long walks home from here.

    Hempstead was the turning point in Texas's battle for independence from Mexico. Sam Houston and his retreating forces camped and regrouped here from March 31 to April 14, 1836, and then began an aggressive march to San Jacinto, site of their ultimate victory over Santa Anna and his Mexican Army. A brief jaunt down FM-1887 today finds a historical marker about the Texian Army camp.

    Hempstead slowly is reawakening to its heritage, but at present all vintage structures remain in private hands and are not open to the

public. A windshield tour of the quiet residential streets on either side of US-290 offers such rewards as Coburn Cottage, 327 Twelfth Street; the Ahrenbeck-Urban Home, 1203 Bellville Highway; and the Houx House, on the corner of US-290/T-6 and New Orleans Street. Another good reason to stop in Hempstead is Dilorio's thriving produce market on US-290 at the southeastern edge of town.

WHAT TO DO

E & B Orchards. From US-290 4 miles northwest of Hempstead, go 4.5 miles north on FM-1736, turn left on Clarke Bottom Road, then go half a mile to the entrance. This 15-acre pick-your-own fruit farm offers peaches, nectarines, apples, Asian pears, plums, and blackberries in season. Open daily during fruit season; ask if pond fishing is available. (409) 826-6303.

Liendo Plantation. From US-290 in Hempstead turn northeast at the FM-1488 signal and then right on Wyatt Chapel Road; the plantation's gate will be 1 mile down on the right. Originally a Spanish land grant of 67,000 acres, Liendo was one of the earliest cotton plantations in Texas, and its large Greek Revival–style home was built by slave labor in 1853. During the Civil War Liendo served as a Union camp for Confederate prisoners directed by George A. Custer, and from 1873 to 1911 it was the home of sculptress Elisabet Ney and her husband, Dr. Edmond Montgomery. Both are buried on the grounds. Now privately owned, this gracious old home has been restored and furnished much as it would have been during its cotton-growing days. Liendo is a Texas Historic Landmark and is on the National Register of Historic Places. Docents give guided tours at specific times on the first Saturday of every month; groups with reservations are welcome at any time. Two wonderful public events, the Liendo Holiday Marketplace (December) and the Old South Festival at Liendo (Spring), show off this handsome and historic home annually. At other times this is a private residence; please do not wander the grounds without an advance appointment. Fee. Call for details. (409) 826-4400.

Liendo's resident owner, Will Detering, also operates Liendo's Restaurant, a charming Texana shop and tearoom in downtown Hempstead, as an extension of the plantation (see below).

Peckerwood Garden. This seven-acre, private experimental garden near Hempstead emphasizes Mexican trees, shrubs, and perennials and their counterparts from Texas, the Southeast U.S., and Asia. Dry land gardens dramatically contrast with lush woodlands and formal topiary. Tours are available by appointment ($60 per hour for one to six persons, $80 per hour for seven to ten persons; two week advance notice required). The nursery is open Thursday–Saturday from February through October; call for directions. The Yucca Do catalogue ($4.00) can be ordered from Yucca Do Nursery @ Peckerwood Gardens, Box 450, Waller, 77484. (409) 826-4580.

WHERE TO EAT

The Hempstead Inn. 435 Tenth Street. (US-290/T-6). This old railroad hotel was built in 1901, 100 yards closer to the train tracks than its present site. It closed in 1968, only to rise to useful life again in 1981. Lunch and dinner are served boardinghouse style, and the simple food is like Grandma used to fix—fresh vegetables from the local markets, fried catfish, pot roast, and so on. Guests help themselves from never-empty bowls, so you can sample or take seconds. Open for lunch and dinner daily. $-$$; (CC). (409) 826-6379.

   Liendo's Restaurant. 306 Tenth Street (US-290/T-6). Delicious and often unusual soups, salads, and sandwiches quickly earned this new eatery a hungry clientele. Expect tasty homemade breads and pastries as well as well as creative entrees at this offshoot of Liendo Plantation. Open Monday–Saturday for lunch, Friday and Saturday for dinner; call to confirm. $-$$; (CC). (409) 826-4400.

WANDERING THE BACKROADS

From Hempstead you have several choices if you wish to journey on. The easiest is to continue on US-290 west to Chappell Hill and do all or part of Day Trip 5, this sector. Or you can swing southwest 16 miles on T-159 to Bellville and pick up Day Trip 5, west sector. If you do the latter, plan a stop midway at the Cochran General Store. Run by Eddy and Sharry Burnham, it's a good place for a cold drink, snacks, and some Texas-style chatting; (409) 865-2544.

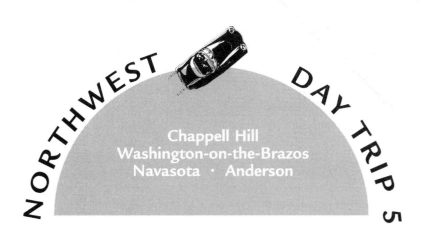

CHAPPELL HILL

From Houston this day trip follows US-290 northwest approximately 60 miles through Hempstead to the intersection of FM-1155. A short jog north takes you to the first stop, Chappell Hill.

This charming village just north of US-290 may seem like the Brigadoon of Texas, so true is it to its time. Settled in 1847 and named for early Texas hunter Robert W. Chappell, Chappell Hill thrived as a stage stop on the Houston-to-Austin/Waco run and became the cultural center of Washington County, the home of two four-year universities. But the fickle tides of progress soon moved on, and visitors today often feel they have stumbled on a quiet place left over from the 1880s.

The universities have long closed, their charters transferred to become the seeds of Southwestern University in Georgetown, Southern Methodist University in Dallas, and the University of Texas Medical Branch in Galveston. But the old Stagecoach Inn is still here, a private home restored to its antique glory, and the Farmer's State Bank, circa 1900, has its original brass teller's cage. *Fun to know:* This was the last bank in the region to register its customers by name instead of magnetic codes and computers.

There's a latchkey library—local folks all have their own keys so they can come and go at will—and more than twenty-five historical medallions are scattered throughout this four-street settlement. Four treasured homes offer B&B accommodations: The Mulberry House (1855), (409) 830-1311; the Stagecoach Inn (1858), (409)

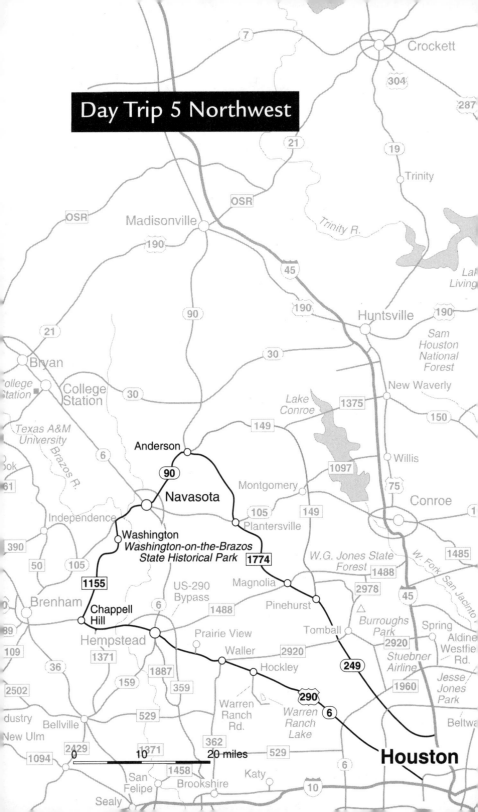

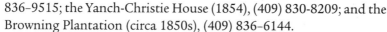

836–9515; the Yanch-Christie House (1854), (409) 830-8209; and the Browning Plantation (circa 1850s), (409) 836–6144.

Buy an ice cream cone at the old drugstore and then take a nostalgic walk through Lesser's Grocery, stocked with kerosene, seed spuds, local sausage, and jams just as it was in great-grandfather's day. Other portions of Main Street and seven additional local sites are on the National Register of Historic Places, and several of them now house antiques shops.

WHERE TO GO

Browning Plantation. One mile south of US–290, off FM–1371. Also listed in the National Register of Historic Places, this three-story wood home was built as the heart of a 2,000-acre plantation in 1856 by Colonel W. W. Browning, a loyal Confederate supporter and one of Chappell Hill's leading citizens. By the early 1980s, however, the house was a teetering ruin surrounded by 170 acres of wild country. Bought and restored in 1983 with love and megabucks by a Houston couple, this 6,000-square-foot house is once again an elegant charmer and filled with antiques. Tours are given by appointment, and four bedrooms are available for classy B&B, as are two bedrooms and two baths in a replica of a Southern Pacific Railroad depot near the swimming pool. Don't miss the "before" photos in the downstairs parlor or the 1.5 miles of model railroad that run around the backyard. Fee. (409) 836–6144 or (713) 661–6761.

Chappell Hill Historical Museum and Methodist Church. On Church Street, 1 long block east of Main. The museum is in the old school and is staffed Wednesday through Saturday and on Sunday afternoons. The church has stained glass windows worth seeing and is open for Sunday services. Donations are appreciated. (409) 836–6033.

Chappell Hill Sausage Co. On westbound side of US–290, 3.5 miles east of Chappell Hill. Six different kinds of sausage are made here, primarily for supermarkets around the state. You can watch the sausage-making process and buy your favorite to take home. Closed Sunday. $. (409) 836–5830.

Old Masonic Cemetery. Turn west at the four-way stop at Main and Chestnut streets in Chappell Hill, then right on the first road for 0.5 mile. At least twenty-four Confederate soldiers are buried here, along with assorted Crocketts and the son and daughter of William Barret Travis. The latter were longtime residents of Chappell Hill. Cemetery lovers also will enjoy the old Atkinson Cemetery, south of town on County Road 87.

Rock Store Museum. East side of Main Street near the bank. The prime display is the town's history, embroidered and appliquéd on two 30-foot cloth panels. Open weekend afternoons or when the local ladies feel like socializing. Donations are appreciated. Special appointments: (409) 836–6033.

Stagecoach Inn. Main and Chestnut streets. This is the public's best look at the past in all of Washington County. Listed in the National Register of Historic Places, this beautiful Greek Revival structure was built in 1850 and was a busy stage stop through the Civil War. Note the Lone Star and 1851 date inscribed on the downspout heads, the detail of the Greek-key frieze on the cornice that encircles the house, and the old-fashioned flower gardens. Groups of four or more can arrange guided tours (fee), and this wonderful old place now is back in the hospitality business as a B&B inn, (409) 836–9515. Through this number you also can arrange tours of other historic homes in the Chappell Hill area. Owner Elizabeth Moore also runs an antiques shop in the historic Weems House behind the old inn.

WHERE TO EAT

Bevers Kitchen. Main Street in Chappell Hill. This combination house, real estate office, and restaurant serves tasty salads and sandwiches, homemade soup and chili, and the best Mexican food in the county. Open for lunch through 3:00 P.M. Monday–Saturday. $–$$; (CC). (409) 836–4178.

Cactus Jack's. At intersection of US–290 and FM–1155 in Chappell Hill. Good Tex-Mex standards in a bright and spacious setting. Open for lunch and dinner daily, but the buffet closes from 2:00–5:00 P.M. $–$$; (CC). (409) 830–0020.

Chappell Hill Restaurant. On eastbound side of US–290 at Chappell Hill (blinking light) intersection. New management has turned what was a forgettable eatery into one of the better country cafes in Texas. BLTs come on bread baked each morning, all veggies served have just been picked from the garden out back, and the fried chicken is better than Mom ever made. The menu also includes shrimp, fish, and steaks. Open breakfast through dinner, Tuesday–Sunday. $. (409) 836–0850. *Nice to* *know:* Floyd's Meat Market next door has outstanding Polish sausage, steaks, and home-cured bacon.

WASHINGTON-ON-THE-BRAZOS

From Chappell Hill continue north 18 miles on FM-1155 to Washington-on-the-Brazos. Early settlers used this same route. This portion of Texas was crossed by countless trails that were the interstate highways of the seventeenth and eighteenth centuries, and numerous historical markers today comment on three major routes. The Old San Antonio Road ran to the Louisiana border and passed to the north of Bryan–College Station. The Coushatta Trail through Grimes County to the north was part of the Contraband Trace, used for smuggling goods from Louisiana into Spanish Texas. A third trail, La Bahia, went from Goliad to the lower Louisiana border, sometimes running in tandem with the Old San Antonio Road.

In 1821 one of Stephen F. Austin's first settlers started a small farm and ferry service where the busy La Bahia Trail forded the Brazos River. In 1835 the settlement was capitalized as the Washington Town Company, lots were auctioned, and the raw beginnings of an organized town began to emerge on the river's west bank. It was to become a pivot point for history.

March of 1836 was a fateful month for Texas. While Santa Anna was devastating the Alamo, fifty-nine men were creating a sovereign nation, the Republic of Texas, at the constitutional convention at Washington-on-the-Brazos. Washington later served twice as the capital of Texas but ultimately lost that honor to Austin. Later bypassed by the railroads, the original settlement faded into obscurity and then literally disappeared after the Civil War. Today, a state park (see below) on the site honors Washington's status as "the birthplace of Texas." A major expansion currently under way will add a second visitor center, interactive exhibits, a restaurant, and a living history farmstead focused on the early Texas frontier.

WHAT TO DO

Antique Co-op. Everything from dolls and quality Texas primitives to general junk is housed in a tin building next to the post office. Open weekends only. (409) 878-2112.

The J.M. Brown Plantation. Built in 1855 and on the National Register of Historic Places, this architectural treasure near Washington-on-the Brazos is now the most elegant antiques shop in the state, open only by appointment on weekends. A venture of R.N. Wakefield and Co. Antiques and Interiors of Houston, this Greek Revival mansion's rooms are filled with 18th and early 19th century English and American formal antiques, all of which is for sale. Serious shoppers should call (713) 528-4677 or (800) 216-3246 for an appointment. Visitors without an appointment will not be admitted.

Live Oak Ranch Family Nudist Resort. Off T-105 in Washington. This pretty, twenty-five-acre facility is dedicated to "the Joy of Natural Living," which means no one wears clothes. All ages are welcome, and first-timers are permitted to remain clothed for a reasonable time until they feel comfortable being in the nude. Facilities include a swimming pool, a hot tub, a water slide, a clubhouse with a big-screen TV, volleyball courts, pool tables, dart machines, and so on. The resort also offers RV hookups, tent campsites, rental cabins, and a full-service restaurant. No overtly sexual behavior is tolerated, and "undue" demonstrations of affection are considered to be in very poor taste. If you've always wondered what it would be like to go skinny-dipping or live without the constraint of clothing, this is the place. After a few tough minutes of wondering where to put your eyes, the scene becomes very natural, almost asexual. Although there are no age limits (families very welcome), those under twenty-one must be accompanied by their parents. A fifteen-minute video ($16.26 including tax and shipping) tells all. Fee; (CC). (409) 878-2216.

Washington-on-the-Brazos State Historical Park. On FM-1155 at the Brazos River in Washington; follow signs. Today only a handful of relatively new buildings mark where the Republic of Texas began in 1836. However, big changes are under way. A $4.3 million legislative grant is expanding this 154-acre park to "living plantation— circa 1830" status. Additional land has been purchased, a restaurant and new visitor's center are planned, and both the Star of the Republic Museum and Anson Jones' historic homeplace, Barrington, will be changing in many ways.

For now visits should start at park headquarters, and do bring a hamper to enjoy the shady picnic grounds along the Brazos River. Considering the planned construction, it would be wise to call ahead to make sure all will be open when you plan to visit. (409) 878-2214.

All of the following are within the park's boundaries.

Barrington. Built in 1844–45 and restored in 1968 and 1971, this was home to Anson Jones, the fourth and last president of the Texas Republic. Guided tours are given daily from March 1 through August; on weekends only from September through February. Fee.

Independence Hall. This simple frame building is a reconstruction of the original structure on this site, in which the signing of the Texas Declaration of Independence took place. Open daily year-round.

Star of the Republic Museum. Start with the video presentation for a good historical perspective, and then take the self-guided tour through displays that include a rare printing press, a collection of frontier medical instruments and medicines, and exhibits on various cultures that shaped the state. The museum also attracts excellent traveling exhibits and is noted for its reference collection of Texana material, including old maps, documents, letters, and rare books. Guided tours can be arranged in advance. Open daily, except major holidays. For more information contact Star of the Republic Museum, P.O. Box 317, Washington 77880, (409) 878–2461.

CONTINUING ON

After exploring Washington, continue north on FM-1155 to the T-105 intersection, and turn right to Navasota.

NAVASOTA

Settlers responding to Stephen F. Austin's advertisements for colonists founded this town in the 1820s. A generation later cotton was king of the plantation economy, thriving here on the rich bottomland of the Brazos River.

The coming of the railroad in the 1850s brought even larger profits, and the wealthy farmers splurged on lavish town homes in Navasota, many of which remain in fine shape today. Some line Washington Avenue (T-105) as it flows through town, and others require short detours onto Johnson, Holland, and Brewer streets. All are private homes, one of which is open to the public as a living history project during Navasota Nostalgia Days the first Saturday of April.

One Victorian mansion (circa 1893), The Castle Inn at 1403 East Washington, welcomes B&B guests and group tours (fee), (409) 825-8051. Another, LaSalle House at 400 East Washington, is an 1897 Queen Anne Victorian that houses an antiques co-op; house tours (fee) are available on weekends, (409) 825-3865. Shoppers will find numerous other antiques shops and malls scattered around town.

Groups of ten or more can tour several other historic structures in and around Navasota by reservation. Information and walking/driving-tour brochures are available from the Grimes County Chamber of Commerce, 117 South LaSalle (P.O. Box 530), Navasota 77868, (409) 825-6600 or (800) 252-6642.

Not too surprisingly, Navasota stood heart and soul with the South during the Civil War, but unpaid Confederate soldiers angrily burned much of the town in 1865. A yellow fever epidemic two years later dealt the final economic blow. Today this quiet community of 7,000 snoozes in the heart of horse farm country, its downtown a National Historic District.

Even fewer traces of the area's Indian and Mexican history survive, and visitors often are startled to find a statue of French explorer La Salle in the center of the main road. It memorializes his death nearby in 1687 at the hands of his own men.

WHAT TO DO

Bank of Navasota. 109 West Washington Avenue. This 1880s building has been restored to its original look and use. Open Monday–Friday and Saturday mornings.

Christmas Tree Farms. After Thanksgiving call Rudolph's Treeland Farm for directions, (409) 825-3052. Amenities include a playground, hayrides, live reindeer, and a lodge with fireplace.

Gibbons Creek Reservoir. On FM-244 in Carlos, approximately 20 miles north of Navasota via T-90. Operated by the Texas Municipal Power Authority, this 2,500-acre lake draws heavy-duty fisherfolk from as far away as Oklahoma and Arkansas. Bass, crappie, catfish, and perch thrive here, stocked by Texas Parks and Wildlife, and while boating and picnicking are allowed, water sports and camping are not. In fact, there's a long list of rules and regulations. Closed Wednesdays and holidays. Fee. (409) 873-2013.

Horlock History Center. 1215 East Washington. Navasota's past is documented in this restored 1892 Victorian house. Open

Friday–Sunday. Fee. (409) 825-7055.

Navasota Livestock Auction Co. Three miles east of Navasota on Highway US-90 (also see Cow Talk Steak House in "Where to Eat" listings). Ranchers from Grimes, Washington, and Brazos counties bring their livestock here for sale, making this auction the state champ in terms of volume and dollars. Visitors are welcome to watch the action, but don't scratch your nose or tug on your ear—you may go home with a live calf as a souvenir. Saturday sales start at 12:30 P.M. (409) 825-6545.

Navasota Theatre Alliance. 104 West Washington. This local theater group uses professional directors and set designers for five or six quality productions by major playwrights each year. Call for schedule. (409) 825-3195.

Navasota Trading Company. 1.5 miles north of Navasota on business T-6. Similar to First Monday at Canton, this 30-acre plot brims with antiques, food, collectibles, crafts and so on the Friday, Saturday, and Sunday preceding the third Monday of every month. Free. (409) 825-8490.

The Wood Factory. 111 Railroad Street. *Victoriana lovers' alert:* This antique millwork business welcomes visitors to its showroom in what was Navasota's old P. A. Smith Hotel. Whether you need any gingerbread trim or not, take a peek; many pieces of their turn-of-the-century equipment are as old as the designs they produce. Open business hours. (409) 825-7233.

WHERE TO EAT

Coffee Cup Cafe. 808 North LaSalle. Locals stash their own mugs at this community gathering place. Good spot to stop if you're hungry for a real country breakfast or lunch; the omelettes are great. Open for breakfast and lunch, Monday–Saturday. $. (409) 825-2208.

Cow Talk Steak House. At the Navasota Livestock Auction Company, 3 miles east of Navasota on US-90. Nothing like going straight to the source for good hamburgers and steaks. Open for lunch Tuesday–Thursday, lunch and dinner Friday and Saturday. $–$$; (CC). (409) 825-6993.

The Golden Palace. 201 North LaSalle. Locals say that this Chinese food is worth the drive from Houston and that the daily lunch buffet is an excellent buy. Open Tuesday–Saturday for lunch and dinner. $–$$; (CC). (409) 825-8488.

Gourmet Delights. 212 East Washington. This full service bakery and lunch shop draws locals with homemade soups, sandwiches, salad bar and delicious desserts. You'll also find gourmet chocolates and coffees as well as a variety of outstanding bakery goods, including turnovers and kolache. Open Monday–Saturday from 8:00 A.M. to 5:00 P.M. $. (409) 825-0416.

Margarita's. 310 East Washington. Tex-Mex in all its unswerving forms is the house specialty. Open for lunch and dinner Monday–Saturday. $. (409) 825-2284.

Must Be Heaven II. 121 East Washington. Shirley Syptac has cloned her successful eatery in Brenham and created this tiny cafe on Navasota's main street. All breads, desserts, and kolache are homemade, and the soups and sandwiches are some of the tastiest in the region. Open Monday–Saturday from 8:00 A.M. to 5:00 P.M. $; (CC). (409) 825-7536.

The Seafood Company. 104 Highway 6 North. Fish fixed all ways, with a good salad bar. Open daily for breakfast, lunch, and dinner. $–$$. (409) 825-7051.

Ruthie's Bar-B-Que Cafe. 905 West Washington. This seemingly undistinguished barbecue place is a Texas classic—six kinds of meat pit-smoked over oak and mesquite. Open Wednesday–Saturday for lunch and dinner. $–$$; (CC). (409) 825-2700.

CONTINUING ON

From Navasota this day trip travels to the tiny town of Anderson, 10 miles northeast via T-90.

ANDERSON

Time stopped here about 1932, and the entire town looks like a stage set for *Bonnie and Clyde*. Fact is, one member of the Barrow gang was tried here in the old courthouse, a tidbit duly noted on the building's historical medallion. But Anderson's history reaches back much farther than the 1930s.

Established in 1834 as a stage stop on the La Bahia Trail, the town became an important assembly point and arms depot during the Civil War. Those days of glory live again during Texian Days in late September, when local folks don period costumes and open their homes to visitors. The entire town—everything you can see from the top of the courthouse—is listed in the National Register of Historic Places. Antiques stores have begun to fill some of the vacant buildings along Main Street, and Sarah's House, (409) 873-2809, now offers B&B accommodations. For information on the town, call Historic Anderson, Inc., (409) 873-2662 or 873-2111.

WHAT TO DO

Baptist Church. Left side of Main Street, 2 blocks south of FM-1774. Built of native rock by slaves in 1855, this handsome church still has regular Sunday services. LBJ's granddaddy once was Anderson's preacher.

Fanthorp Inn. South end of Main Street on the left. One of the first stage stops in Texas and the seed that started the town, this old inn was built in 1834 and led to Anderson's being, for a time, the fourth largest town in Texas. Owned by the Texas Parks and Wildlife Department since 1977, the inn has been restored and returned to a somewhat rumpled 1850s appearance; visitors have a sense that one stage has just departed and another is on its way. A barn of that period has been reconstructed to house a Concord stagecoach (reproduction) as well as exhibits discussing the early stage routes across Texas. Staffed with an interpreter, the inn is open Friday through Sunday for self-guided tours. If you want to tour on Wednesday or Thursday, call ahead; there's usually someone there. Want to ride through the streets of Anderson in a horse-drawn stagecoach? Come for Stagecoach Days on the second Saturday of every month. And for a look at what holiday travel was like in the mid-1800s, don't miss the candlelight festivities on the Saturday of Thanksgiving weekend. *Note:* No overnight or dining facilities are available at the inn. Fee. (409) 873-2633.

Grimes County Courthouse. Top of Main Street. Built in 1894 of hand-molded brick with native limestone trim, this oldie has its original vault. Note the handsome pressed-tin ceilings with rounded cove moldings in the main hall. Open weekday business hours. (409) 873-2111.

Historic Anderson Park. South of the intersection of FM-1774 and T-90. Several architectural relics of Anderson's past are preserved here, including the Steinhagen Log Cabin, built in 1852 by slaves and notable for its walls of unspliced hand-hewn timbers; the Steinhagen Home, with a wing furnished to its 1850s period; and the Boggess Store, filled with turn-of-the-century merchandise. These old buildings can be toured only during special events or by arrangement. (409) 873–2553.

New York Row. Parallels Main Street 1 block east. This lane is where the town swells lived during Anderson's heyday.

WANDERING THE BACKROADS

For those who like country drives, getting home from Anderson via FM–1774 south is pure pleasure. While spring is prime because of the wildflowers, an autumn drive recalls the rolling hills of western Massachusetts. The oaks turn color with the first frost, and Anderson's lone church steeple pokes up through the landscape like a sentinel on a hill.

BRENHAM

If it wasn't a 72-mile commute on US-290 each way, Brenham would be overrun with refugees from Houston. This thriving community of slightly more than 12,000 is close to the ideal American small town— old enough to be interesting but enterprising enough to keep up with the times.

Shaded residential streets still sport a number of antebellum and Victorian homes, and many of the turn-of-the-century buildings downtown are spiffed up and in use. Just blocks away it's open country again—thousands of acres of beautiful farmland. In the spring the bluebonnets and other wildflowers are magnificent, a carpet of color rolling to all horizons.

Founded in 1844 and settled by German immigrants over the ensuing two decades, Brenham was occupied and partially burned by Union troops during the Civil War. Most of the town's surviving history can be seen on a windshield tour, courtesy of a free map and visitor's guide available from the Washington County Chamber of Commerce, 314 South Austin, Brenham 77833, (409) 836-3695 or 1-888-BRENHAM. Call in advance to arrange a guided tour of the downtown historic district. Groups should inquire about tours and use of the Citadel, a former country club (circa 1924) that has been restored to *Great Gatsby* elegance. Highly visible on the westbound side of US-290, it looks like a massive plantation house sitting in the middle of a young vineyard 3 miles east of town.

Should you enjoy Brenham too much to leave, there are a number of B&B establishments in town, among them Ant Street Inn, (409)

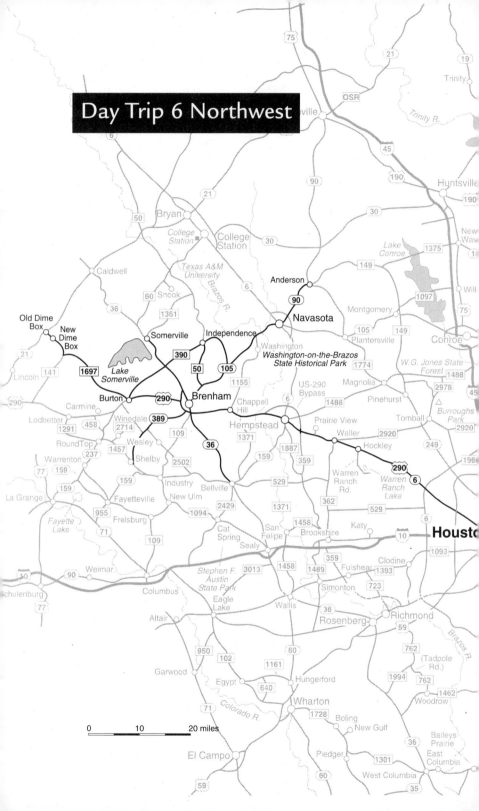

Day Trip 6 Northwest

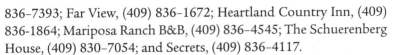

836-7393; Far View, (409) 836-1672; Heartland Country Inn, (409) 836-1864; Mariposa Ranch B&B, (409) 836-4545; The Schuerenberg House, (409) 830-7054; and Secrets, (409) 836-4117.

Nearby Burton (next stop on this day trip) also has B&B accommodations.

WHAT TO DO

Ant Street Historic District. This downtown section of Brenham has been undergoing a colorful renovation for several years and now sports several fresh exteriors. The historic district extends to the old Savitall Market at Commerce and Baylor streets, now handsomely renovated into the Ant Street Inn and Gallery, a fourteen-room B&B hotel similar in quality to the Tremont House in Galveston. If you're planning a big party or wedding, check out the ballroom; that space also is used for frequent antiques auctions. (409) 836-7393.

Bassett & Bassett Banking House. Corner of Market and Main streets. This vintage bank has been freshly restored as part of a Main Street revival program and is open during normal business hours.

Blue Bell Creameries. Loop 577 (Horton Street). Weekday tours and tastings, but call ahead to confirm space. Fee. (409) 836-7977.

Brenham Heritage Museum. 105 South Market. Housed in the refurbished and quite grand Federal Building (1915), this museum offers artifacts and memorabilia dating from 1844, the year Brenham was founded. Displays change monthly, and an 1879 Silsby steam-powered fire engine resides permanently in an exterior showcase, and a train exhibit that depicts Brenham in the early 1900s is under way. Open Wednesday–Saturday; call for hours. Donation. (409) 830-8445.

Christmas Tree Farms. Mockingbird Hill Christmas Tree Farm also offers hayrides as well as B&B. For directions, call (409) 836-5329.

Ellison's Greenhouses. 2107 East Stone, 0.75 mile south of Blue Bell Creameries on Loop 577. Whatever the holiday, celebrate it early by touring this colorful wholesale nursery. Seasonally, some five acres of greenhouses are filled with poinsettias, tulips, Easter lilies, hydrangeas, and much more. Retail trade is welcome, and visitors love the wildflower-motif T-shirts sold in the gift shop. Tours Monday through Thursday only by appointment; drop-ins welcome only on Friday and Saturday. Closed days prior to major holidays. Fee; (CC). (409) 836-0084.

Fireman's Park. 900 block of North Park Street. This shady city park has a fully restored C.W. Parker carousel, manufactured for carnival touring prior to 1913 and one of only a few antique merry-go-rounds remaining in Texas today. Now visible behind protective glass panels, this wonderful antique operates by appointment and whenever Brenham has a civic celebration in the park. (409) 836–3695.

Gerson Artworks. 307 West Alamo. Only the colorblind will have trouble finding artist Alan Gerson's multitoned purple house with its front yard filled with crazy sculpture. Look closely, and you'll see that one of the huge pieces on display began its useful life as a Volkswagen trunk lid. Not sure if you've found the right place? Watch for a fried egg on the front walk and slashes of red and blue neon in the windows. Gerson also sculpted the horses that pull the city's old steam fire engine outside the Brenham Heritage Museum, 105 South Market. Gerson's gallery usually is open daily; call to make sure he'll be there. (409) 836–4935.

Giddings-Stone Mansion. 2203 Century Circle, near South Market and Stone streets. This twelve-room Greek Revival home with its imposing galleries was built in 1869 on a hill in what was then south of town. Now owned by the local Heritage Society, it is being restored as funds become available and is considered by historical architects to be one of the ten most significant old homes in Texas. You may walk around the grounds but not enter the house except during special festivals and events. Group tours by appointment. (409) 836–1690.

Giddings-Wilkin House. 805 Crockett. Built in 1843, this is thought to be the oldest house still standing in Brenham. Now the property of the Heritage Society, it sometimes is open as a museum and can be toured by appointment. (409) 836–1690.

Miniature Horses at the Monastery of St. Clare. Nine miles northeast of Brenham via T-105 and FM-2193 East. The breeding, training, and sale of miniature horses are self-support ventures of this cloistered order, the Franciscan Poor Clares, and three of the nuns are permitted to show the public around this outstanding ninety-eight-acre facility. Although the convent and chapel are open from 2:00 to 4:00 P.M. daily, visitors have a good chance of viewing training on Monday, Wednesday, and Friday. Spring visitors see twenty to thirty foals, each about 18 inches tall, cavorting in fields filled with wildflowers, and there are public shows in May and September. Individuals and families are welcome year-round, bus tours only by advance reservation from mid-March through mid-October.

You'll also find a gift shop and a picnic area here. Fee for guided tours; self-guided tours are free. (409) 836-9652.

Nueces Canyon Ranch Resort and Equestrian Center. 9501 US-290 West, 8 miles west of Brenham. This well-designed horse show and training complex has something going on—cutting horse competitions, hunter/jumper shows, barrel racing, and so on—nearly every weekend. Passersby are welcome to watch the action and walk through the training barns, and there's a pretty area where you can picnic. Groups with advance arrangements can tour this working ranch (fee), which also offers B&B for both humans and horses. (409) 289-5600 or (800) 925-5058.

WHERE TO EAT

Country Inn II. 1000 East Horton, across from the Washington County Fairgrounds on Loop 577. Beef steaks with all the trimmings are the house specialty, generously cut with good ol' boys' hearty appetites in mind. The menu also offers fish, shrimp, and hamburgers. Open for lunch and dinner Monday–Saturday. $–$$; (CC). (409) 836-2396.

The Fluff Top Roll Restaurant. 210 East Alamo. The staff at this gingham-decked cafe bakes fresh yeast rolls daily, and the blue-plate specials are substantial and popular with the downtown Brenham business community. Open for breakfast and lunch Monday–Saturday. $–$$. (409) 836-9441.

Garden Alley. 202 Commerce, inside The Pomegranate shop. Need a coffee fix or snack? This tiny spot serves cappuccino, espresso, latte, etc., along with biscotti, baklava, and a variety of gourmet foods and candies. Open Monday–Saturday, 8:30 A.M. to 5:30 P.M. $; (CC). (409) 836-1199.

Glissman's. 106 West Main. In addition to a 1950s-era soda fountain where you can chow down on homemade soups and sandwiches, you'll also enjoy the authentic 1924 fixtures of this vintage pharmacy. Open Thursday–Tuesday. $. (409) 830-9100.

Manuel's Mexican Restaurant & Taqueria. 409 West Main. While handy with all the standards, this place is well liked locally for its weekday lunch buffet and chicken, pork, and beef fajitas. Open daily for lunch and dinner. $–$$; (CC). (409) 277-9620.

Must Be Heaven Ice Cream and Sweet Shop. 107 West Alamo in downtown Brenham. These folks have a strong local following for their tasty kolaches, pies, and other pastries. There's Blue Bell ice cream, along with homemade soups, salads, sandwiches, and quiche. Open Monday–Saturday for breakfast and lunch (until 5:00 P.M.). $–$$. (409) 830–8536.

Trace Cappuccino Caffe. 101 South Baylor. Whether you fancy home-baked pies, banana nut bread, sandwiches, or 26 varieties of coffee, this gourmet coffee bar and deli has it. Open Monday–Saturday. $. (409) 836–3991.

BURTON

Continue west from Brenham on US–290 to visit the reviving small town of Burton, population 325. One of the few vintage cotton gins in Texas is under restoration here as a National Historic Landmark, and there's an interesting old shoe repair shop next door. Tours of both are available for groups of five or more by appointment Wednesday–Sunday. Donation. For information call (409) 289–2863 or 289–3849. You also can tour these pieces of the past during Burton's Cotton Gin Festival, held annually on the third weekend of April.

Burton also has at least three vintage B&Bs: Long Point Inn, (409) 289–3171; the Knittel Homestead, (409) 289–5102; and the Cottage at Cedar Creek, (409) 278–3770. There's also one B&B in Independence.

WHERE TO EAT

Brazos Belle Restaurant. 600 North Main. Andre Delacroix, a French-born chef at the Four Seasons Hotel in Houston, and his wife, Sandy, serve deliciously untrendy country food with French touches in one of Burton's most venerable buildings. Expect blue-and-white checkered place mats, fresh vegetables, exceptional breads, and a changeable feast of professional-quality art on the walls, most of which is for sale. Open for dinner Friday and Saturday, brunch on Sunday. Reservations suggested. $$. (409) 289–2677.

The Burton Cafe. 12513 Washington Street, on FM–390, behind the post office. Homespun vittles and charm carry the day at this friendly place, considered by many to be one of the best country cafes in the state. The roast beef platters are great, the homemade bread and veggies are locally produced, the pies are made from scratch, and the breakfasts are humongous. Want to know what's going on in the Brenham-Burton neighborhood? Just sit a spell and listen; you'll soon know as much as the locals. Open Monday, Thursday, Friday, and Saturday for breakfast,

lunch, and dinner; Tuesday and Wednesday for breakfast and lunch. $-$$. (409) 289-3849.

CONTINUING ON

From Burton you can complete this day trip by swinging northwest on FM-1697 and FM-141 to Dime Box and some areas of Lake Somerville. Or you can bypass Dime Box and reach Somerville by following FM-390 northeast to its intersection with either FM-1948 (turn north) or T-36 (turn northwest).

An alternative route follows T-105 northeast from Brenham to Navasota (Trip 5, this sector), or you can jog south from Brenham on FM-389 (Trips 4 and 5, west sector).

DIME BOX—OLD AND NEW

The name alone of these two separate communities brings some explorers. Perhaps this explanation will save some time, gasoline, and tempers.

Old Dime Box is on T-21, sort of around the corner a few miles from new Dime Box on FM-141. The only things of visitor interest in both places are the historical plaques explaining that the town name comes from the old custom of leaving dimes in the community mailbox on the Old San Antonio Road (T-21) in return for items brought by rural delivery from Giddings.

If you do explore in and around Dime Box, you can get back on your original day-trip route by following T-21 northwest to Caldwell and then T-36 south to Somerville. Continuing on T-21 northeast from Caldwell brings you to College Station, Trip 3 in this sector.

SOMERVILLE

Who would think that three little creeks could combine to form a 24,000-acre lake? Dammed in the early 1960s as a flood control and water conservation project, Lake Somerville has become a favorite water playground 88 miles northwest of Houston on T-36.

The town itself serves only as a gas and grocery supply depot—the lake is the big attraction. Popular with boaters, this lake offers excellent fishing for largemouth and white bass, white crappie, and channel catfish. Deer and other wildlife abound, particularly on the islands within this relatively shallow lake. Birding is varied enough to warrant a special brochure and field checklist, available free from the Texas Parks and Wildlife Department, Resource Management Section, 4200 Smith School Rd., Austin 78744, (800) 792-1112. Cyclists also should contact Bicycle Country in regard to their Tour of The Other Dimension, a popular off-road night ride conducted in the park every spring. For information, call (409) 542-0964.

Campers, picknickers, boaters, hikers, and equestrians should investigate the following:

Rocky Creek Park, Yegua Creek Park, Overlook Park, and *Big Creek Park,* operated by the U.S. Corps of Engineers, (409) 596-1622 or 596-2383; for campsite reservations 60-90 days in advance, call (800) 284-2267.

Welch Park, operated by the City of Somerville, (409) 596-1122.

Birch Creek Park, (409) 535-7763, and *Nails Creek Park,* (409) 289-2392, operated by the Texas State Park system, (800) 792-1112.

WHERE TO EAT

Magnolia House Restaurant. On the west side of T-36 on the northwestern outskirts of town, opposite the Exxon Station, Somerville. Good to know about after a day on the lake, this spot serves authentic Cajun food because owner Wanda Cantrell learned her kitchen skills back home in Morgan City, Louisiana. Another Louisiana tradition called lagniappe means dinner customers get complimentary dessert if there's any left over from lunch. Come for lunch and you'll be served on one of the many gift plates brought to Wanda by the ladies of Somerville—now that would happen only in Texas. *Tip:* The quarter-pound crawfish étouffée dinners ($5.25, including salad) are huge. Menu also includes standard Texas homestyle food. Open for lunch on Sunday and Monday; lunch and dinner Tuesday–Saturday. $-$$; (CC). (409) 596-1828.

CONTINUING ON

Your day trip continues south on T-36 from Somerville to FM-390. Turn northeast (left) to Independence.

INDEPENDENCE

As far as Washington County is concerned, Independence is where it all started. Originally called Coles' Settlement for its first pioneer, John P. Coles, the town changed its name in 1836 to celebrate Texas's independence from Mexico. Coles was a member of Stephen F. Austin's original 300 families, and his cedar log and frame cabin, built in 1824, stands just east of town at the entrance to Old Baylor Park. The town's interesting cemetery is equally old, about 2 miles north of the park entrance on County Road 60.

When Brenham won election as the county seat by two votes, Independence began a century-long slide into obscurity. Today it is a mecca for Texana lovers because of its old stone church and historic ruins. The second house east of the T-50/FM-390 intersection was the last home (circa 1863) of Mrs. Sam Houston; unfortunately, it currently is closed to the public. A second Houston homesite across from Old Baylor Park has a granite marker. For B&B contact The Captain Tacitus T. Clay House, (409) 836-1916, or Campbell's Country Home, (409) 830-0278.

WHAT TO DO

The Antique Rose Emporium. One-half mile south of the T-390 intersection on T-50. More than 200 varieties of old garden roses, documented to have grown in Texas during its years as a republic, thrive here on the site of the Hairston-McKnight Homestead, settled in the 1840s. The remains of an old stone kitchen (circa 1855) have been restored as the center of a typical cottage garden of those times, a converted barn is now the office and bookstore, and an old corn crib has become a gift shop featuring rose-related items. There's also a selection of native Texas trees, shrubs, vines, wildflower seeds, and other plant species appropriate to our climate and locale. Open daily. A catalog ($3.00) is also available: Route 5, Box 143, Brenham 77833, (409) 836-9051 (weekday catalog sales), (409) 836-5548 (retail).

Independence Baptist Church. At the intersection of FM-50 and FM-390. Organized in 1839, the church's present stone building was finished in 1872 and still hosts services every Sunday. Sam Houston saw the light here and was baptized in nearby Rocky Creek. (409) 836-5117.

Old Baylor Park and Ruins of Old Baylor University. One-half mile west of the church on FM-390. This birth site of Baylor University now is marked only by a few ghostly columns and some old oaks and is a good place to enjoy a picnic. The Coles Cabin has been relocated here and can be toured by appointment, (409) 836-1690, or on weekend afternoons in March and April. Donation.

Texas Baptist Historical Center. Adjacent to the Independence Baptist Church, this museum houses pre-Civil War artifacts as well as old church and family records. Mrs. Sam Houston (Margaret Moffet Lea) and her mother are buried in a somewhat unlovely site across the street. Open Wednesday–Saturday, Sunday afternoon by reservation. Free. (409) 836-5117.

WHERE TO EAT

Independence Kountry Kitchen. On T-50, opposite Antique Rose Emporium. A retirement venture by Houstonians Carl and Lori Crafton, this spiffy place offers a full menu but specializes in rib eyes, sirloins, chicken-fried steak, shrimp, half-pound hamburgers, and catfish. Carl mixes his own seasonings and keeps them secret, having learned his lesson years ago: "I lost a good fishing hole that way." Open Wednesday–Sunday for lunch and dinner. $-$$. (409) 277-0316.

WANDERING THE BACKROADS

Independence is the last stop on this day trip, but you can easily extend your travels. Following FM-390 east brings you to T-105. Turn northeast (left) and you can tour Washington-on-the-Brazos, Navasota, and Anderson (Trip 5, this sector). An alternative is to continue south from Independence on FM-50 to T-105 and Brenham, connecting there either with FM-389 and Trips 4 and 5 in the west sector or with T-36 south to Bellville and home.

WEST HOUSTON

Because this day trip begins with a drive west on I-10, consider stopping on the western outskirts of town for one of the following activities:

WHAT TO DO

Albert Alkek Velodrome. 19008 Saums Road in Cullen Park. Take the Barker-Cypress exit from I-10 and go north 1 mile to the park. Built for the 1986 U.S. Olympic Festival, this is one of only nineteen Olympic-quality velodromes in the country and often the site of the Junior National biking championships. The overall program includes general riding sessions, developmental cycling classes for beginners, races for graduates of that program, and a Friday night racing series open only to USCF-licensed riders. Helmets and track bikes can be rented on site; spectating is free. For a brochure and seasonal schedule, either call the track, (281) 578-0693, or write Alkek Velodrome, Houston Parks & Recreation Department, 18203 Groeschke, Houston 77084.

Flying at West Houston Airport. 18000 Groeschke Road. Take Barker-Cypress exit from I-10 and follow the airport signs north to Groeschke Road. You too can discover the wonder of flying in a two- or four-seat Cessna; discovery flights (thirty minutes) are $30 and $42, respectively, in these high-winged planes. Sightseeing and photography flights also can be reserved, starting at $90 per hour in the four-seater. Reservations required. (281) 492-2130.

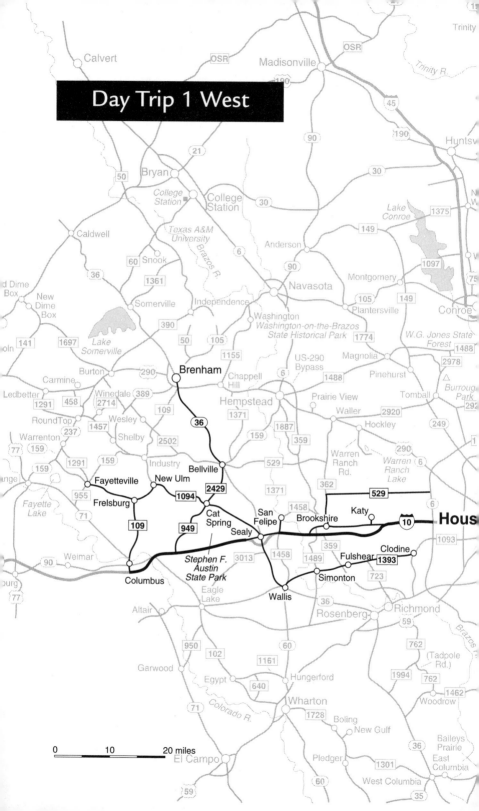

Hot Air Ballooning. Several companies will take you silently floating over Houston for sixty to ninety minutes in a three-person basket suspended below a giant hot air balloon. Most liftoffs are at sunrise to take advantage of the still air, and costs are in the range of $200–$300 per couple, including champagne at the end of the trip. Get the particulars from Above It All Balloons, (281) 341-5550; Adventure Ballooning, (713) 774-2359; Better Way to Fly, (281) 493-2048; Pretty Balloons Unlimited, (713) 463-0080; or Soaring Adventures, (800) 762-7464.

CONTINUING ON

To continue this day trip, take I-10 West to the Katy exit.

KATY

Founded as a rice and railroad town, Katy now is of interest to day trippers primarily as a great spot to eat, play, shop, and experience China. You'll find a smattering of gift and antiques shop in "Old Towne" and several places to picnic. It's also a good food stop Tuesday through Saturday if you're returning to Houston on I-10 from points west.

WHAT TO DO

Forbidden Gardens. 23500 Franz Road, Katy. From Houston, take the Grand Parkway exit from I-10, turn north, then west on Franz road; watch for orange pagoda roofs. A day trip destination in itself, this handsome, 80-acre open air museum authentically replicates major scenes from China's history, starting in the Third Century, BC. Handmade in China by gifted artisans who then installed their work on the Katy prairie, the exhibits include a huge and intricate scale model of Beijing's Forbidden City; detailed models of Chinese palaces; a half-scale reproduction of the entire 6,000 piece terra-cotta army (no two soldiers are alike) found in burial pits of China's first emperor; and replicas of the weapons used by that first emperor to conquer and meld several warring states into one empire. Future exhibits will include a scale model of the Great Wall of China and a reproduction of the beautiful city of Quilin, complete with canals and river boats for visitor enjoyment. Also under way is a 100-foot-long model of Su Zhou, a city known as the Venice of China, detailed with various types of houses, shops and temples as well as miniature figures of people going about their daily routines. Hourly guided tours are included in admission fee ($10 per adult, $5 for students and seniors, five and under free); Parking is free; no credit cards. Open Wednesday–Sunday, 10:00 A.M.–dusk, weather permitting (call ahead to confirm times). (281) 347–8000.

Katy VFW Veterans Memorial Museum and Community Park. George Bush Drive and Avenue D. This oak-shaded retreat offers picnic tables, a small playground, and indoor exhibits focused on America's participation in foreign wars. Park is open daily; museum is open Saturday and Sunday, noon to 5:00 P.M. (281) 391–8387.

Mary Jo Peckham Park and Katy City Park. Franz Road and Avenue D. These blended play spaces offer miniature golf, playgrounds, picnic areas, a caboose and the old Katy Railroad depot; a lake is under construction. Open daily. (281) 496–2177.

Waterfowl Hunting Trips. For guided hunts on the Katy and Eagle Lake prairies, call (281) 392–8999 or 391–6100.

WHERE TO EAT

Jill's. 5800 Fifth Street. Starting with a vintage house (a historic plaque out front tells all), this pleasant eatery has expanded to include a banquet hall, party caboose, and a patio shaded by five huge oaks planted in 1904. The extensive menu ranges from Cajun offerings to steaks and seafood, the latter truly the specialty of the house. Open Monday for lunch only; Tuesday through Saturday for lunch and dinner. $-$$; (CC). (281) 391–1442.

John & Ann's Pie Shoppe. 5608 Fifth Street. Need a box lunch to eat here or to go? For $6.50 you get a great sandwich, chips, drink, and a slice of their super homemade pie. This tiny spot also makes a special quiche on Thursdays as well as fruit, cream, and specialty pies to order. Prefer sugar-free? Just let them know. Open Tuesday–Saturday, 10:00 A.M. to 5:00 P.M. $-$$. (281) 391–8088.

BROOKSHIRE

Brookshire's history is brief. This small community was established in the early 1880s by the MKT Railroad to serve a rich agricultural area. Its ethnic past ranges from Polish to German, Greek to Czech, Swiss to Armenian. The Waller County Festival is an energetic melding of these cultures every October.

WHAT TO DO

Blue Barn Fun Farm. On FM-1458 near Pattison, approximately 0.75 mile west of FM-359. This ten-acre country learning experience is run with loving care by longtime farmers Clyde and Maudine Brubaker to educate children about country life. Following a basic program set up with the assistance of Texas A&M, the pint-size visitors learn how to milk a cow and get to try the hands-on method themselves. They also pet calves, baby chicks, and a soft shell turtle; jig for crawfish; and get up close to doves, bullfrogs, pigs, deer, geese, ducks, quail, golden pheasants, bobwhite quail, guinea hens, ring-necked pheasants, rabbits, goats, chickens, and turkeys. A small plastic horse is used to teach children how to mount and rope. A tractor-drawn hayride then hauls everyone to a picnic area shaded by 200 oaks, so pack a hamper when you come; cold drinks are sold on premises. July visitors are given free watermelon, August visitors get stone-ground cornmeal and a recipe for corn bread, October and November visitors receive free pumpkins, and December visitors go home with candy canes. Cost is $5.00 per person in groups of twenty or more; $6.00 per person (including children) for individuals. Open daily October to December 15 and March through August. Absolutely no admittance without advance reservations. (281) 375-6669.

The Brookwood Community. 1752 FM-1489, in rural Brookshire, 1 mile south of I-10 (signs). This handsome, 475-acre country facility is a privately funded, self-supporting community for functionally disabled adults (mentally and/or physically handicapped), aided in part by a volunteer staff largely made up of retirees. Institutional gloom is not found here, however. Brookwood looks like a country club, feels like the home most people only dream about, and functions like a successful company. Last year the 112 persons in the program produced $1,300,000 worth of horticultural and/or crafts products. Their bedding and potted plants, trees, and art are sold not only on the premises but also through Brookwood's five retail outlets in Houston. Tours are given the first Wednesday of every month or by appointment; call in advance in either case; (281) 375-2100. Visitors can purchase Brookwood's original ceramics, garden sculptures, silk-screened notes and cards, plants, and trees at the Garden Center, open Monday–Saturday 9:00 A.M. to 4:30 P.M.; Sunday noon to 4:30 P.M. (281) 375-2149.

Lilypons Water Gardens. Just south of I-10 on FM-1489. Where else in Houston can you find acres of exotic goldfish amid blooming lotus and water lilies? The shop sells everything needed to create your own water garden, but visitors are welcome to just browse among the twenty-five production ponds out back. These folks also publish a large color catalog (fee) and even mail goldfish. Open daily in summer, Monday–Saturday in winter. (CC). (281) 391-0076.

The Waller County Historical Museum. 4026 Fifth Street, at Cooper. Built in 1910, this nice old home houses period furnishings, historical artifacts and documents, and some interesting vintage photos. Free, but donations are welcome. Open Wednesday, Friday, and Saturday; call for hours. (281) 934-2826.

WHERE TO EAT

The Cotton Gin. 907 Bains Street, at the intersection of US-90 and FM-359. Fine food is reason enough to come to this restaurant, but the building itself also rates a look. Built in 1936, this cotton gin hummed with activity for a decade before closing down in 1946 due to a decline in area cotton production. Much of the equipment had come from an earlier Brookshire gin built in the 1920s. Today that old equipment is part of the restaurant's authentic decor. Expect outstanding steaks, seafood, and chicken entrees. Open Tuesday–Friday for lunch, Tuesday–Saturday for dinner, and there's an extensive Sunday buffet noon to 8:00 P.M. Call to confirm hours of operation. $-$$; (CC). (281) 375-5841.

WANDERING THE BACKROADS

If you are coming from the FM-1960/T-6 area of Houston and prefer backroads, swing west on FM-529 and then south on FM-362 to Brookshire. Going home, just reverse those directions to miss the traffic crunch on T-6 near Bear Creek.

If you love country drives, save some time for wandering south of I-10 on FM-1489. This is horse and cotton-growing country, and the ranches and farms are beautiful. The road passes through the small communities of Simonton, Wallis, and East Bernard, an excellent route into the southwestern section of this book.

CONTINUING ON

To find San Felipe, either drive west from Brookshire on I-10 for 8 miles and watch for the exit signs to Stephen F. Austin State Park, or follow the country route via FM-359 northwest to Pattison and then west on FM-1458. The latter is a great country ramble along the route of the pioneers.

SAN FELIPE

Alas, how fleeting is fame. From 1823 to 1836 San Felipe collected enough "firsts" to secure its niche in Texas history. Then known as San Felipe de Austin, it was the original settlement and capital of Stephen F. Austin's first colony. It also was the site of the first Anglo newspaper and postal system in the territory and the founding spot of the Texas Rangers. The town was burned in 1836 to prevent its use by the advancing Mexican Army. Although rebuilt later in that decade, San Felipe never regained its earlier momentum.

In addition to visiting the oldest post office in Texas, visitors today find some pieces of San Felipe's past in and around the state park. Stop first at the small historical park where FM-1458 crosses the Brazos and search for the still visible traces of wagon ruts that lead to the old ferry crossing. A dog-trot log cabin replicates Austin's headquarters, and the J. J. Josey Store, built in 1847, has been restored as a museum; unfortunately, neither is open very often. Bring a lunch; there's a shady picnic ground along the river on the other side of the road.

Stephen F. Austin State Park is nearby and open daily, year-round; watch for Park Road 38 turnoff from FM-1458. This park offers an outstanding eighteen-hole golf course, as well as picnicking, camping, swimming, fishing, and numerous other family activities. As an oak-shaded retreat, it's wonderful on warm weather weekends. Fee. (409) 885-3613 or (800) 792-1112.

WHAT TO DO

Willow River Farms. Take exit 723 from I-10, go north 2.7 miles on FM-1458; after crossing the Brazos River, turn left on FM-3318 and go 2 miles to the farm. This 310-acre farm is home to sixty mentally retarded adults who contribute to their keep by producing herbs, ceramics, handmade papers, woven goods, produce in season, potted plants, and hanging baskets. Their products are for sale at the community hall near the front gates. Visitors are welcome weekdays from 9:00 A.M. to 4:30 P.M.; on weekends by appointment. (409) 885-4121.

CONTINUING ON

After enjoying San Felipe and the park, resist the temptation to take backroads to Sealy; the route that forks to the right immediately outside the park gate is frustrating and nonscenic. Instead, return to I-10 and continue west to the Sealy exit.

SEALY

San Felipe sold a portion of its original 22,000-acre township to the Gulf, Colorado, and Santa Fe Railroad in the 1870s to create the town of Sealy in 1879. That town now bills itself as the "Best Little Hometown in Texas" and collects a few more refugee Houstonians every month.

Is there any connection with the Sealy mattress? Yes, indeed. A Sealy businessman named Haynes made the first tufted mattress early in this century, and folks referred to it as "that mattress from Sealy." Haynes later sold the patent and the name, but his factory with its original equipment is still intact, awaiting an "angel" to finance its refurbishment as a museum sometime in the future.

Visitors enjoy a drive down Sealy's oak-shaded Fifth Street with its turn-of-the-century homes and a walk around the downtown sector, which is being restored to its original appearance. There are numerous antiques shops, most of which have free walking maps of the town.

For information on Sealy, San Felipe, or Frydek, contact the Sealy Chamber of Commerce, 311 Fowlkes Street, Sealy 77474, (409) 885-3222.

WHAT TO DO

Christmas Tree Farms. Call the Hilltop Christmas Tree Farm, (409) 865-3049, for directions.

Port City Stockyards. North of Sealy on T-36. This is one of the largest cattle auction operations in America, and visitors are welcome. Hogs are auctioned on Monday mornings and cattle on Wednesday mornings, year-round. (409) 885-3526.

Santa Fe Park Museum. On Main Street. Artifacts from the early days of Sealy and Austin County are shown in this museum. Just look for the small tin building with bright flowers, a flagpole, and a grader in the front yard. Open by appointment. (409) 885-3571 or 885-3222.

Sealy Outlet Center. On I-10. Westbound, take exit 721; eastbound, take exit 723. More than 30 stores offer direct-from-manufacturer savings at this mall, a sister to the outlet mall in Conroe. Most are names you know: Spiegel, Jones New York, Mikasa, Van Heusen, Florsheim, and so on. Discount coupons for groups. Open daily; call for seasonal hours. (409) 885-3200.

WHERE TO EAT

The Front Porch. 101 Fifth Street. If you want a light lunch—salads, sandwiches, and/or soups—while enjoying Sealy, this is the place. Ask about the daily specials. Open weekdays for lunch. $. (409) 885-4998.

The Sportsman's Restaurant. 615 Highway 90 West. A clone of the very successful Sportsman's Restaurant in Eagle Lake, this cafe has already been voted one of the best hometown restaurants in the state. In addition to a full menu, there's an all-you-can-eat seafood buffet on Friday and Saturday night ($13.95), and a Mexican buffet ($7.99) on Wednesday night. Open daily for lunch and dinner, breakfast on weekends. $-$$; (CC). (409) 885-6665.

Tony's Restaurant. 1629 Meyer (T-36). Breakfast anytime, and a full menu and noon buffet make this a popular eatery. Open daily for breakfast, lunch, and dinner. $-$$; (CC). (409) 885-4140.

CAT SPRING

When the wildflowers bloom in late March and early April, this tidy crossroads community looks like a calendar picture. From Sealy take FM-1094 north toward New Ulm. Just past the intersection with FM-949 (to Columbus), watch for an unusual twelve-sided building on a rise to your right. This is the Cat Spring Agricultural Society Hall, built in 1902 and still the heart of community activities.

The Cat Spring Agricultural Society was founded in 1856 and is considered the forerunner of today's Texas Agricultural Extension Service. Early German and Czech farmers pooled their knowledge through this society, keeping explicit planting and production records of their small cotton and grain farms in a central book. All entries were written in German until America entered World War I; the practice was then deemed unwise, and all records thereafter were written in English. They are still used as a reference by local farmers.

If you want to use Cat Spring as a touring base, consider overnighting at Southwind Bed and Breakfast, (409) 992-3270. This also is a working spread for registered Texas Longhorns and Arabian horses. If you have a horse and would love some country riding, bring it with you; Southwind has an old restored barn with twelve stalls. Other pets are also welcome, as are day visitors who call ahead for an appointment.

WHAT TO DO

Austin County Vineyards. On FM-1094, one-half mile west of FM-949. This commercial vineyard sells grapes only to wineries—sorry, no tasting!—but Jerry and Cozette Watson also have two acres of high bush blueberries available on a pick-your-own basis on weekends during June and early July. You'll pay $1.25 per pound, and they provide the buckets. There's also a picnic area, as well as local honey for sale. Call ahead to be sure they are open. (409) 992-3748.

Rancho Texcelente. This 250-acre working ranch holds open house on Saturdays for visitors interested in Paso Fino horses (appointments preferred). They love to show off their beautiful stock and even offer riding lessons ($30 per hour) to those who would like to saddle up for a guided trail ride. Also here: stock tank fishing and bed and breakfast accommodations for those who want to experience ranch life. Call for directions. (409) 865-3975.

WHERE TO EAT

Cross Roads Tavern. At the corner of FM-949 and FM-1094. This gasoline station also sells hamburgers at lunch daily and puts on super, all-you-can-eat catfish frys on Friday nights. $. (409) 357-4808. **Whistle Stop Cafe.** On FM-949, one mile south of FM-1094 in Cat Spring. Like German potato salad? Bratwurst? Schnitzel? Marinated steaks? All are on the menu here along with hamburgers, chicken, sandwiches, homemade pies, malts, and shakes. Open for lunch and dinner (closed from 2:00-5:00 P.M.) Wednesday–Saturday; from 11 A.M.–3 P.M. on Sunday $-$$. (409) 865-0461.

WANDERING THE BACKROADS

From Cat Spring you have several choices. A turn southwest on FM-949 at its intersection with FM-1094 will scoot you through pretty country to I-10. A turn west then takes you to Columbus (Trip 3, this sector); a turn east returns you to Houston.

An alternative route takes you northwest to New Ulm on FM-1094 (Trip 3, this sector) and then southwest into Frelsburg via FM-109. From Frelsburg you can either continue south on FM-109 to Columbus or go northwest on FM-1291 to Fayetteville (Trip 4, this sector).

If you haven't yet explored to the north, consider taking FM-949 and FM-2429 from Cat Spring northeast to Bellville (Trip 5, this sector). Continue north on T-36 to Brenham (Trip 6, northwest sector).

The area around Cat Spring is threaded with small country roads, and rambling is a joy. Be sure, however, that you have a good state highway map in hand if you care where you end up.

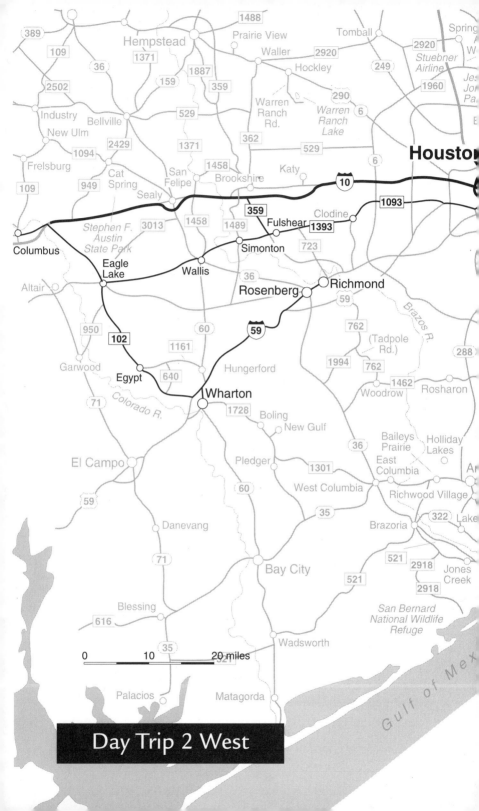

Day Trip 2 West

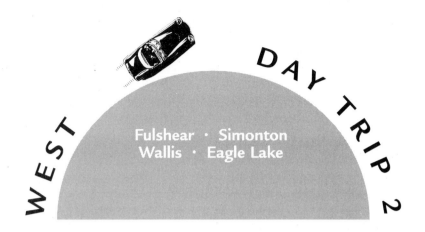

FULSHEAR

This day trip via I-10 West is ideal if you enjoy beautiful country, rodeo, good hunting, and meat—not necessarily in that order. The first stop is the crossroads town of Fulshear, and you have a choice of two routes. From I-10 West take FM-359 South about 7 miles, or from west Houston you can continue out Westheimer to Fulshear and turn right at the blinking light that marks the FM-359 intersection.

Folks generally come to Fulshear for one reason—good barbecue at Dozier's, 8222 FM-359. You can buy it either by the pound or as a sandwich to go, and the help will be glad to take you out back and show you how Dozier's makes sausage and smokes its meats; house specialties include pecan-smoked turkeys, peppered hams, and venison. Lest you should think this place is just another BBQ joint, be aware that it sells more than 3,000 pounds of brisket, 300 pounds of sausage, and 500 pounds of pork ribs every week. Closed Monday. $-$$; (CC). (281) 346-1411.

WHERE TO EAT

Moore's Double Horn Grill. 8506 FM-1093. This clean spot is ideal for a quick hamburger, sandwich, shrimp basket, or similar type of meal. There's even a special menu for children. In addition to indoor seating and a drive-thru, you'll find picnic tables on the pleasant front deck. Open lunch and dinner, Monday–Saturday. $; (CC). (281) 346-2544.

The Shade Tree Country Restaurant. 11511 FM-1464, Clodine. From T-6 take Westheimer 3.6 miles, then left 4.5 miles on FM-1464. This candy shop and restaurant serves up authentic East Coast-style crab cakes, along with "heavy beef" steaks. In the mood for Mexican? The enchiladas are made from scratch. Do you love vegetables? You'll munch on ten different kinds in the giant "Shade Tree" salad. There's always a good variety of entrees on the menu as well. No smoking, except when you're lucky enough to sit under the shade trees out back. Open for lunch and dinner Wednesday–Sunday. $–$$; (CC). (281) 277-1331.

CONTINUING ON

From Fulshear continue west on FM-1093 5 miles to Simonton. From I-10 west take the FM-1489 exit in Brookshire south for 10 miles to Simonton.

SIMONTON

For years Simonton's big (and only) draw was the Roundup Rodeo, held every Saturday night year-round. Any young buck with the entry money in his jeans could compete in anything from bareback riding and barrel racing to roping and bulldogging, and some C&W boot-scooting to polish off the evening. Unfortunately this classic slice of redneck Texas life was fading into the sunset at last inquiry. If you're headed this way on a Saturday, call to see if the rodeo is again loading up its chutes; (281) 346-1534.

WALLIS

Known as Bovine Bend when first settled in 1859, this richly fertile area blossomed when the railroad arrived in 1879. Visitors today enjoy Wallis for its numerous antiques shops and old-time atmosphere while traveling from Simonton to Eagle Lake on FM-1093.

WHERE TO EAT

Cliff's Country Kitchen. 6535 Commerce (T-36). Homemade chili and chicken soup are the big draws here, along with hamburgers and sandwiches. Open for lunch and early dinner (until 6:00 P.M.) daily except Wednesday. $. (409) 478-6193.

EAGLE LAKE

Continuing west from Simonton on FM-1093 about 27 miles brings you to Eagle Lake. As to how this community got its name, you can go Gothic or plain vanilla. The Gothic version says that a Karankawa Indian maiden named Prairie Flower had two suitors, Light Foot and Leap High. Unable to decide between them, she challenged them to bring down a young eaglet from a nest in a cottonwood by a natural lake. Light Foot did and won the fair maiden's hand, whereupon poor Leap High decamped in high dudgeon to the nearby Colorado River.

The less romantic tale is that two of Austin's first settlers shot an eagle on the shores of this lake in 1823, and it was thereafter known as Eagle Lake. Whatever, the lake still is the main feature of this small town. Unfortunately, it is mostly private, and only hunters on guided trips can see or use it.

The Eagle Lake community actually was settled in 1851, and today it thrives as the "Goose Hunting Capital of the World." Day-trippers can arrange hunts through a number of guides; a list is available from the Eagle Lake Chamber of Commerce, P.O. Box 216, Eagle Lake 77434, (409) 234-2780. That mailing address translates to the old train depot next to the Prairie Edge Museum (see below) if you already are in town (open weekdays only). This also is wonderful wildflower territory in the spring; contact the chamber of commerce for maps to the best-color areas. Ask also about the progress of the proposed public birding trail along the shores of Eagle Lake.

WHAT TO DO

Attwater Prairie Chicken National Wildlife Refuge. Six miles northeast of Eagle Lake on the west side of FM-3013. A refuge for many species of birds, this 8,000-acre preserve also is the happy "booming" grounds for the nearly extinct Attwater prairie chicken. Best time to go is during the booming season, mid-February through April, although rangers may restrict public access to protect the birds. Each male prairie chicken has his own domain and protects it with a war dance. Day visitors can drive 5 miles of road through the prairie preserve, and there are two walking trails; binoculars are highly desirable. The refuge also has a high resident bird population and harbors migratory flocks in winter as well. More than 250 species of flowering plants have been recorded here, making a spring visit exceptional. Open year-round with some picnic facilities, but please call in advance for advice. P.O. Box 519, Eagle Lake 77434. (409) 234–3021.

Blue Goose Hunting Club. For directions see Blue Goose Restaurant, in "Where to Eat" section. From November through mid-February, owner John Fields offers outstanding day hunts on private lands stretching from Richmond to Victoria and year-round clay shooting at his own range near Eagle Lake.

Fishing. There is some good fishing in assorted gravel pits around Eagle Lake, but most are on private property and hard to find. Permits to fish in one of the largest pits are available Monday through Saturday at Johnny's Sport Shop, 101 Booth Drive, Eagle Lake 77434, (409) 234–3516. Overnight guests at Riverlake Farms outside of town can fish for bass, perch, and catfish in two lakes, (409) 234–2492 or (281) 589–0562.

Prairie Edge Museum. 408 East Main. Many antiques and mementos having to do with the development of Colorado County are housed in the spacious quarters of an old motorcar company. Check out the 1924 Star, a four-cylinder Continental automobile in nearly mint condition, and the stuffed remains of a state-record alligator, 13 feet, 8 inches long and 900 pounds. If you want to know what's going on in town, this is a good place to ask. Open Saturday– Sunday afternoons or by appointment. Donation. (409) 234–7442 or 234–2662.

WHERE TO EAT

Blue Goose Restaurant. At the intersection of T–71 and alternate US–90, 8 miles west of Eagle Lake. Expect outstanding game dinners in this restaurant, as well as a varied menu that may include beef, frog legs, and soft shell crab in season. Open for lunch and dinner daily during hunting season, for dinner only on Friday and Saturday the rest of the year. $$–$$$; (CC). (409) 234-3597. *Bonus here:* The dining room's large dioramas are filled with a rich variety of beautiful trophy birds, all locally caught.

The Farris 1912. 201 North McCarty at Post Office Street. Constructed as the Hotel Dallas in 1912, this building flourished until the Great Depression and then floundered into disrepair and virtual abandonment. Thanks to the restoration efforts of Bill and Helyn Farris, who bought it in 1974, and current owner Phil Ramsey, that former flophouse now is a pleasant hotel and restaurant catering primarily to hunters as well as company seminars, weddings, retreats, and so on. Stop in for a look, even if you can't stay. All-you-can-eat breakfast, lunch, and dinner are served daily during goose hunting season (November, December, and January). $–$$$; (CC). From February through October the hotel's antiques and gift shop remains open weekdays, but meals are served only to tour groups, clubs, and private parties. *Nice to know:* There is no tipping at either the restaurant or the hotel. (409) 234-2546.

The Sportsman's Restaurant. 201 Boothe (US–90–A). Don't be put off by the mountain lion in the entry—he's an import from Laredo. The rest of the trophy menagerie is local stuff. This busy place has the atmosphere of a hunting lodge and the menu of a cafeteria, offering more than sixty items ranging from steaks to Mexican and Cajun. Open for breakfast and lunch daily, dinner also on Friday and Saturday. Days and hours of operation change seasonally; call for specifics. $–$$; (CC). (409) 234-3071.

WANDERING THE BACKROADS

From Eagle Lake you can return to Houston by reversing your entry route: FM–1093 east to home. *Alternatives:* Take FM–102 north to I-10 and jog west a few miles to Columbus (Trip 3, this sector), or take FM–102 south to Wharton (Trip 1, southwest sector) and turn north on US–59 to Richmond-Rosenberg (Trip 2, southwest sector).

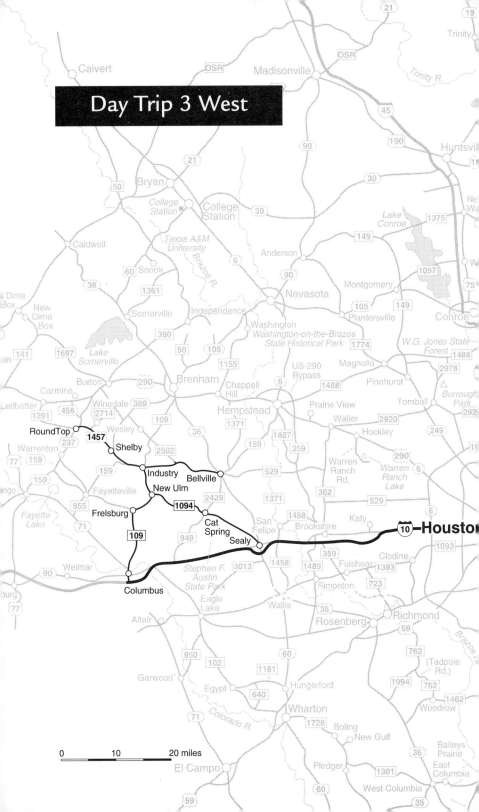

COLUMBUS

Some 56 miles west of Houston's city limits via I-10, Columbus is in one of the oldest inhabited areas of the state. The early Spanish maps of Texas marked this as a sizable Indian village known as Montezuma, and Stephen F. Austin's first colonists called it Beason's Ferry. Today, as Columbus (population 4,800), it is one of the prettiest and most historic towns in Texas. As you stroll through the shady town square, it's hard to believe that the busy interstate zips by less than 1 mile to the south.

Back in 1823 Stephen F. Austin brought a survey party to this fertile land looped by the Colorado River, thinking it would make a fine headquarters and capital for his first settlement. The river was deep enough for commerce, and the busy Atascosito Trail crossed the river nearby. But this was Karankawa country—the Karankawas were a fierce Indian tribe labeled by history as cannibals—and the threat made San Felipe a better choice.

Some of Austin's colony did settle here, however, and a tiny village named Columbus was laid out in 1835. Its life was brief. In March 1836 General Sam Houston and his Texian forces retreated from Gonzales and camped in Columbus on the east bank of the Colorado River. The pursuing Mexican Army settled in on the west bank, where it soon was reinforced by additional troops.

Knowing his position was weak and that an attack on the Mexicans would be suicide for both his men and the cause of Texas independence, Houston elected to retreat farther. Moving on to Hempstead (Trip 4, northwest sector), he ordered all the buildings in

89

and around Columbus burned so that they would be of no use to the Mexicans. Caught in the middle, the local residents fled east to safety, a migration termed by history as the "Runaway Scrape."

Houston's strategy was vindicated by his victory over Santa Anna and the Mexican Army at San Jacinto the following month, and slowly Columbus began to build again. Today it is a delightful small town full of live oak and magnolia trees; if you're into superlatives, drive by the massive oak at 1218 Walnut, the second largest in the state. Thanks to large natural deposits of sand and gravel, Columbus literally is where Houston comes from—approximately 90 percent of the aggregate used to construct Houston's skyscrapers was excavated nearby.

The town's mainstay always has been the river on its doorstep. Early settlers floated their construction lumber downstream from pine forests near Bastrop, and by the middle nineteenth century paddlewheelers were making regular runs between Columbus, Austin, and Matagorda. Dressed up with names like *Moccasin Belle, Flying Jenny,* and *Kate Ward,* these flat-bottom boats also carried cotton from large plantations south of town to the shipping docks at Matagorda Bay (Trip 1, southwest sector).

Today the river still figures in the town's life but with a lighter touch. Columbus children grow up "floating around the bend," and local high school seniors traditionally celebrate graduation with all-night float trips. The most popular stretch for recreation starts at the North River Bridge (T-71 North) to the East River Bridge (US-90), a distance of about 0.5 mile by land and 7 miles (about four hours) by water. Canoe rentals and livery service come and go in Columbus; check with the chamber of commerce for current status. You may need your own canoe and two cars, one of which should be parked at the East River Bridge take-out.

Wide and smooth (and usually opaque with sediment), with only a few small rapids, the Colorado River at Columbus is relatively safe for novice canoeists. The numerous long sandbars make night floats a timeless experience. Moonlight glows from these freshwater beaches, and the wildlife show is fascinating as the river comes alive with beaver, deer, and raccoons.

Exploring Columbus and its numerous heritage medallion homes is easy with the *Historical Trailguide,* published by the Columbus Chamber of Commerce. It is available weekdays at the chamber offices on the ground floor of the Stafford Opera House (435 Spring

Street, across from Courthouse Square) or by mail: P.O. Box 343, Columbus 78934, (409) 732-8385. The chamber also can advise you in regard to the many historical homes offering B&B and on the best wildflower routes in spring.

WHAT TO DO

Alley Log Cabin. 1230 Bowie. Built in 1836 by Abraham Alley, one of Stephen F. Austin's original "Old Three Hundred" colonists, this square-notch oak cabin was moved into town in 1976 from its original site at the Atascosito crossing of the Colorado River. Open for viewing Thursday, Friday, and Saturday.

Canoeing. Colorado River Longhorn Canoes offers trips "from three hours to three weeks" on the Colorado from Austin to the Gulf. Maps and shuttle service available for renters. (409) 732-3723.

Christmas Tree Cutting. Call Raondo Christmas Tree Farm for directions, (409) 732-5596.

Colorado County Courthouse. Bounded by Spring, Milam, Walnut, and Travis streets on Courthouse Square. Built in 1890-91, this is the third courthouse on the same site and still the county seat. The four-faced clock is original, but its steeple fell in a 1909 hurricane and was replaced by a neoclassic dome. A full restoration completed in 1980 uncovered a handsome stained glass dome above the district courtroom, hidden for generations behind a false ceiling. The courthouse is open Monday–Friday.

Take special note of the stump of the famous Courthouse Oak, 2,000 years old and the site of the first district court held in 1837. At that time the first courthouse on this site had been burned by Houston's forces, and a second one had yet to be built. Judge R. M. Williamson, known as "Three-Legged Willie" because of his false leg, elected to hear cases under this tree.

Columbus Opry. 715 Walnut (The Oaks Theatre). Named the best of its kind in the nation in 1996 by the Country Music Association, this bit of Nashville in the heart of Texas showcases outstanding local and regional C&W talent and regularly draws professional scouts every Saturday night. There's lots of audience-performer interaction and a wholesome "no alcohol, no smoking" environment suitable for families. $; children under six are free. (409) 732-9210 or 732-6510

Confederate Memorial Museum and Veterans Hall. On the southwest corner of Courthouse Square. This old water tower was built 400,000 bricks strong in 1883. Dynamite didn't dent it in a later demolition attempt, so the United Daughters of the Confederacy decided it was a safe repository for their treasures. The exhibits feature clothing, small possessions, articles, documents, and pictures of early Columbus, including artifacts from the "Old Three Hundred," as Stephen F. Austin's first colony was known. Donation. Open during the May homes tour and for groups by prior arrangement. (409) 732-8385.

Dilue Rose Harris House. 602 Washington. Built of tabby in 1858, this house museum is filled with Texas primitives and early Victorian furniture. Open during May homes tour and by private arrangement. (409) 732-8385.

Fishing. Bass and catfish await in the Colorado River. You'll find a public boat ramp at the North River Bridge.

Grave of the Infidel. Odd Fellows Cemetery on Montezuma Street. Like all frontiers, the Columbus area attracted characters. Back in the 1890s Ike Towell made a name for himself as an outspoken atheist. The town marshal, he also was instrumental in the establishment of Jim Crowism in the area. He wrote his own funeral service, and his tombstone reads "Here lies Ike Towell, an infidel, who had no hope of heaven or fear of hell."

"Gunsmoke" at the Brune Land and Cattle Company. Take the T-71 (Austin) exit from I-10 for 7 miles, turn left on FM-1890, and watch for signs. A nonprofit organization that promotes the sport of cowboy action shooting and safe gun handling, the Texas Historical Shootist Society holds cowboy shoot-outs here every third Sunday of the month. The society also hosts "Trailhead," a yearly shoot-out and gathering for society members on the fourth weekend of March that includes a trail ride through bluebonnet country, shooting competitions, a vendors' row, games, crafts, a campfire-sing-along-liar's contest, and so on. Visitors are welcome to come and watch, but no children under eight, please. For information, contact the Texas Historical Shootist Society, P.O. Box 216, Barker 77413, or call the Columbus Chamber of Commerce, (409) 732-8385.

Hunting. Colorado County is happy hunting grounds for deer, quail, dove, and geese. Every winter it becomes the goose capital of the world because of its location on the central flyway. In addition to the Blue Goose Hunting Club (Trip 2, this sector), arrangements to hunt can be made through Clifton Tyler (goose and wild duck guide, day and season hunting), 1139 Fannin, Columbus 78934, (409) 732-6502. Guided hunts for large white-tail Texas bucks are offered by J. W. Golla, Route 2, Alleyton 78935, (409) 732-5280.

Live Oak Arts Center. 1014 Milam. Housed in a historic building, this gallery's exhibits change monthly and feature both local and internationally known artists. Open Wednesday through Saturday. (409) 732-8398.

Mary Elizabeth Hopkins Santa Claus Museum. 604 Washington. Push Santa's nose on the doorbell of this nice old home and you're greeted with "Santa Claus is coming to town!" Actually, he's already here, more than 2,000 strong and in every form imaginable. This lady's lifelong collection fills several rooms and includes jewelry, paperweights, cookie jars, music boxes, samplers, and more, in addition to the expected ornaments and mantel decorations. Open Thursday, Friday, and Saturday. Fee.

Nesbitt Memorial Library. 529 Washington. Root-tracers prize this library's new archives room for its regional genealogical information; children and collectors love it for its antique doll and toy collection. Open weekdays, Saturdays until 2:00 P.M. (409) 732-3392.

Preston Kyle Shatto Wildlife Museum. 1000 block of Milam. Animal trophies from around the world are shown here in simple dioramas. Donation. Open during May homes tour and by appointment. (409) 732-8385.

P. T. Ranch Exotics. On T-71, approximately 5 miles north of downtown Columbus. In addition to commercial breeding programs focused on top quality trophy animals, this seventy-acre exotic game ranch specializes in bottle-raising many critters (pure Nubian ibex, spotted fallow deer, northern whitetail deer, blackbuck antelope, axis deer, and nilgai antelope) for customers desiring domesticated stock. During tours (reservations required), visitors hand-feed many of the above, and children are welcome; bring your camera. (409) 732-8280.

Restored 1886 Stafford Bank and Opera House. 425 Spring Street, across from Courthouse Square. Built by millionaire cattleman R. E. Stafford in 1886 for a reputed $50,000, this elegant old building originally housed Stafford's bank on the first floor and a 1,000-seat theater upstairs where such headliners as Lillian Russell and Al Jolson performed. Today the show-biz names may not be so grand, but the theater is, thanks to an eighteen-year, $1.5 million restoration financed entirely by local residents. The original 15-foot chandelier and the first elaborate stage curtain have been reproduced, and a variety of entertainments once again bring up the footlights. There's usually one performance a month September through June. Don't miss either the museum on the first floor or the unusual marble cornerstone. The opera house also is open to visitors Monday–Friday and during the homes tour in May. Fee for tours. (409) 732-8385.

WHERE TO EAT

Hackemack's Hofbrau Haus. On FM–109, 10 miles north of Columbus and 1 mile south of Frelsburg. You can't miss this place—it's a Bavarian chalet in the middle of a small pasture, surrounded by flying flags. And you shouldn't miss it, because the German food is great (as are the steaks, seafood, and hamburgers), and there's lots of live oom-pah-pah when the yodeling house accordionist is joined by other local talent on the guitar, a "squeeze box," or the rhythm rake 'n bench. Their Friday and Saturday night repertoire ranges from Bavarian tunes through C&W to rhythm and blues; call ahead to see what's going on fun-wise if you are coming this way on a weekend. Open for dinner Thursday–Saturday throughout the year and for lunch and dinner on Sundays from March–May. $-$$; (CC). (409) 732-6321.

    Mikeska's Barbeque. On I-10, one mile east (exit 698). Known as the BBQ king of the Southwest to local folks, Jerry Mikeska not only sells his tasty ribs, sausage, and brisket at two locations in Columbus but he also caters for events as far away as Washington, D.C. Open for lunch and dinner daily, with a buffet on Sunday morning. $. (409) 732-3101.

    ...of the day/A Cafe. 1114 Milam, on Courthouse Square. There's a New Orleans feeling to this small place, thanks to imaginative restoration of a vintage building. Chef-owner Penny Miekow explains her cafe's unusual name by saying she not only uses what's freshest that day but also changes the menu to fit trendy things going on in the cooking world. That means you may find the latest fad food or some old-fashioned favorites on the blackboard specials at noon, something a bit more sophisticated at dinner. One of her standards is Columbus sausage (from the butcher next door) braised in Shiner bock beer. For the timid she excels at sandwiches, home-made breads, and soup of the day. Open Tuesday–Friday for lunch. $–$$. (409) 732-6430.

Picnic Basket Sandwich Shop and Cafe. 1221 Bowie Street. Good lunch spot for freshly made soups, salads, sandwiches, and daily specials. Open weekdays for lunch. $. (409) 732-9119.

Schobel's Restaurant. 2020 Milam. Convenient from I-10, this family restaurant cuts its own steaks, grinds its own hamburger meat, and makes its own pies. The menu also includes seafood and Mexican dishes, and there are large buffets at the daily lunch and on Friday night. Open daily for lunch and dinner. $–$$; (CC). (409) 732-2385.

CONTINUING ON

Columbus is the gateway to all of Austin and Fayette counties, rolling farmland that still looks much as it did when it was settled by Polish, German, and Czech immigrants in the 1800s. FM-949 North continues this day trip through that territory to the small German communities of Frelsburg and New Ulm.

FRELSBURG

When you stop to chat in this region, don't be surprised to hear strong German accents. The ethnic heritage of this community, 12 miles north of Columbus via FM-109, runs deep. The town is named for John and William Frels, who settled here in the 1830s.

You'll see Saints Peter and Paul Catholic Church on a hill as you approach on FM-109. Although this particular Catholic sanctuary was built in 1927, the parish it serves was organized in 1847 and is the oldest in Texas. Visitors are welcome either to celebrate Mass or to view the three carved wood altars. Nearby and a bit more humble in its architecture, St. John's Lutheran Church (1855–56) and its churchyard look like New England transplants.

Heinsohen's General Store has served this area for generations. If you stop in to buy a cool drink, you'll find it stocks everything from the latest in electronic games to pegged pants. Don't leave without buying some of the home-done pickles.

The big doin's in Frelsburg is the annual Fireman's Picnic on the second weekend in June. A fundraiser, it also is an enjoyable look at a small, still very German community in the heart of Texas.

WHAT TO DO

Texas Falls Golf and Country Club. Three miles east of FM–109 via Dr. Neal Road, between Frelsburg and New Ulm; watch for signs. The golf course of this large real estate development is ranked fifth in Texas among golf pros, a demanding eighteen holes designed by Jay Riviere and Dave Marr. Expect bentgrass greens, a series of clearwater lakes, and numerous waterfalls. Golf fees vary; call for tee times three days in advance if possible. The resort's restaurant is open for breakfast on weekends, lunch Wednesday–Saturday. $–$$; (CC). Two-bedroom villas with kitchens and swimming pool privileges also are available for overnight guests. Closed on Tuesday. (409) 992–3123 or (281) 578–5550.

CONTINUING ON

From Frelsburg continue north on FM–109 to the more sizable community of New Ulm, population 650.

NEW ULM

Also founded by Germans, Czechs, and Poles in the early 1800s, New Ulm soon may be in for its second golden age. Back in the 1940s the entrepreneurial Glenn McCarthy made some Texas-size bucks in the nearby Frelsburg oil field and brought lots of his Hollywood friends to the quiet streets of New Ulm. Today new wells are hinting at another wave of prosperity sometime in the future. In the meantime enjoy the simplicity and old-time rural architecture of this crossroads settlement as part of a country drive. This also is spectacular wildflower territory in the spring.

WHAT TO DO

Green Gate Ranch. Owned by Roberta Ellis, this forty-acre spread breeds, trains, and sells Peruvian horses, a relatively rare breed that's noted for its even temperament and smooth gait. Please, do not enter the grounds of this ranch without advance arrangements, However, visitors who call ahead are welcome; during spring foaling is a great time to come. (409) 992-3441.

WANDERING THE BACKROADS

To reach Houston from New Ulm, go east 23 miles on FM-1094 to Sealy (Trip 1, this sector) and then east on I-10 to home.

If you want to extend this day trip, you have several choices. From New Ulm take FM-109 north to Industry and its intersection with T-159. A turn west (left) and then a jog northwest on FM-1457 takes you to Round Top (Trip 5, this sector). A turn east (right) on T-159 brings you to Bellville (also Trip 5, this sector).

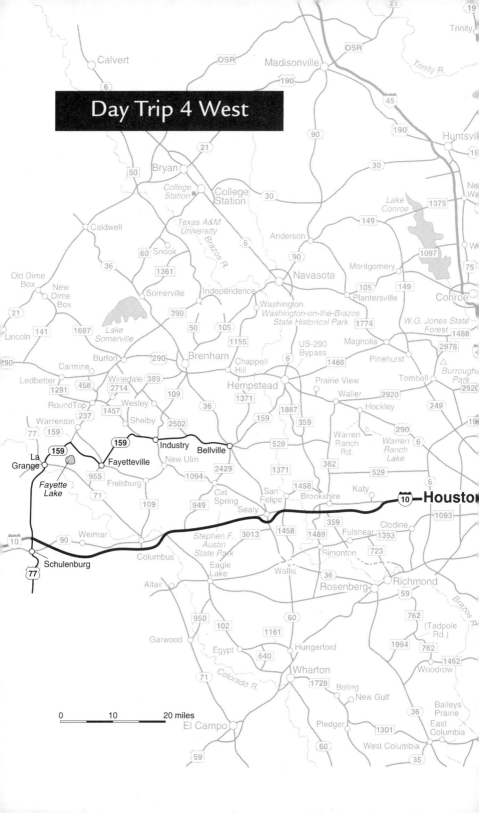

Day Trip 4 West

SCHULENBURG

Begin this trip by driving due west from Houston on I-10 to the Schulenburg exit and turning south on T-77.

Like Sealy, this is a railroad town, created in 1873 when the fledgling Galveston, Harrisburg, and San Antonio Railroad purchased a right-of-way across Louis Schulenburg's farm and built a station. Folks living in nearby High Hill used log rollers pulled by oxen to move their homes and business buildings 3 miles south to the new town site, and Schulenburg began to thrive.

Today local residents still tell time by train whistles, and daytrippers find an architecturally interesting Main Street (particularly the 400–600 blocks), numerous historic sites, and a string of "painted churches" beautifully representative of the area's strong Czech, Austrian, and German heritage. Another local oldie, the 1930s Schaefer Observatory, has been featured on the television show "The Eyes of Texas." Open only to serious amateur astronomers, this working observatory has a 14-inch telescope. (409) 743-3448 (weekdays only).

Strong ethnic traditions make the Schulenburg Festival a big event the first full weekend in August. For additional information and a driving-tour map, contact the Schulenburg Chamber of Commerce, 101-B Kessler Avenue (P.O. Box 65), Schulenburg 78956, (409) 743-4514.

WHAT TO DO

Itsy Bitsy Burro Company of Cedar Grove Farm. North of Schulenburg; call for an appointment and directions. Dr. Seuss would have loved this place—it has green eggs (courtesy of Aracana chickens) and ham (on the hoof)! Basically a breeding farm for miniature donkeys, it also has potbellied pigs and a llama, and cattle fields line the long drive up to the 1860s ranchhouse. Visitors sometimes get free green eggs! This is an ideal place to show off the best of country life to children. (409) 247-4965.

The Old Anderson Place. 510 South Main Street. Built before 1857 and later the home of Louis Schulenburg, this is thought to be the oldest occupied house in the area. Privately owned, it is not open for tours.

Painted Church Driving Tour. An interesting map to the rural countryside around Schulenburg is available from the chamber of commerce. It will lead you to the tiny Czech settlement of Dubina and its beautifully frescoed Sts. Cyril & Methodius Catholic Church; to Ammannsville and the unusual stenciled Gothic interior of St. John the Baptist Catholic Church; to Praha and the painted murals of the Blessed Virgin Mary Catholic Church; and to High Hill and the painted murals of St. Mary's Catholic Church. En route and worth seeing are a Russian-styled house and (near Dubina) a hundred-year-old iron bridge over the Navidad River. Most of the churches are still in use and may or may not be open; best consult in advance with the Schulenburg Chamber of Commerce, which also provides guided tours by advance appointment. (409) 743-4514.

Schulenburg Historical Museum. 631 North Main. Visiting this old store-turned-museum is wonderful on Sunday afternoons. There are few cars around, and the atmosphere is that of a quieter time. Lots of old stuff here, and it's fun to poke around. Donations welcome. Also open by appointment. (409) 743-4887.

WHERE TO EAT

Guentert's BBQ Restaurant and Meat Market. One-half mile north of I-10 on T-77. A super place to stop after touring the painted churches, this chef-owned eatery smokes its own sausage, ham, bacon, beef, ribs, and such. There's a daily all-you-can-eat barbecue buffet ($4.95 at last notice), lunch specials, and a full menu. The market side of this place sells jerky, sausage, ham, and bacon, and it'll cut to order fine-quality meats, so come prepared to haul some home. Open daily for breakfast and lunch; Tuesday–Sunday for dinner. $–$$; (CC). (409) 743–4688.

Kountry Bakery. Highway 77 North in Schulenburg. While a great spot for homemade breads, cookies, pies, sweet rolls and so on, this fragrant place also serves salads, breakfast tacos, stew, chili, soups, burgers, sandwiches, and daily specials. Check the blackboard for the cook's selections. Closed on Wednesday. Open other weekdays from 5:30 A.M. to 5:00 P.M., Saturdays until 2:00 P.M. $. (409) 743–4342.

Nannie's Biscuit & Bakery. 3401 East US–90 at I–10 (use exit 677). In addition to super baked goods for take-out, this modest place offers blackboard menus for breakfast, lunch, and dinner. *Shoppers:* A gift shop and Fostoria factory outlet are in this same complex. Kids love the livestock out back. Open Tuesday–Sunday; call for hours. $. (409) 561–8535.

Oakridge Restaurant & BBQ Smokehouse. At the intersection of T–77 and I–10 (use exit 674). This long-established family restaurant smokes its own meats and makes its own sausage, but you'll find chicken, burgers, fish, and buffet offerings here as well. In addition to patio dining on nice days, there's a small playground for children and a gift shop. Open daily for breakfast, lunch, and dinner. $–$$; (CC). (409) 743–3372, (800) 320–5766.

Pat's Sweet Shop. 617 North Main, Schulenburg. Housed in one of the town's oldest business buildings, this fragrant bakery also has a good sandwich/salad bar lunch. Some 185 cookie jars dominate the decor. Open Tuesday–Saturday. $. (409) 743–4060, (800) 814–5490.

WANDERING THE BACKROADS

If you want to explore further, consider deviating briefly from this day trip itinerary to visit Flatonia, 12 miles farther west and well beyond the 110-mile limit of this book. While I–10 and US–90 are hardly backroads, they are timesavers and the most direct routes. Another railroad town, Flatonia was established in 1875 and is where many of the eggs sold in Houston are laid. Prime sights include a historical museum in the old Flatonia Bank Building and livery stable out back (both open Sunday afternoon and by appointment), an 1886 mercantile (open daily except Sunday), and the oldest operating newspaper (1875) in the county. For information call (512) 865-3920 on Monday, Wednesday, or Friday morning.

While you're in the territory, visit Praha on FM-1295, off US-90, 3 miles east of Flatonia. The first Czech settlement in Texas, this tiny community and its large church host Czechs from all over America for homecoming in mid-August, a festival that began in 1856.

LA GRANGE

There are two ways to get to La Grange from Houston, but they both follow I-10 West some 56 miles to Columbus. There you can either take T-71 northwest 26 miles to La Grange or continue on the interstate another 21 miles to the US-77 exit, then go north 16 miles to your destination.

Long before TV personality Marvin Zindler focused the bright lights of TV publicity and traditional morality on Miss Mona and her Chicken Ranch on the outskirts of town (Best Little Whorehouse in Texas) some years ago, La Grange had a colorful personality. A bear of a man known as Strap Buckner was running an Indian trading post here by 1819, and local legend says he cleared the site of La Grange in a wild wrestling match with Satan.

Whatever the truth, a small community began about 1831 where the La Bahia Trail crossed the Colorado River, and some of Stephen F. Austin's first colony helped tame the land. By 1837 the town known as La Grange was the seat of government for Fayette County. Today the courthouse, built in the 1890s, stands in the town square, and its original clock still chimes the hour.

Pause for a moment under Muster Oak on the square's northeast corner. Through six conflicts starting with the Mexican attack of 1842, La Grange's able-bodied men have gathered here with their families before leaving for battle. The tradition took a 1990s twist during Iraq's occupation of Kuwait. When area army reserve units came through La Grange, they found Muster Oak wrapped with a giant yellow bow.

La Grange is a nerve center for wildflower tours in the spring, and the local chamber of commerce will help you plan a driving route.

Whenever you come, spend some time exploring the city's historic square, slowly being restored to historic character via the Main Street Program. Walking tour brochures as well as guides to area antiques shops and cemeteries are available at the chamber of commerce, 171 South Main. To contact them in advance, call (409) 968-5756 or (800) LA GRANGE. Should you decide to linger, you'll find B&B at The Blue Caboose, (409) 968-5053 or (800) 968-5053; Live Oak, (800) 438-2281; and Y Knot, (409) 247-4529.

WHAT TO DO

N. W. Faison Home and Museum. 822 South Jefferson Street. The nucleus of this gracious frontier home is a two-room cabin built of pine around 1845. Bought in 1866 by N. W. Faison, a Fayette County clerk and land surveyor who survived the Dawson Massacre, the home remained in the Faison family until 1960. Open only for group tours by prior arrangement. Fee. (409) 968-5756.

Fayette County Heritage Museum and Library. 855 South Jefferson Street, across from the Faison home. A local bicentennial project, the museum has changing exhibits and special humidified archives to preserve historic documents. Open Tuesday–Sunday, but hours vary. (409) 968-6418.

Hermes Drug Store. 148 Washington, across from the courthouse. Established in 1856, this is the oldest drug store in continuous operation in Texas. Visitors expecting a vintage sight will be disappointed, however; although many of the original fixtures and beveled mirrors remain, the interior otherwise is very much of our times. Open Monday–Friday, Saturday until noon. (409) 968-3357.

Holy Rosary Catholic Church in Hostyn. From La Grange take US-77 South approximately 5 miles; then turn west on FM-2436 for 1 mile. Even non-Catholics enjoy strolling on this hilltop, noted for its large stations of the cross, grottoes, shrines, Civil War cannon, and replica of the first log church on this site.

Monument Hill and Kreische Brewery State Historical Park. Two miles south of town off US-77. Even after the Texans' historic victory at San Jacinto, the Mexican Army continued to raid this portion of Texas through the following decade. The tragic 1842 Dawson Massacre near San Antonio and the ill-fated Mier Expedition are the focus of this memorial. Both are lesser-known but interesting chapters of Lone Star history. This popular picnic site, high on a bluff overlooking the Colorado River, features a nature walk through the woods and one trail designed for the handicapped. The view north from the overlook includes the old La Bahia Trail crossing on the river.

In 1978 the adjacent Kreische Brewery and homesite were added to the facility and subsequently restored. Kreische was a skilled stonemason and brewer from Europe who established this first brewery in Texas between 1860 and 1870 below his home on what is now Monument Hill. Ultimately it became the third largest brewery in the state, and his product, a dark beer called Frisch Auf, was sold at his beer garden. The restoration has cleaned out the springs that provided water for the brewery and stabilized the old buildings. Guided tours down to the brewery are given on weekends. Open daily. Fee. (409) 968-5658.

Mountain Biking at Bluff Creek Ranch. Owl Creek Road, Warda. From the Columbus exit on I-10 west take T-71 north to La Grange, turning north on US-77 10 miles to Warda. Turn right on Owl Creek Road (Fayette County Road 152) and go 0.5 mile to a green gate with cattle guard; follow signs to barn. This private, 200-acre Longhorn cattle and Arabian horse ranch offers nine miles of challenging mountain bike trails through meadows and creeks as well as forested and hilly terrain. Rated intermediate to expert, some of the hard dirt trails are easy enough for new riders. Bluff Creek hosts several major races annually. Bikers also can camp here— there's a restroom with showers. Fees. Do not come without calling first to make sure the ranch and trails are open. (409) 242-5894.

St. James Episcopal Church. 156 North Monroe. Built in 1885 and still painted its original rust and cream, this small church has retained its original furnishings, handmade by the first rector and his congregation. Visitors are welcome at the 10:00 A.M. Sunday service and by appointment. (409) 968-3910.

WHERE TO EAT

Boss' House of Steaks. 710 West Travis. This Victorian home with its three-story fireplace has more to offer than just outstanding steaks, seafood, and Mexican entrees. Well-done on a western theme, it also sports a massive antique bar and collections of guns, barbed wire, and Indian arrowheads. Open for dinner Tuesday–Saturday. $-$$$; (CC). (409) 968-8886.

Cedar Creek BBQ Place. 1612 T-71 Bypass, La Grange, west of the T-159 intersection. Although owners Robert and Claire Land offer an extensive menu (lots of great nibbles), the house specialties are huge chicken-fried steaks and some of the best barbecued ribs and steaks in the region. Open for lunch and dinner Thursday–Sunday. $-$$. (409) 968-8033.

Frank's Place. 235 West Travis. A varied selection of steaks and seafood here, with a salad bar. Although no mixed drinks are sold, take note of the 200-year-old bar. Open for breakfast and lunch on Monday and Tuesday; breakfast, lunch, and dinner Wednesday–Saturday. Reservations are recommended on weekends. $$; (CC). (409) 968-3759.

Holman Valley Steakhouse. On FM-155, 9 miles south of La Grange in the crossroads community of Holman. Judy and David Hajovsky have turned this old country store and meeting house into an excellent and much needed eatery for the region. In addition to steak, the menu includes seafood and chicken. Open for dinner Wednesday–Saturday. Reservations advised. $-$$. (409) 263-4188.

La Cabana. 658 South Jefferson (T-77 South). Ever had a Greek taco? You can here, along with a wide selection of Mexican and American standards. Open daily for lunch (buffet) and dinner. $-$$; (CC). (409) 968-6612.

Prause's Market. 253 West Travis on the town square. Fresh and smoked meats here, as well as barbecue to eat on-site or take out. Open Monday–Friday and on Saturday morning. $. (409) 968-3259.

WANDERING THE BACKROADS

Before continuing on from La Grange to Fayetteville and the conclusion of this day trip, consider a detour north/northwest to the tiny community of Serbin. Settled from 1854 through 1900 by Wends (Sorbs) from Lusatia in East Germany, this is the only Wendish village in Texas where you can still occasionally hear the Wendish language. Sights include St. Paul's Lutheran Church, completed in 1871 and still in use, (409) 366-9650; and the Texas Wendish Heritage Museum, open Sunday through Friday afternoons (fee), (409) 366-2441. The latter exhibits old country folk dress, manuscripts, personal papers, photographs, and painted Easter eggs in addition to two log buildings built in the 1850s. Group tours that include a Wendish meal can be arranged by calling the museum. To reach Serbin, take US–77 north from La Grange for approximately seven miles and turn west (left) on FM–153 for eight miles. Turn north (right) on FM–448 and go nine miles to FM–2239; Serbin then is two miles west (left). You'll be driving through lovely countryside all the way.

If hunger strikes, you're out of luck in Serbin. Closest food source is a true taste of rural Texas: the Warda Store (and post office, gas station, restaurant, and bar). Located in Warda on US–77 about halfway between La Grange and Giddings, this spot is locally famous for its "Warda-burgers." Open daily but only after 4:00 P.M. on Sunday; (409) 242-3366.

Delaying an exploration of Fayetteville for another day, you'll also find road food as well as a picturesque 1899 octagonal courthouse in Giddings, about five miles northeast of Serbin via FM–448. From Giddings, it's a straight shot home to Houston via US–290 east, unless you detour just east of Carmine onto T–237 south which connects you with Day Trip 5, this sector.

CONTINUING ON

If you do not jaunt off to Serbin, your next stop on this day trip is Fayetteville. From La Grange follow T–159 northeast 15 miles on its zigzag course through the countryside.

FAYETTEVILLE

If you like the big time and bright lights, move on. This small town keeps a low profile, tucked away in the rolling farmland east of La Grange. If too many folks fall in love with it, it's bound to change, and that would be a pity.

Some of Austin's first colony were sharp enough to settle here in the early 1820s, and by 1833 the tiny community was a stage station on the old San Felipe Trail, with service to Austin via Round Top and Bastrop. The town officially was mapped in 1847, and the next decade saw extensive German and Czech immigration, an ethnic blend that continues here today.

In the town's settlement days, free food was served to all comers, but occasionally the vittles ran out before the customers did. Late arrivals were told to "lick the skillet," and Fayetteville was nicknamed Lickskillet as a result. Today the town celebrates the Lickskillet Festival the third weekend of October with parades, fun, and a big meal (not free!) in the town square.

Fayetteville looks much as it did at the end of the last century: a series of 2- and 3-block streets in a grid with a central square. The town's pride and heart is the rare Victorian precinct courthouse in the center of that square, a small wooden structure built in 1880 for the heady sum of $800. The four-faced clock in the steeple resulted from a ten-year fundraising effort by the Do Your Duty Club and was installed with much civic horn-tooting in 1934.

City folks cherish this small town as a wind-down place. The best way to get on Fayetteville time is to pick up a walking map from one of the stores and take a slow stroll around town. While Fayetteville still retains its sleepy charm, its days of relative obscurity are definitely numbered. In just one three-month period in late 1994, more than a dozen of its old homes were sold to Houstonians as country getaways, and many of the vintage buildings around the square are metamorphosing into Victorian-style shops, galleries, or lodgings.

Fayetteville's shops usually are open Tuesday–Sunday, but Friday and Saturday are the best times to come to town and stay late. That's when Baca's Historic Saloon and Confectionery on the square swings with live music ranging from Czech and German polka tunes to contemporary country. This is a good-old-boy country band, the likes of which are rare in rural Texas today. Bring your dancing shoes and plan to stay over via an advance reservation at one of Fayetteville's 12 bed and breakfast establishments. For reservations and maps call (800) 256-7721. For additional overnight options in the region consult the Round Top (page 112), Brenham (page 61), and La Grange (page 102) sections of this book.

WHAT TO DO

Chovanecs. Corner of Live Oak and Fayette streets, on the square. In what must be termed a gargantuan case of overstocking, this old store still has dry goods typical of the 1940s and 1950s. Incidentally, the name is pronounced Ko-VAHN-itz. Open Monday–Saturday. (409) 378-2248.

Country Roads Bicycle Tours. This Houston-based outfit offers excellent guided trips through this part of Stephen F. Austin's Cradle Country. (713) 666-8444, (800) 366-6681.

Fayette Area Heritage Museum. On the Square in Fayetteville. Lots of local lore here, with docents to add the human commentary. Open weekends, sometimes on weekdays, or by appointment. (409) 378-2231.

Fayette Artist Colony. Around the square. Many of the town's 19th century buildings now house artists' studios and galleries, most of which are open Wednesday–Sunday. Same story on antiques shops.

Lake Fayette. From T-159 bass fishermen may want to detour east on County Road 196 to 2,400-acre Lake Fayette, the cooling pond for the Fayette Power Project. Open year-round, it offers fishing, camping, swimming, and power boating from both Park Prairie and Oak Thicket parks, with a multimillion dollar upgrading under way at this writing. Bait and tackle shops dispense necessities and advice at the entrances to both. Fee. (409) 249-5208 or 249-5322.

WHERE TO EAT

Hackemack's Hofbrau Haus. Between La Grange and Frelsburg on FM-109. (See Trip 3, this sector.)

Keilers Restaurant. On the square in Fayetteville. Take your pick: In addition to daily lunch specials, this menu offers fried catfish, steaks, hamburgers, and seafood platters. Save room for the home-made pies. Open for lunch and dinner Wednesday–Saturday. Lodging rooms upstairs. $–$$. (409) 378-2578.

Orsak's Cafe. On the square in Fayetteville. There's nothing fancy about this clean and basic cafe, but the food is acceptable and affordable. In addition to daily lunch specials and a regular menu, Wednesday night brings fried chicken; Thursday night, pork chops; Friday night, seafood; and Sunday, barbecue. You'll want to linger long enough to visit with local residents; nearly everyone who comes to town drops in for at least a cup of coffee, to pick up messages, and otherwise to stay in touch. Open Tuesday–Sunday for breakfast, lunch, and dinner; until 2:00 P.M. on Monday. $–$$. (409) 378-2719.

The Painted Lady Tea Room. 209 West Main, Fayetteville. Just off the square and serving far more than finger sandwiches, this handsome old home (circa 1880s) was considered the ugliest structure in town until its 1994 renovation by a Houston couple. Now a Victorian beauty filled with antiques (for sale), it serves delicious soups, salads, sandwiches, breads, and desserts as well as creative entrees. The first Friday and Saturday of every month are candlelight dinner nights; reservations advised. Otherwise it's open for lunch Wednesday–Sunday from March through November; and Friday–Sunday from December through February. Inquire about additional dinner hours. $-$$; (CC). (409) 378-4281.

WANDERING THE BACKROADS

After touring Fayetteville, you can continue east on T-159 to Bellville and then home (Trip 5, this sector). Or you can reverse the order of this day trip, touring Fayetteville first and then continuing to La Grange. See the map with this section for your route options. It's also easy to connect with tours of Round Top and Winedale (Trip 5, this sector) or Brenham (Trip 6, northwest sector), if you prefer.

If you are traveling in any part of this territory from late March through May, contact the La Grange Chamber of Commerce in advance. It scouts the best routes for color during the wildflower season. Information: (800) LA GRANGE.

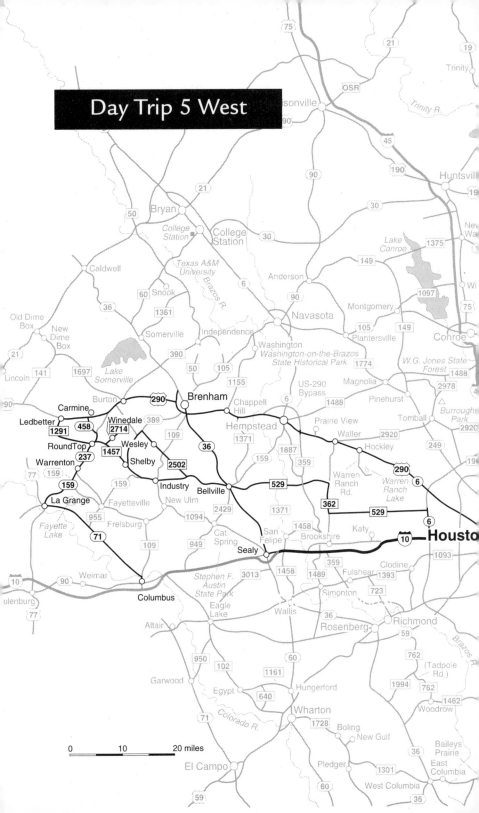

Ledbetter
Round Top
Winedale and Industry
Bellville

LEDBETTER

Begin this day trip by driving northwest from Houston on US-290 to Ledbetter, 25 miles west of Brenham. If it's Saturday, antiques shoppers will want to spend some time in the whistle-stop town of Carmine, a few miles east of Ledbetter.

Both Carmine and Ledbetter are railroad towns, the latter platted in 1870 by the Texas and New Orleans Railroad. Folks anticipated big things—those old plats show a big depot from which wide streets with pretty names stretched in all directions. The depot did become a reality, the first and largest in Fayette County. The town, however, maxed out at about 1,000 residents in 1900 and began a steady decline after World War II. The last passenger train whistled through in 1952, the last freight in 1979. Now even the tracks are gone, and Ledbetter has a permanent population of approximately 100 souls. Perhaps the town is best defined by what it doesn't have: gas stations, fast-food franchises, supermarkets, traffic lights, noise, and crowds—in short, Ledbetter is a perfect pause in another era.

WHAT TO DO

Stuermer's General Store and Working Museum. At the intersection of US-290 and FM-1291. No one knows exactly when this old place was built, but the two antique bars (one dated 1836 on the back) were part of a saloon established here by the owner's great-grandfather in 1890. Today Chris Jervis and her mother, Lillian Stuermer Dyer, sell sandwiches and Blue Bell ice cream from those bars, and the rest of the two-story store is filled with memorabilia and antiques (not for sale), along with those sundry items no one can do without. Kids love this place; the jukebox, pool table, and pinball machines are free. This is the oldest flag stop on the Kerrville bus route, and when the shutters are closed, the store is closed (usually Sunday except during wildflower season); when the shutters are open, come on in.

Jay and Chris Jervis also have seven B&B lodgings, one in a charming 1880s country cottage known as Granny's House, the others in a refurbished 1860s hotel on the north side of the highway. All the units have private baths and include full country breakfasts in their basic $55–$70 nightly rate. Guests also have access to a party house, complete with indoor swimming pool and numerous free mechanical and electronic games. (409) 249-5642 or 249-3066.

Ledbetter Buggy Shop. Two doors down from the general store on US-290. Jay Jervis sells traditional Amish buggies here and, with his wife, puts on horse-drawn chuckwagon cookouts at a nearby ranch throughout the year. Open by appointment. (409) 249-3066 or 249-5642.

Alice Darnell Studio. Between the buggy shop and general store. This artist specializes in spinning local wool into thread on antique equipment and then hand-looming that thread into handsome cloth. She also restores and sells antiques and artworks. Open by appointment. (409) 249-5234.

CONTINUING ON

To reach Round Top, take either FM-1291 South from Ledbetter or T-237 South from Carmine.

ROUND TOP

When it comes to vintage Texas villages that have retained the essence of their past, Round Top is the champ. Officially founded in 1835 by settlers from Stephen F. Austin's second colony, it was first called Jones Post Office and then Townsend, after the five Townsend families who established plantations in the area. The name of Round Top originally applied to a stage stop 2 miles north, a landmark by 1847 because it had a house with a round top. When the stage line between Houston and Austin moved its route slightly south, the town and the name followed.

Driving into Round Top is like passing through a time warp. A small white meeting house in the middle of the village green is part of the town's charm. In fact, Round Top is so small, so compact and neat, that visitors often feel like giants abroad in Lilliput.

Those first Anglo settlers were followed by Germans, many of whom were intellectuals oppressed in their native country. Others were skilled carpenters and stonemasons whose craftsmanship marks numerous area buildings that survive today. A drive on the lanes around Round Top is a lesson in enduring architecture.

Nice to know if you hate to leave: There are numerous B&B lodgings in the Round Top area, including Briarfield at Round Top, (409) 249-3973; Broomfields, (409) 249-3706; Ein Kleines Haus and Ginzel Haus, (409) 249-3060; Heart of My Heart Ranch, (800) 327-1242 or (409) 249-3171; Leonhardt Haus, (409) 249-3144; Outpost at Cedar Creek, (409) 836-4975; Round Top Inn, (409) 249-5294; The Settlement House, (409) 249-5015 or (888) ROUND TOP; Sun Flower Cottage, (409) 249-3593; and Tricklecreek Farms, (409) 249-3060.

With its current population of eighty-seven, Round Top holds two distinctions. Not only is it the smallest incorporated town in the state, it has what many think is the oldest Fourth of July celebration west of the Mississippi. Local folks have been kicking up their heels on Independence Day since 1826, and the annual tradition now runs to orations, barbecues, a trail ride, and the firing of the cannon in the town square.

Whenever you visit, just park your car near the square and walk around. Round Top folks welcome visitors and have lots of tales to tell, so stop and chat as you explore. Unless you are passionate about country antiques and/or folk art and don't mind major crowds, avoid coming to Round Top on the first full weekend of both April and October when literally thousands of people attend the Round Top Antiques Fair, one of the finest events of its kind in the world. More than 270 dealers from all parts of the country participate in this blue chip show, but that's not all. Riding the fair's coattails is a seemingly endless antiques and flea market scene along many of the region's roads. Farmers rent field space to all comers, and hunting for bargains and treasures is the rule of the day. Nerve center for the latter scene is Warrenton, three miles south of Round Top on T-237 (toward La Grange), and the action begins the weekend prior to the Round Top show.

For information on the area, contact the Round Top Chamber of Commerce, P.O. Box 216, Round Top 78954, (409) 249-4042.

WHAT TO DO

Bethlehem Lutheran Church. Up the hill from Moore's Fort and 1 block southwest. This sturdy stone church was dedicated in 1866 and is in use still. The front door usually is unlocked, so enter and climb the narrow wood stairs to the loft. Not only will you get a strong feeling for the simplicity of the old days, but you'll see an unusual cedar pipe organ, one of several built by local craftsman Johann Traugott Wantke in the 1860s for area churches. The old churchyard cemetery is charming and ageless, enclosed by a hand-laid stone wall reminiscent of New England.

Henkel Square. On the square. Back in 1852 a German immigrant named Edward A. Henkel bought twenty-five acres in Round Top to establish a mercantile store. The following year he built a two-story home that today is the keystone of Henkel Square, a historical open-air museum operated by the Texas Pioneer Arts Foundation.

Dedicated to preserving the history of this region, Henkel Square is a collection of sixteen historically important structures scattered across eight acres of pasture in the heart of town. The docents are local women who explain each home or building, its furnishings, and how it fit into early Texas life. Don't miss the old Lutheran church, which doubled as a school. Its painted motto translates from German to "I call the living to my church and the dead to their graves," a reference to its two-clapper bell. One rings, the other tolls.

Five of the buildings were moved to Henkel Square from sites in surrounding communities, and the lumber needed for restorations was cut in the local woods, just as it was in pioneer times. Using old tools and techniques, today's craftsmen have kept each structure faithful to its period, an attention to authenticity that has won Henkel Square awards for restoration excellence.

The entrance is through the Victorian building that once housed Round Top's apothecary, and several of the homes have outstanding wall stenciling and period furniture. Open Thursday–Sunday afternoons year-round, except for major holidays. Fee. (409) 249-3308.

International Festival-Institute at Round Top (Festival Hill). On Jaster Road, off T-237, one-half mile north of the town square. What once was rolling open pasture graced only by bird song is now a mecca for music lovers throughout the world. Back in 1968 noted pianist James Dick performed near Round Top and fell victim to its bucolic charm. Returning in 1971, he held the first of his musical festival-institutes in Round Top's tiny town hall, a venture that has grown into permanent quarters on Festival Hill. Every summer sixty young professional musicians from various parts of the world attend master classes taught by a professional guest faculty and perform with internationally known musicians in a series of public concerts.

Two handsome old homes have been moved onto the Festival Hill grounds. The William Lockhart Clayton House, built in 1870 in La Grange, is now staff living quarters, and the C. A. Menke House, originally an old ranchhouse in Hempstead, is used as a conference center.

An Early Music Festival on or near Memorial Day weekend kicks off a series of summer concerts (through mid-July) in the new and air-conditioned Festival Hall, and monthly afternoon performances are offered from August to April. Tickets can be ordered in advance or purchased at the box office prior to curtain. There usually is a free concert for children in mid-June, as well as assorted educational museum forums at various times of the year.

Picnic facilities are free for the summer concerts, and you can even leave the food packing to someone else. Both Royers' Round Top Cafe, (409) 249-3611, and Klump's Country Cooking Restaurant, (409) 249-5696, prepare box picnics to go if you call in advance. During the August-to-April series you can reserve a Saturday night pre-concert dinner at Festival Hill ($$$). Limited overnight accommodations also are available by advance reservation during those months. P.O. Box 89, Round Top 78954, (409) 249-3129. Extensive herb gardens amid rock and cloisters are under construction and open daily adjacent to Menke House under the supervision of herb gurus Madalene Hill and Gwen Barclay. For a guided tour (fee), call (409) 249-5283. Those ladies also offer monthly "Herb Days at Festival Hill" which include a guided tour of the gardens, a three-course luncheon, and a short lecture on the use and enjoyment of herbs. Cost, at last notice, was $25 including tax and gratuity. They also teach educational workshops on various "herb" topics and organize the Round Top Herb Festival annually in the spring. For information and/or program reservations, write Gwen Barclay, Director of Food Service, P.O. Drawer 89, Round Top 78954; or call the number above.

Moore's Fort. Across T–237 from Round Top's square. This double log cabin with an open dog-trot center was the frontier home of John Henry Moore. Built about 1828 near the Colorado River in La Grange, it was used primarily as a defense against Indians.

Round Top General Store. On the T–237 side of the town square. Stop at this circa 1847 store for antiques, gifts, and fudge. Open Friday–Sunday afternoons. (409) 249–3600.

WHERE TO EAT

Calico Bakery. On the Square in Round Top. This small spot sells croissants, kolache, pastries, doughnuts, "pigs & wraps," and other baked goods for a quick breakfast or light lunch. Open Thursday–Sunday. $. (409) 249–5950.

Klump's Country Cooking Restaurant. On the west side of the square in Round Top. House specials run to Mexican food on Wednesday night, fresh catfish filets on Friday night, and fried chicken at Sunday noon. Owner Liz Klump also offers memorable apple pie, barbecue, steaks, and hamburgers for lunch and dinner Wednesday–Saturday, breakfast and lunch (until 2:00 P.M.) on Tuesday and Sunday. $–$$; (CC). (409) 249–5696.

Mad Hatter Tea Room and Old Brewery Cafe. On the Square in Round Top. A comfy adaptation of an old brewery, this interesting restaurant does as well by steaks, pasta, fish, and chicken at dinner as it does by quiche, salads, and sandwiches at lunch. Very much a hands-on enterprise of owners Kathleen and Kirk Whatley, you'll find wonderful desserts here as well as an eclectic collection of antiques, including vintage hats. English cream teas are served by reservation to four or more persons. Open Thursday–Sunday. $–$$; (CC). The Whatleys also operate a two-room B&B within walking distance of Round Top's heart. (409) 249–3331.

Royers' Round Top Cafe. On the north side of the square in

Round Top. Owned by Bud and Karen Royer and written up in *Country Living* magazine, this small place features "the kind of food you come to the country for." Frills run to Blue Bell ice cream cones (vanilla only) and homemade desserts. Real apples and pumpkins go into the pies—no canned fillings are used—and if you are lucky, it will be dewberry cobbler day. Open for lunch and dinner Wednesday–Saturday, Sunday from noon to 4:00 P.M.; expect to wait a spell on the front porch. $–$$. (409) 249-3611 or (800) 624-PIES.

CONTINUING ON

To visit Winedale, take FM-1457 north for 4 miles to FM-2714 and turn northeast.

WANDERING THE BACKROADS

If you have lingered too long in Round Top and now must head home, why not take the scenic route? T-237 South (connecting to T-159 South) to La Grange (Trip 4, this sector) is one of the nicest country rambles in the state. Take a few minutes to travel east or west of the highway on the many graded county roads. You'll pass gracious old homes, log cabins, churches flanked by tiny cemeteries, and numerous historical landmarks. As you enter Warrenton on T-237 South, watch for a large two-story rock house on the west side of the road. This is the Neece House, built in 1869 and currently being restored as a private residence. You'll also pass St. Martin's, locally called the smallest Catholic church in the world; it holds only twelve people. Concurrent with the Round Top Antique Fair on the first full weekends in April and October, Warrenton blossoms into a giant antiques, crafts, and collectibles market, with plenty of hearty country food on the side. Warrenton's old grocery store has been renovated into a B&B, Warrenton Inn, (409) 249-3074.

From La Grange follow T-71 southeast to Columbus (Trip 3, this sector) and I-10 east to Houston.

WINEDALE AND INDUSTRY

Winedale provides another look at yesterday's Texas. The settlement is blink-small: a gas station and a few homes tucked into a valley threaded by Jack's Creek. That old-style split-rail fence on the right, however, encircles one of the most ambitious restoration projects in the state, the Winedale Historical Center.

Administered by the University of Texas, this 225-acre outdoor museum illustrates many pages of the past. The basic farmstead was part of a Mexican land grant to William S. Townsend, one of Austin's second colony. He built a small house on the land about 1834 and in 1848 sold the farm to Samuel Lewis. He in turn expanded the home and the plantation, and by the mid-1850s this old farmhouse was a stage stop on the main road between Brenham and La Grange.

Although Winedale's grounds are open daily for wandering, guided tours (fee; weekends or by appointment only) are the only way to access the buildings. Starting at the visitor center, the first stop is a simple 1855 farm building known as Hazel's Lone Oak Cottage, often used as a gallery for special exhibitions. From there the tour moves to the focal point of the entire museum complex, the Sam Lewis House. This two-story farmhouse is notable for its authentic Texas primitive furnishings and beautiful wall and ceiling frescoes painted by a local German artist of the time, Rudolph Melchoir. Other rare examples of Melchoir's art can be seen in several of the Henkel Square houses in Round Top.

The Winedale complex also has assorted dependencies, such as a smokehouse and pioneer kitchen. The old barn, built in 1894 with cedar beams salvaged from an early cotton gin, now rings with the ageless words of Shakespeare in July and August, courtesy of University of Texas English students. The performances are Thursday–Sunday evenings, seats must be reserved in advance ($), and an inexpensive hunter's stew dinner is served before the Saturday evening show. You also are welcome to bring a picnic basket and blanket and feast in the field. For picnics to go contact either Klump's or Royer's eateries, listed in the Round Top section of this trip (pp. 112–117).

A ten-minute trek through the back pastures of Winedale leads to the McGregor-Grimm House, a two-story Greek Revival farmhouse built in 1861 and moved to Winedale from Wesley in 1967. As the

Lewis House represents the earlier, rather simple plantation home of the area, the McGregor-Grimm House is more gracious and elaborate, typical of pre–Civil War cotton-boom wealth.

Winedale hosts numerous special fests, symposia, and exhibitions throughout the year, many of which focus on early Texas antiques and crafts. New additions to the complex include a nature trail and herb garden. Picnickers are welcome. For more information call (409) 278-3530.

CONTINUING ON

From Winedale turn southeast (left) on FM-1457 and go approximately 9 miles to the intersection with T-159. Turn east (left), and it's then 19 miles to Bellville—beautiful country all the way.

En route take a few minutes to explore Industry, settled in 1831-33 and the oldest German community in Texas. An 1838 Republic of Texas post office still stands, now surrounded by Friedrich Ernst Memorial Park just north of the FM-159/FM-109 intersection. Stop also at Lindemann's General Store, in business since 1884 and a great place to buy local sausage, custom-cut meat, and cold drinks (open daily). Two other bits of the past are open by appointment: a 1920s doctor's office, (409) 357-2772, and Welcome Hall (1899), (409) 357-2729. Originally called Halle Das Welcome Maennerchor (Hall of the Welcome Men's Choir), the latter was the community's social center for years.

WANDERING THE BACKROADS

As an alternative, follow FM-1457 only as far as the tiny town of Shelby and swing north (left) on FM-389. At the intersection with FM-2502, turn right to Wesley. This was an early Czech-Moravian settlement and includes the first church of the Czech Brethren faith built in North America (1866). The rock foundation is original and utilizes a huge oak log to support the center of the building. The interior has some unusual hand-painted decorations more than a century old.

From Wesley continue south on FM-2502 to T-159 and turn east (left) to Bellville. Should you rather explore part of the northwest sector from Wesley, go north on FM-2502 and then northeast on

FM-389 into Brenham (Trip 6, northwest sector). From here it's US-290 East back to Houston.

BELLVILLE

Settled in 1848 and the Austin County seat, Bellville was named for Thomas Bell, one of Stephen F. Austin's "Old Three Hundred," as his first colony has been labeled by history. The best time to visit is during the spring Country Livin' Festival, when nature lines the routes into the town with bluebonnets and Indian paintbrush. During that festival the chamber of commerce sets up roadside booths where you can get maps and directions to the best flower displays. They also sell packets of bluebonnet seeds in the hope that you will sow some of next year's color yourself. For information on Bellville, including antiques shops, galleries, and such, contact the chamber of commerce, 4 North Holland (P.O. Box 670), Bellville 77418, (409) 865-3407.

Restoration is bringing back the architectural integrity of the old town square. Numerous building fronts have been returned to their original design, and more than a dozen housed antiques stores at last count. There also are new boutiques and art galleries, most of which open on Sunday afternoons. Plan your trip to take in Market Day on the Square on the first Saturday of every month (March–December). *Also fun:* Trash or Treasure Day on the third Wednesday of each month (March–November), when many residents place salable items in their front yards. Maps for the latter event are available at local convenience stores and the chamber of commerce on the day of the sale.

Although there are many historical markers in town, no vintage homes currently are open for scheduled tours. For a modest donation, however, members of the Bellville Historical Foundation can open some of those doors for you on a private guided tour. One of the special sites they have access to is Sam Houston's Texian Army encampment at Raccoon Bend on the west bank of the Brazos, currently undergoing an archaeological dig.

The following offer B&B: Banner Farm, (409) 865-8534 or (800) 865-8534; Cedar Creek Bed & Breakfast, (409) 865-9607 or (800) 481-1951; and High Cotton Inn, (409) 865-9796.

WHAT TO DO

Bluebonnet Farms. This hundred-acre farm near Bellville breeds, raises, and trains American saddlebred horses and has several national champions in its paddocks. Visitors are welcome only if they have a sincere interest in the riding and training of horses; no sightseers or casual drop-ins, please. Appointments required. (409) 865-5051.

Christmas Tree Farms. You can choose your own and haul it home at Fortune's Farm, (409) 865-5826.

The 1896 Jailhouse Museum. 36 South Bell. The sheriff's office and county jail (with original gallows) have been furnished to their turn-of-the-century look, and monthly exhibits include artifacts from the Texian Army encampment at Raccoon Bend as well as assorted weapons, many of which were confiscated from prisoners during the jail's serious years. Open Fridays from 1:00–3:00 P.M., Saturdays 10:00 A.M. to 2:00 P.M. Call to confirm hours. Fee. (409) 865-3407 or 865-3325.

The Turnverein (Dance Hall). On FM-529 in the city park, immediately east of Bellville. Now celebrating its centennial, Bellville's dance hall was the first (1897) of five wooden pavilions in Austin County attributed to Joachim Hintz, a German immigrant carpenter. Still in continuous use, this quaint, 12-sided hall has hosted many an oom-pah band and Schottische as well as countless county fairs, antiques shows, and so on. Other examples of Hintz's dance halls include the Sealy Liedertafel Hall on Main Street in Sealy (circa 1914 and under restoration); Peter's Hacienda Schuetzen Verein (circa 1900), five miles north of Bellville on T-36, then 1 mile west on Trenckman Road; the Coshatte Turnverein (circa 1928; call the Bellville Historical Society at 409/865-9116 for directions); and the Cat Spring Landwirth Schaftlide Verein (circa 1902), on FM-1094 in Cat Spring.

WHERE TO EAT

Bellville Restaurant. 103 East Main, across from the courthouse. The building dates from 1885, the restaurant from the 1930s. Lunch here is a daily ritual for Bellville's business community. The steam table with its multichoices of entrees and vegetables is popular, and there are daily specials and a regular menu. Open for breakfast and lunch Tuesday–Sunday. $-$$; (CC). (409) 865-9710.

Granny's Bar-B-Q. 515 E. Hellmuth St., one-half block off T-36. Real pit barbecue here, with all the fixings. Open for lunch and early dinner Monday–Saturday. $–$$. (409) 865-5752.

Manuel's Mexican Restaurant. 1416 S. Front (T-36 south). Fajitas and shrimp enchiladas are two of the house specialties. Open daily for lunch and dinner. $–$$; (CC). (409) 865-8408.

Newman's Bakery. 504 E. Main. This coffee shop is a local favorite for breakfast as well as soup and sandwiches for lunch. Open daily, 6:00 A.M. to 5:00 P.M. $. (409) 865-9804.

Sillavan's Restaurant. 472 T-36, between Bellville and Brenham. Good old American standards like chicken-fried steaks, hamburgers, and seafood are served here, including a blue-plate special at lunch. Open for lunch and dinner Tuesday–Saturday. $–$$. (409) 865-5066.

Stagecoach Barbecue. 239 FM-2429. This is a good place for those two Texas favorites, barbecue and baked potatoes, along with a game of horseshoes or washer-pitching. Open for lunch and dinner Tuesday–Sunday. $–$$. (409) 865-8433.

WANDERING THE BACKROADS

To return to Houston from Bellville, you again have a choice. FM-529 east is a rural route that intersects T-6 north of the Bear Creek business area on the northwest side of Houston. If you live in south Houston, your best bet from Bellville is T-36 south 15 miles to Sealy (Trip 1, this sector), then east on I-10 toward home.

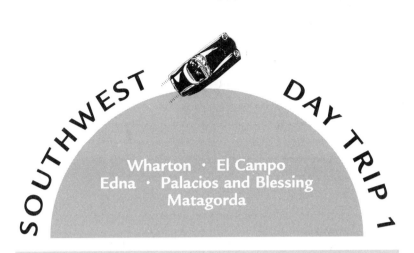

Wharton · El Campo
Edna · Palacios and Blessing
Matagorda

WHARTON

The trip through Wharton, El Campo, Edna, Palacios and Blessing, and Matagorda covers a lot of territory, so you may want to make a weekend out of it with an overnight at the Luther Hotel in Palacios. Take your fishing and crabbing gear and have fun.

Start your trip via US–59 south to Wharton. While not a gee-whiz destination in itself, Wharton has several pleasures. This rich agricultural land drew Stephen F. Austin's early settlers, and the town of Wharton began about 1846. Fun to know: Playwright Horton Foote, winner of the 1995 Pulitzer Prize for *The Young Man from Atlanta* as well as two Academy Awards at various times in his career, is a Wharton native and still maintains a home here. Many of his plays take place in "Harrison," a thinly disguised stand-in for his home town.

Although no homes are open to the public on a regular basis, it's interesting to drive down Wharton's oak-shaded streets. For information on local events as well as a list of antiques shops and an interesting driving map of "the Caney Run" through Wharton, Colorado, and Matagorda counties, contact the Wharton Chamber of Commerce, 225 North Richmond Road, Wharton 77488, (409) 532–1862.

WHAT TO DO

Cotton Ginning. There are not many places left in Texas to watch a cotton gin do its thing. If you are interested and plan to visit

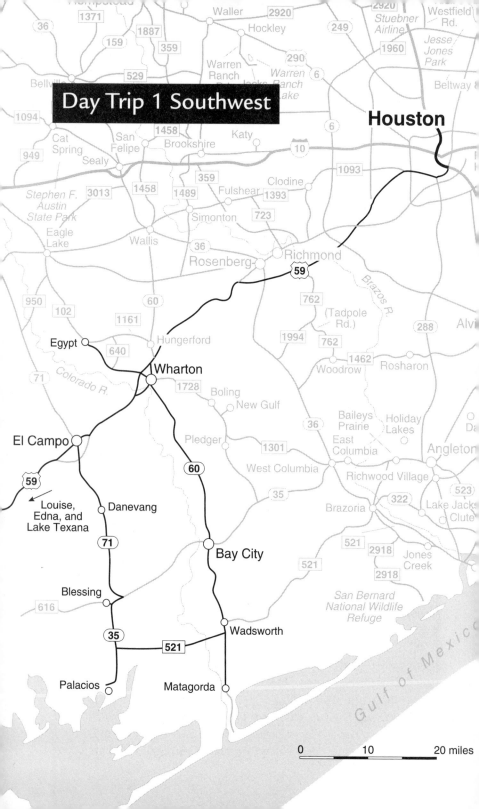

Wharton during the August–September ginning season, you can visit the Moses Gin through advance arrangement with the Caney Valley Cotton Co., Box 470, Wharton 77488, (409) 532–5210 or 532–3522.

Egypt Plantation. On FM–102 north between Wharton and Eagle Lake. The tiny crossroads town of Egypt was settled by Austin's second colony. Park at the old frame general store and go in for a chat and a cool drink. Then walk to the new post office with its two vintage gas pumps before looking around the rest of this tiny town. A one-lane road, FM–1161, leads to the Heard-Northington family cemetery, and just beyond is the family's old homeplace, Egypt Plantation. Normally open only to groups of twelve or more, this durable pink-brick plantation home (circa 1849) welcomes individuals and families in October, November, and during the summer. The house tour includes the Northington-Heard Museum, a remarkable collection of Texana housed in the old Egypt–Santa Fe Railroad depot behind the plantation house. Reservations required. Fee. Box 277, Egypt 77436, (409) 677–3562.

James G. Martin Nuts. 117 South Sunset. This local pecan broker has six mechanical pecan crackers that rarely stop during the harvest months of October through January. You are welcome to stop in and watch. He sells both wholesale and retail, so you can pack some home. Open Monday–Friday; Saturday until noon. (409) 532–2345.

Peachland (Gundermann's) Orchard. Take the Eagle Lake exit from US–59 South and follow FM–102 North into Glen Flora. Watch for signs. If tornados, freezes, and droughts have left the crops intact, visitors are welcome to pick Brazos blackberries, tomatoes, squash, pickling cucumbers, green beans, and peas here, starting in mid-May. This farm is notable for its extremely limited use of pesticides. Country arts and crafts and sometimes cider also are sold here. Call for crop information. (409) 677–3319.

The Real McCoy Hunting Club. Guided or unguided duck and geese hunting on 900 acres of prime rice-growing land at the edge of the Lissie-Egypt prairie. Fee. Contact Hudg Ansley, 425 Croom Drive, Wharton 77488, (713) 485–0081.

Riverfront Park at the Port of Wharton. This seventeen-acre civic project has a playground, picnic tables, walking trails, restrooms, and a deck overlooking the river. Concessionaires are often here during summer, offering rental canoes, paddleboats, and bicycles; check the current situation with the Wharton Chamber of Commerce. Stop here with your picnic, and then tour the nearby Monterey Square in front of the 1888 courthouse. The square is one of the Main Street projects fostered by the National Trust for Historic Preservation.

Wharton County Museum. 3615 Richmond Road. Some interesting bits and pieces of Wharton's past are gathered here. Open daily Tuesday–Friday and on Saturday afternoon. Donations appreciated. (409) 532-2600.

WHERE TO EAT

Hinze's Bar-B-Que. 3940 Highway 59 Loop. Local folks think this family-run place has the best barbecue in the region, not to mention the homemade chocolate, coconut, and pecan pies. Try Hinze's on a take-out. Open for lunch and dinner daily. $-$$; (CC). (409) 532-2710.

Mama John's. 814 East Milam. The "Home-burgers" are flavorful and juicy here because John grinds his own chuck meat; the buffet lunch on weekdays is an equally tasty buy. Everything is fresh—and in season—not even the buffet vegetables come from cans—and John makes 90 percent of his own seasonings. Test those out on the blackened fish of the day; all his seafood is bought off the boats in Matagorda or Palacios. Open for breakfast, and lunch daily. $-$$. (409) 532-8761.

Must Be Heaven. 100 S. Houston. This is a good spot for lite lunches, soups, sandwiches, pies, and a snack on Blue Bell ice cream. Open Monday-Saturday, 8:00 A.M. to 5:00 p.m. $. (409) 532-4504.

WANDERING THE BACKROADS

Wharton is surrounded by vast cotton, corn, and rice fields, and the early spring months along any rural road in the area produce a vision of fresh green punctuated by bright wildflowers. Local folks think there is no prettier drive in Texas than FM-102 from Wharton north to Eagle Lake.

Another nice rural drive is along the Spanish Camp Road, FM-640. Watch for the Glen Flora Plantation home (private) on your left, a hint of the Old South. To continue this day trip, follow US-59 south to El Campo, Louise, and Edna.

EL CAMPO

This spreading town, 68 miles south of Houston on US-59, sits in the middle of a vast coastal grass plain used for open cattle range from the early 1800s. By the 1850s this area was the starting point for cattle drives across east Texas on the Opelousas and Atascosito trails, heading for the railroad terminals at New Orleans and Mobile.

The railroad eventually made it to this part of Texas, and by the early 1880s the area had an official railroad name, Prairie Switch. Mexican cowboys handling the large herds would camp nearby—thus the name El Campo, which was officially adopted in 1902 when the town was incorporated. Early settlers came from Germany, Sweden, Czechoslovakia, and Ireland, an ethnic mix celebrated on El Campo Grande Day every August. For information contact the El Campo Chamber of Commerce, Box 446, El Campo 77437, (409) 543-2713.

WHAT TO DO

El Campo Museum of Art, Science and History. 2350 North Mechanic, in the Civic Center on T-71 North at FM-2765. The main local attraction is the big-game trophy exhibit at this elaborate and extensive museum, originally a private collection of a local family. Shell and rock displays have been added, along with a waterfowl exhibit and a clown collection. Temporary shows are mounted four times a year. Open Monday–Saturday. Donation. (409) 543-2714.

WHERE TO EAT

Churchill Downs. 101 South Mechanic. This antiques store serves homemade soups and sandwiches. Open Tuesday–Saturday. $. (409) 543-5611.

The Front Porch. 111 West Calhoun. This comfy old home-turned-restaurant serves home-style food with fourteen choices of veggies. Everything is made from scratch. Open weekdays for lunch. $. (409) 543-1881.

Greek Bros. Oyster Bar and Saloon. 133 South Mechanic. One of the most popular eateries in the region, this large and lively place puts some tasty twists on seafood, chicken and other Texas standards. Oysters are always on the menu, prepared several different ways, and the Blue Plate Special at lunch ($5.95) changes daily. Although there's a full bar as well as dancing (live band on Thursday and Saturday nights), this is a family kind of place. Open weekdays for lunch and dinner; dinner only on Saturday. $-$$$; (CC). (409) 543-1757.

Mikeska's Bar-B-Q. 218 Merchant. Centrally located, this is a good spot to pick up some picnic sandwiches or take a road break. Open daily. $. (409) 543-5471.

Prasek's Smokehouse. On US-59, 4 miles west of El Campo. Using an old family recipe, Mike and Betty Jo Prasek turn out memorable smoked sausage and both beef and turkey jerky, as well as baked goods. If you call ahead, they'll have a gift box or sandwiches ready to go when you arrive. Open daily from 7:00 A.M. until early evening. $-$$; (CC). (409) 543-8312.

LOUISE

First established in 1881 as a station on the "Macaroni" line (the New York, Texas and Mexican Railroad that ran between Victoria and Rosenberg; see information on Edna that follows), this tiny settlement today lies at the heart of a major rice growing region, 24 miles west of Wharton. Visitors who take the quick jog off US-59 south (exit 1160) find a few antiques shops, an old cemetery (good gravestone rubbings; ask locally for directions), an outstanding vintage hardware store, and some good eats. Fun to know: the towns of Louise, Inez, and Edna (all on US-59) were named after the daughters of one of the railroad's financial backers, D.E. Hungerford.

WHERE TO EAT

The Antique Eatery. 700 North Old Highway 59. The building and the food share top billing here. Built in 1908 as a store and Wells Fargo agency, this false-fronter has been moved at least three times and has had more lives than a cat. Twin sisters Jane Smith and Judy Peter now operate an excellent country cafe within its venerable walls. Known especially for its outstanding breads, pies, and cakes, this eatery also offers hamburgers, shrimp, steaks, and chicken (when was the last time you saw a fried gizzard platter on a menu?), and most of the antique furnishings are for sale. Open for lunch Monday-Friday, dinner Friday and Saturday. $-$$. (409) 648-2550.

EDNA

Once known as "Macaroni Station," because that's all the New York, Texas and Mexican Railroad commissary on this site stocked, Edna today is home to some 5,556 people and is a commercial center for livestock, oil, and agriculture. It's important to day trippers primarily as the gateway to beautiful Lake Texana (see below).

Interesting to know: That lake now covers the old town site of Texana, which was a well-established Indian village at the time of La Salle's expedition in the area in 1685. In 1832 it became the first town founded in Jackson County, and a few years later the Allen brothers decided Texana would be the ideal location for their dream city because of its location on the Navidad River, which provided deep-water access to the Gulf of Mexico. Anticipating that it would be a great port, they offered $100 in gold for the land. When the owner demanded $200, the Allen brothers moved northeast and ultimately bought a tract of land in Harris County upon which they founded their dream city—Houston.

Artifacts from Texana's early days were uncovered by archaeologists before the site was inundated with water; they now are on display at the Lavaca-Navidad River Authority headquarters, north of Palmetto Bend Dam on FM-3131. Free and open weekdays.

The Jackson County Chamber of Commerce has area bird lists as well as information on Lake Texana, the town of Edna, and assorted historical sites, more than thirty of which have historical markers; P.O. Box 788 (317 West Main), Edna 77957, (512) 782-7146.

WHAT TO DO

Lake Texana. Twenty-one miles southwest of El Campo via US-59; 6.5 miles east of Edna via T-111 South. Formed by the Palmetto Bend Dam, which backs up the Navidad River for 18 miles, this 11,000-acre lake is noted for its catfish and bass, plus there are good camping, fishing, and picnicking under shady oaks. Much of this mixed oak-and-pecan woodland is usually kept neatly trimmed by resident deer. All water sports are here, either at Lake Texana State Park, (512) 782-5718 or (800) 792-1112, or at Lake Texana Marina and Brackenridge Plantation Campground, (512) 782-7145; you can rent paddle boats and canoes. Birding is excellent in the state park, so much so that it's a stop on the recently developed Great Coastal Birding Trail. For information on the latter, contact the Houston Audubon Society, (713) 932-1392.

Texana Museum. 403 North Wells (T-111 North). Exhibits here include old volumes of medicine formulas, a rosewood Chickering piano more than 130 years old, a much older violin, artifacts pertaining to the settlement of Jackson County, and a jail out back, built in 1922 and complete with hangman facilities. The museum is open Tuesday–Friday afternoons. The jail can be toured by appointment. (512) 782-5431.

WHERE TO EAT

The Brown Boar Saloon & Grill. In the ghost town of Blair on T-111, 5 miles north of US-59 overpass in Edna. Housed in a ninety-year-old brick schoolhouse surrounded by century-old oaks, this combination nightclub and eatery is owned by national recording artist Jimmy Lee Huff, who often entertains the patrons. Expect Victorian decor, special activities on weekends, and a live brown boar named Baby. The menu ranges from bar food to seafood and steaks. Open daily; call for hours. $-$$; (CC). (512) 782-7905.

Dos Hermanos Mexican Restaurant. 106 East Houston Highway (US-59 frontage road; exit 111), Edna. If you hanker for Tex-Mex while roaming this way, try here. Open for lunch and dinner daily. $-$$: (CC). (512) 782-3372.

Frontier Barbecue. 608 North East Street, Edna. This local favorite does the standards well. Open for lunch daily, dinner Thursday–Saturday. $-$$. (512) 782-5270.

Palmetto Restaurant. 906 West Main, Edna. American and Mexican standards here, along with a good noon buffet and salad bar. Don't pass up the homemade rolls. Open for breakfast, lunch, and dinner Monday–Saturday; breakfast and lunch on Sunday. $-$$; (CC). (512) 782-2471.

CONTINUING ON

To reach Blessing and Palacios from Edna, take T-111 east from Edna for 29 miles (you'll cross Lake Texana) to T-71; turn south (right) four miles, then west (right) on T-35 for two miles to Blessing, 13 miles to Palacios.

PALACIOS AND BLESSING

When you want to get away from it all, take T-71 south from El Campo to the sleepy fishing community of Palacios. Whatever you want to escape, it isn't here. The big activity for visitors is walking from the Luther Hotel to Petersen's Restaurant, with a short stroll along the recently refurbished bayfront thrown in for excitement. The hotel also is a popular haven for boaters.

The area was named Tres Palacios several centuries ago by shipwrecked Spanish sailors who claimed they saw a vision of three palaces on this bay. Although the tiny town that began here around the turn of the century doesn't quite live up to the vision, for daytrippers Palacios is the perfect low-key escape.

There are two lighted fishing piers (bring your own bait and gear), numerous other wood jetties out into the bay, a new shell beach, plus several public playgrounds, marinas, piers, and boat ramps. A 1.5-mile lighted walkway curves along the seawall (ideal for rollerblading), and a new, rather grand public beach area starts just south of the Luther Hotel.

The old town of Blessing, 13 miles north of Palacios via T-35, is a real piece of the past. When the tracks of the New York Central (Missouri Pacific) Railroad and the Southern Pacific Railroad finally crossed on the Texas prairie in 1902, legend says that developer J. E. "Shanghai" Pierce said, "Thank God," and set aside 640 acres for a town of that name. The post office demurred, and "Blessing" was chosen as a compromise. Pierce's burial site is here in Hawley Cemetery, along with his likeness atop a 10-foot column so that he could continue to oversee his lands even after death.

WHAT TO DO

Birding. More than 450 bird species, including brown pelicans and black skimmers, have been spotted along this portion of the Texas coast, making Palacios an important stop on the Great Texas

Coastal Birding Trail; there are five birding sites in the city and six others nearby. For a map to major birding sites, contact the Palacios Chamber of Commerce, 312 Main, Palacios 77465, (512) 972-2615, (800) 611-4567.

Charter boat excursions aboard the 30-passenger *Spoonbill Express.* One good reason to overnight in Palacios is the chance to continue on to the Port O'Connor area the next day for a boat tour of the coastal sanctuary islands in southern Matagorda Bay. Captain-guide Robbie Gregory's tours ($15) cover marine ecology, several centuries of history, and birding. From October through March twelve whooping cranes winter within 1.5 miles of Port O'Connor, and countless other species nest here from January through June. (512) 983-2862.

WHERE TO EAT

Blessing Hotel Coffee Shop. Avenue B and Tenth Street, Blessing. Built in 1906, the hotel now is owned by the Blessing Historical Foundation and is under slow restoration; its twenty rooms are simple and inexpensive. What was the hotel's ballroom is now a coffee shop with a well-earned reputation of its own. You pay your money and fill your plate from pots of delicious country-style food lined up on top of old stoves. The breakfasts are incredible, and the lunches are large enough to satisfy a hardworking field hand. No cutesy quiches here; the noon meal on Sunday is like Thanksgiving all year long. Open daily until 2:00 P.M. $. (512) 588-6623.

Petersen's Restaurant. 420 Main Street, Palacios. Almost everything edible that swims in the gulf ends up on the table at Petersen's, and the toasted homemade French bread is in a high class by itself. Open for lunch and dinner Tuesday-Sunday. $-$$; (CC). (512) 972-2413.

WHERE TO STAY

The Luther Hotel. 408 South Bay Boulevard, on the bay between Fourth and Fifth streets in Palacios. Quality lasts, and this rambling white frame hostelry has survived many a storm since its construction in 1903. Sited with dignity on a large lawn, this is the kind of place where you contentedly watch twilight creep across

Palacios Bay while lounging in a chaise on the front porch. Resort it isn't; relaxing it is. Members of the Luther family still run this historic hotel and suggest you have reservations, as they hang out the NO VACANCY sign with regularity. The rooms are plain but comfortable, with air conditioning and/or ceiling fans and private baths. Several have kitchens, plus there's a third-floor "penthouse" if you feel like splurging. Except for a complimentary Continental breakfast, no food is served at the hotel. (512) 972-2312.

WANDERING THE BACKROADS

The main route into Palacios is T-71 and T-35 south from El Campo. En route a short turn east on County Road 46 (11 miles south of El Campo) brings you to Danevang Lutheran Church and a memorial to the Danish pioneers who settled here in 1894.

T-60 is an alternate route to Palacios through neat and orderly Bay City. Take a break here at the Matagorda County Museum, 2100 Avenue F, and examine its collection of early Texas maps, carpenter's tools, and other Matagorda-related archival material. There's also an outstanding historical children's museum in the basement. "Our Town" focuses on the turn of the century from a child's point of view. Kids play "dress-up" in vintage-style clothing, write on slates in a one-room school, shop in a general store, and so on. Open Friday mornings and weekend afternoons. Fee. (409) 245-7502.

CONTINUING ON

To reach Matagorda from Palacios, take T-35 north approximately 6 miles. Then turn east (right) on FM-521 for 17 miles to the T-60 intersection at Wadsworth. Turn south (right) on T-60 for approximately 11 miles to Matagorda. Plan a stop en route at the Houston Light & Power Company's South Texas Nuclear Plant on FM-521. The free visitor center (open Monday–Saturday) explains all, but tours of the project (weekdays only) must be reserved in advance; (409) 245-1477 or (512) 972-5023. While driving FM-521 near the power project, watch on the north side for tiny St. Francis Catholic Church and cemetery. An early Polish settlement, only the church was rebuilt after the 1895 hurricane swept all else away.

MATAGORDA

Founded in 1829 with Stephen F. Austin as one of its original proprietors, Matagorda thrived as the Colorado River's port on the Gulf of Mexico and was the third largest town in Texas by 1834. One of the early freight routes that supplied central Texas with the basics of life ran between Matagorda and Austin; wagons left both cities on the first and fifteenth of every month.

The railroad steamed across Texas by 1853 and bypassed Matagorda in favor of Bay City. A hurricane in 1854 dealt another blow, and Matagorda never regained its early prominence.

Visitors today find two historic churches (1838 and 1839; both thought to be the first of their denominations in Texas), an 1830 cemetery, several homes with historic markers, and a double lock system operated by the U.S. Army Corps of Engineers on the Intracoastal Canal.

If it's crabbing, seining, picnicking, or beaching you want, turn south on FM-2031 (locally called River Road) in the center of town and follow it to the Gulf. There are many fine crabbing and fishing holes along the way, and the road ends at a new county park (picnic and restroom facilities) and 20 miles of beach stretching as far as you can see. Pink granite jetties poke out into the Gulf, ideal for fishing. There are several charter fishing operations on River Road, among them Allen's Landing, (409) 863-7729, and Raymond Cox, (409) 863-7434. Catches change with the season but generally include trout, flounder, and redfish.

WHERE TO EAT

Seabreeze Restaurant. Corner of Market and Matagorda streets. It's a good thing this is a good place to eat, because it's nearly the only game in town. The shrimp salad holds its own against the best of the coast, and the seasonal oysters come from nearby shoals. Contrary to the general rule of "Don't order beef in a seafood restaurant," the burgers and steaks win local raves. Open Tuesday-Sunday for lunch and dinner. $-$$; (CC). (409) 863-7905.

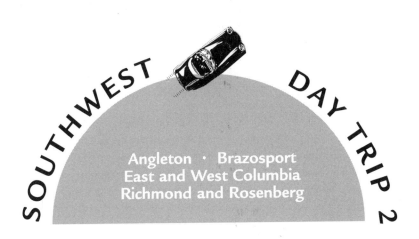

Angleton · Brazosport
East and West Columbia
Richmond and Rosenberg

ANGLETON

Two routes—T-288 and T-35—come south from Houston and meet in Angleton before continuing to the Brazosport area as T-288. You'll pass the old Brazoria County Courthouse in Angleton, built in 1896 and expanded in 1916 and again in 1927. It now houses the Brazoria County Historical Museum.

If you enjoy canoeing, explore Bastrop Bayou, about 5 miles south of Angleton via either FM-523 or T-288. The best put-in for this 5-mile float is at the FM-2004 bridge, south of the intersection with FM-523. The best take-out is 2 miles (by road) farther at the old T-288 bridge (watch for a railroad track). Even better, float as far as you want and then turn around and paddle back to your car. The current generally is not a problem.

WHAT TO DO

Brazoria County Historical Museum. 100 East Cedar, at intersection with T-288 (Velasco Street). A general store and a doctor's office from Brazoria County's past are re-created here, along with a plantation bedroom, dioramas, and economic exhibits. Well worth a stop, if only to shop in the museum's interesting store. Free. Open Tuesday–Saturday. (409) 849-5711, ext. 1208.

Brazos River County Park. From T-288 north of Angleton, turn west on County Road 44, south on FM-521, then west on County Road 30. This seventy-five-acre park on the banks of the Brazos River

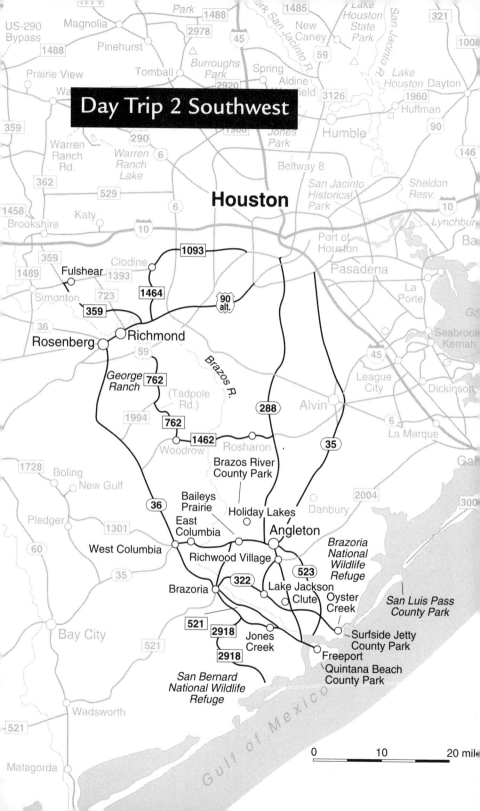

has picnic sites with grills, pavilions for groups, 0.5 mile of surfaced trail, a man-made lake with a duck island, a two-story observation tower, and a large, well-equipped playground. Lots of small wildlife here, including rabbits, squirrels, and deer. For information or group reservations, call (409) 849-5711, ext. 1541.

Chenango Peach Orchards. Beginning in early May and continuing through June, you can pick peaches, nectarines, blackberries, apples, and other produce at reasonable cost at this farm near Rosharon. Take the first Angleton exit from T-288 south, turn west and go 1 mile to FM-521, turn south for 0.5 mile, and watch for signs. (281) 431-2138.

CONTINUING ON

From Angleton T-288 South takes you into the heart of Brazosport.

BRAZOSPORT

It's rare to find the name Brazosport on current maps, but that's because it really is nine communities: Brazoria, Freeport, Lake Jackson, Quintana, Richwood, Surfside, Oyster Creek, Jones Creek, and Clute. Their common bond is the mighty (and usually muddy) Brazos River as it empties into the Gulf of Mexico.

Local folks say that the name has its origins on seventeenth-century nautical charts to mark where the Brazos meets the sea, and Brazosport today is the only mainland community actually on the gulf-front coast of Texas.

This is historic country—many from Stephen F. Austin's first colony settled here—but there is little physical evidence left to provide tourist interest. The area's biggest draws are the free and unrestricted beaches. Any sunny weekend finds thousands of cars lined up on the sand, boom boxes and barbecues going full blast. Most of the beach-related businesses shut down after Labor Day, and Brazosport quickly reverts to the industrial and refining community it basically is.

There's something going on in at least one of the nine towns nearly every month of the year. For a schedule of special events as well as information on marinas, vacation rentals, deep-sea charter and party-boat fishing, and so on, contact the Southern Brazoria

County Visitor and Convention Bureau, 420 West Highway 332B, Clute 77531; (409) 265-2508 or (800) 938-4853. For local weather information call (409) 798-1212; for surf and tide conditions, call (409) 233-5301; for a fishing report call (409) 233-7351.

WHAT TO DO

Annual Christmas Bird Count. Because of its diversity of habitats, Freeport often leads the nation in number of species spotted during this annual volunteer activity (196 in the 1996 count). Call the visitor and convention bureau above for information.

Antique Dental Museum. 115 North Dixie Drive, Suite 200, Lake Jackson. A former antiques dealer and now a noted endodontist, Dr. Kim Freeman collects old tools of his trade and shows them off in a 500-square-foot minimuseum adjacent to his waiting room. Virtually a building-within-a-building, this precisely reproduced Victorian setting houses five operatories covering the 1860s to 1925 and includes some extremely rare cabinets and unusual furnishings. In all, this is the largest antique dental museum in the Southwest. Open weekdays; weekends by appointment. (409) 297-0633.

The Beaches. The old mouth of the Brazos River becomes, through engineering, the Brazos Harbor Channel and is framed by two jetties ideal for free fishing and crabbing. This channel also divides the beaches. Northeast to San Luis Pass via FM-3005 and the Bluewater Highway (County Road 257) are Surfside and Follet's Island beaches (14 miles of sand). Southwest of the channel are Quintana Beach and Bryan Beach State Park; both are accessed via T-288 South (Brazosport Boulevard) and FM-1495.

The latter's 878 acres are undeveloped but good for fishing, beachcombing, and birdwatching; use four-wheel drive and keep a wary eye on the tide or you may be stranded by rising water. Quintana Beach has an excellent county park that includes two restored historic houses, a shore ecology lab, picnic pavilions, restrooms with showers, a fishing pier, a playground and sports courts, World War II gun mounts, and both primitive camping and RV sites. The latter require reservations. Fee. (409) 233-1461 or (800) 8-PARK-RV. Take notice, however, of the park's warning signs regarding snakes, and be aware that the beach often wears storm debris.

With the exception of Quintana and a small section of Surfside, automobile traffic is allowed on all beaches. Camping generally is where you wish. There are no hookups, and public restroom facilities are extremely limited. Surfside has the most commercial development. If it's solitude you seek, Bryan Beach is your best bet. For additional beach information, call (409) 265-2508.

Anglers and RV devotees note: Two new county parks have been designed with you in mind. San Luis Pass County Park and RV Campground is one of the hottest fishing spots on the gulf coast. Day-use facilities include fishing piers, a boat ramp, a playground, and a visitor center with a deck overlooking the water. The RV area has full hookups as well as a bathhouse with showers and laundry facilities (fee); for reservations call (800) 3-PARK-RV. Fisherfolk, birders, and picnickers also find good facilities at Surfside Jetty County Park on the Brazos River Harbor Channel. This gulf-front park features a deck and patio with picnic tables, restrooms, showers, lighted volleyball courts and parking, a paved walking trail along a bird-rich lagoon, and an observation tower. Handrails and a concrete walkway allow easy fishing from the jetty.

Big Boggy National Wildlife Refuge. On the northern shore of East Matagorda Bay. Difficult to get to, this wild area is open for seasonal wildfowl hunting only. (409) 849-6062.

Brazoria National Wildlife Refuge. On the north shore of West Galveston Bay. From T-288 South in Lake Jackson, turn east on FM-2004 for 5 miles, right on FM-523 for 8 miles, and follow signs. This 42,338-acre reserve is the winter home to some 40,000 snow geese and small populations of Canada and white-fronted geese. It's open the first full weekend of every month for birding and nature photography, and there's also seasonal access by water only for wildfowl hunting. Visitors find hiking trails and a 6-mile auto tour through numerous habitats. (409) 849-6062.

Brazosport Center for the Arts and Sciences. 400 College Drive, Lake Jackson, on the Brazosport College campus off T-288. This 40,000-square-foot cultural complex is of interest to day visitors primarily for the gem of a natural science museum it contains. Exhibits at the Brazosport Museum of Natural Science interpret this coastal region through shells, plants, animals, fossils, minerals, and Indian artifacts. The shell exhibit, the most extensive in the southern United States, is particularly well done and will turn your beach trips into expeditions. The Brazosport Nature Center and Planetarium has star shows for the public on Tuesday evenings. A self-guided nature trail along Oyster Creek reveals more than 200 species of riverbottom vegetation. Closed Monday. (409) 265-7661.

Fishing Charters and Party-Boat Rentals. Captain Elliott's Party Boats offers daily deep-sea fishing trips to the snapper banks 30–60 miles offshore year-round, nine-hour trips on Friday and Saturday nights from May through September, and a twenty-four-hour safari May through October. The company also has (by private charter only) two-hour sightseeing trips on the Old Brazos River. Fee; (CC). Reservations advised. (409) 233-1811.

Two Surfside firms also offer deep-sea charters. Action Charters operates four boats for parties of four to sixteen people. Call for brochure and rates, (409) 265-0999 or (800) 456-6984. Johnston's Sportfishing has three "six-pack" yachts (for up to six people), (409) 233-8513. In both cases all you bring is food and drinks. The charter firms provide equipment, bait, and expertise.

Girouard's General Store. 626 West Second Street, Freeport. When Texas Monthly magazine labels something the best in the state, it's worth a good look. You'll find the wrenches over the bread, plumber's helpers near the piñatas, and nearly everything else tucked somewhere. This is an outstanding example of a nearly extinct type of store. If you forgot your crabbing or seining gear, just stop here. Open daily except Sunday. (409) 233-4211.

Industrial Tours. Dow USA offers free guided bus tours of its operations on Wednesdays by appointment only (no children under ten), (409) 238-9222. It's also possible to tour the Port of Freeport, including a close-up look at a working cargo ship if one is in port. (409) 233-2667.

San Bernard Wildlife Refuge. Ten miles west of Freeport. From T-36 South turn southwest on FM-2611, left on FM-2918, then right on County Road 306. This 24,455-acre prairie and marsh preserve can be reached by boat from the Intracoastal Waterway and by car via FM-2004 West from T-288 in Lake Jackson. Established as a quality habitat for wintering migratory waterfowl and other birds, the refuge has recorded more than 400 species of wildlife and is the winter home to more than 90,000 snow geese. Birding, wildlife observation, hiking, photography, fishing, and waterfowl hunting are the major activities. One loop road encircles Moccasin Pond, and a new walking trail leads to a woodland area usually rich with birds. For on-site assistance try the maintenance facilities on County Road 306, inside the refuge boundaries. The gates are always open; no fee. Information: P.O. Drawer 1088, Angleton 77516, (409) 849-6062.

Scuba Diving. For two- and three-day diving trips in the gulf from Freeport aboard the M/V Fling or the M/V Spree, see any local dive shop.

Sea Center Texas. 300 Medical Drive, Lake Jackson. Technically the largest red drum (redfish) hatchery in the world, this free, $13 million facility is reason enough to journey to Brazosport. The 15,000-square-foot Visitor's Center has a large touch pool where folks can handle marine animals such as clams, snails, anemones, crabs, starfish, and urchins; an impressive coastal bay aquarium where gulf species such as red drum, speckled trout, and snook cruise through 2,200 gallons of water; a 5,000-gallon jetty exhibit with a variety of fin fish zipping in and out of wooden pilings and rocks; a 5,000-gallon artificial reef that replicates those found in the open gulf; a 1,000-gallon salt marsh where crabs, shrimp, periwinkles, and other aquatic denizens scurry around a simulated natural habitat; and a 50,000-gallon Gulf of Mexico aquarium where 500-pound Gordon the Grouper swims amid tarpon, redfish, and circling sharks.

Visitors also can tour the broodfish tanks in an adjacent hatchery building and explore several outside culture ponds and a five-acre marsh area. The latter has elevated walkways, interpretive signing, and viewing platforms. Open Tuesday-Friday from 9:00 A.M. to 4:00 P.M.; Saturday from 10:00 A.M. to 5:00 P.M., and Sunday from 1:00 to 4:00 P.M. (409) 292-0100.

WHERE TO EAT

Cafe Laredo. 403 This Way, Lake Jackson. The chef makes his own tortillas and hot sauce, two reasons why this Mexican place is a hands-down local favorite. Open for lunch and dinner Monday–Saturday. $; (CC). (409) 297-0696.

Dido's. From FM-521 in Brazoria turn left on T-36, right on FM-311, and right on FM-519 to the river. Dido runs his own shrimp boats, which makes for good eating, either in the air-conditioned dining room or on the outside deck. In summer open for lunch and dinner daily except Wednesday; in winter open weekdays (except Wednesday) for dinner, weekends for lunch and dinner. $-$$; (CC). (409) 964-3167.

D.J.'s Bar-B-Que. 906 West Plantation, Clute. A longtime local favorite, this place is open Monday for lunch only, Tuesday-Saturday for lunch and dinner. $. (409) 265-6331.

On the River. 919 West Second Street, Freeport. The fried, boiled, blackened, or baked fish is great here (particularly the stuffed shrimp and catfish), plus there are plenty of steaks and chicken offerings as well. The location is a 1910 building, cozied up with antiques. Open for lunch and dinner Monday-Saturday, dinner only on Sunday (5:00 to 9:00 P.M.). $-$$; (CC). (409) 233-0503.

Red Snapper Inn. 402 Bluewater Highway, Surfside. Locals love this place for its inventive way with fresh fish. Try snapper à la grecque, the shrimp baked with feta cheese and fresh tomatoes, or the sautéed filet of fresh flounder topped with fresh mushrooms and artichoke hearts, and you'll probably agree. Save room for a slice of house-made cheesecake or apple pie. Open daily for lunch and dinner. $-$$. (409) 239-3226.

Windswept Restaurant. 105 Burch Circle in Oyster Creek. One of the favorite seafood restaurants in the Brazosport area, this place specializes in fresh shrimp dinners and whole flounder. To get here, drive east on T-332 in Surfside, left on FM-523, right on Linda Lane, right on Duncan Drive, and right again on Burch Circle. The restaurant is behind the Oyster Creek water tower. Open for lunch and dinner Sunday-Friday, dinner only on Saturday. $-$$$; (CC). (409) 233-1951.

CONTINUING ON

From Brazosport and environs this day trip continues north to East and West Columbia. Although T-36 is the swiftest route, you might prefer to mosey awhile along the old river road that runs beside the Brazos from Jones Creek to Brazoria. To do the latter, start north on T-36 at Freeport, turn east (right) on County Road 400, and continue northwest along the river. At the intersection with FM-521, turn west (left) for about .75 mile to intersect T-36 and the original routing for this trip.

WANDERING THE BACKROADS

As you pass through Brazoria, take time to explore. Most of the original town has been flooded by the river, but there are a growing number of antiques stores as well as several historical markers worth a read. As an alternative to continuing on T-36 to the Columbias, you can follow FM-521 west and T-60 south to Matagorda (Trip 1, this sector).

EAST AND WEST COLUMBIA

As you drive into these two small towns on T-36 and T-35, it's hard to believe they were among the most thriving communities in the state in 1836. East Columbia originally was Bell's Landing, a small port on the Brazos River established in 1824 by one of Austin's first colonists, Josiah H. Bell. Today East Columbia is almost a ghost town, with only a few fine old homes to hint at its early importance.

West Columbia was another enterprise of Josiah Bell. In 1826 he cut a road across the prairie on the west side of the Brazos and created a new town called Columbia. Within three years it was one of the major trading areas in Texas, and by 1836 some 3,000 people lived here, the rich river bottomland nurturing a thriving plantation economy.

After Sam Houston's victory over Santa Anna at San Jacinto, West Columbia really came into its own. The most powerful men in Texas came here, designated it the first state capital, created a constitution, and elected Sam Houston the first president of the new republic.

Such glory was short-lived. The town wasn't big enough to house everyone who came to the governmental proceedings, and in 1837 the legislature moved to Houston. But West Columbia had snagged its place in history, and visitors today can visit several interesting sites as well as antiques shops along Brazos Street. For maps and advance information, contact the West Columbia Chamber of Commerce, 247 East Brazos, West Columbia 77486, (409) 345-3921 (weekday mornings only).

WHAT TO DO

Ammon Underwood House. On the river side of Main Street in East Columbia. Built about 1835 and enlarged twice, this stately old home has been surprisingly mobile. It has been moved three times to save it from tumbling into the Brazos. Currently owned and under restoration by the First Capitol Historical Foundation of West Columbia, this is the oldest house in the East Columbia community. Many of the furnishings and some of the wallpaper are original, and one room has been left unfinished to show early construction techniques. A log cabin built prior to 1850 has been moved onto the land beside the Underwood home and is being restored and furnished as a kitchen. Open during the San Jacinto Festival and by appointment through the West Columbia Chamber of Commerce. (409) 345-3921.

Columbia Historical Museum. 247 East Brazos, West Columbia. Local antiques, plus exhibits on area ranching, the oil boom days of the 1920s, and present times. Open Thursday-Sunday; call for hours. (409) 345-3921.

Hanson's Riverside Park. On the San Bernard River, 2.5 miles west of West Columbia on T-35. This picnic spot has grills, a playground, a fishing pier, and an old-fashioned swimming hole.

Replica of the First Capitol. On Fourteenth Street, behind the First Prosperity Bank. This successful bicentennial project re-creates the small clapboard building that served as the first capitol of Texas. The original building was a store, which subsequently had a variety of tenants before it was destroyed in the 1900 storm that devastated much of the Texas coast. The shed room to the right as you enter is thought to replicate Stephen F. Austin's office when he served as the first secretary of state for the republic, and the furnishings of the building, while not original, are antiques from that period. Open Monday-Friday by appointment. (409) 345-3921.

The Varner-Hogg State Historic Park. One mile north of T-35 on FM-2852. This land was one of the original land grants from Mexico, part of approximately 4,500 acres given to Martin Varner in 1824. Varner built a small cabin, began running stock, and in 1826 built a rum distillery on his holdings. Stephen F. Austin termed the results of this last enterprise the first "ardent spirits" made in the Texas colonies.

Varner sold his holdings in 1834, and the following year the new owner built a two-story brick house that survives today. Varner's original cabin is believed to be incorporated into the house. The bricks of the existing house were made by slaves from clay found in the nearby Brazos riverbed. By the late 1800s this plantation was prospering with sugar cane, cotton, corn, and livestock. In 1901 the first native-born governor of Texas, James Hogg, bought the old plantation and regarded the house as the first permanent home his family had. In 1920 the four Hogg children began remodeling the old house. Donated to the state in 1958, it was further restored in 1981. There is a shady picnic area, and guided tours are given whenever a small group forms. Closed Monday–Tuesday and from noon to 1:00 P.M. Wednesday–Sunday. Fee. (409) 345-4656.

WHERE TO EAT

Hard Tack Cafe. 817 South Seventeenth Street, West Columbia. Owner Scott Leopold's a junkman at heart, so expect nostalgic decor. The house specialty is barbecue cooked slowly over live oak coals, and the results must be good; some 3,000 pounds of barbecue is sold each week in what is essentially a very small town. Breads are homemade, so the sandwiches are super. There's also a noon buffet. Open Tuesday–Sunday. $; (CC). (409) 345-6162.

Lucy's Mexican Food. 1017 South Columbia Drive, West Columbia. The Tex-Mex here is so popular with local residents that you may have to wait for a table. Both the fajitas and the chicken-fried steak come highly recommended. Open for lunch and dinner daily. $–$$; (CC). (409) 345-5300.

My Cousin's Place. 521 South Seventeenth Street, West Columbia. Far more than a sandwich is available here. The weekday lunch and dinner buffets are all-you-can-eat, and the menu ranges from chicken-fried steak to Philly steak sandwiches. All the desserts are made in-house, so save room. Open daily, with varying hours. $; (CC). (409) 345-2816.

Simple Simon Pizza. 118 East Brazos Ave., West Columbia. Great for a day-trip lunch stop, this small place serves memorable pizzas, calzones, stombolis, pasta, hot wings, and barbecue sandwiches, plus there's a salad bar. Open daily for lunch and dinner. $–$$. (409) 345-7821.

RICHMOND AND ROSENBERG

Enjoy Richmond while you can. Within a decade it may be swallowed by Houston's urban creep, a historic oasis amid acres of subdivisions. For now, just getting to Richmond and its sidekick city of Rosenberg is a pleasure, whether you come north via T-36 from the Columbias or west on US-90A from Houston. The countryside primarily is farms and ranches, shaded by mature pecan trees and pleasant to ride by any time of the year.

Richmond flows into Rosenberg, the larger of the two towns. An early shipping site on the Brazos, Rosenberg really boomed in 1883, when the railroad came to town. While it remains the commercial center, the two towns have shared a common history for the past century; for day-trippers Richmond is the more historically interesting destination.

In Texas time Richmond is very old, one of the first permanent settlements of Stephen F. Austin's original 300 colonists. For centuries the Brazos River had made a big bend here, each flood leaving more rich soil in its wake. Shortly after Christmas Day 1821, five men staked their fortunes on this fertile land, building a two-room fort just below the bend, thus the name Fort Bend County. Today a marker stands on this site, almost lost between the eastbound and westbound bridges of US-90A as they span the Brazos.

The settlement thrived with the addition of Thompson's Ferry, northwest in the bend of the river, and in 1837 the town of Richmond was formally laid out on the site of the old fort. By 1843 a sugar mill was in operation at nearby Sugar Land, the forerunner of today's Imperial Sugar plant, and sugar cane plantations were thriving throughout the area by the 1860s.

Richmond had some now-famous residents, among them Mirabeau Lamar, Deaf Smith, and Jane Long. Carrie Nation ran a hotel on the corner of Fourth and Morton streets before she took up her hatchet-wielding crusade against demon rum.

Visitors today find several reminders of Richmond's colonial past, but the overriding feeling is that of exploring small-town America, circa 1940. Somehow it is reassuring to discover a corner drugstore and other small businesses within the shadow of an old-fashioned courthouse. A walk along Richmond's main drag, Morton Street, is a visual antidote to Houston's skyscrapers.

A detailed map guides you along the oak-shaded streets to all the historic sites, courtesy of the Fort Bend County Museum. The maps are available at the museum (see "What to Do" section) or from the Richmond-Rosenberg Chamber of Commerce, 4120 Avenue H, Rosenberg 77471, (713) 342-5464. A strong Czech population leads to the annual Czech Fest on the first weekend of May at the Fort Bend County Fairgrounds. The Fort Bend County Fair livens things up again in early October.

WHAT TO DO

Brazos Bend State Park. 21901 FM-762 (Tadpole Road) in Needville, 20 miles south of Richmond. Turn south on the Crabb River Road exit from US-59 South and follow signs. One of the newest parks in the system, this is 5,000 acres of wild beauty along Big Creek, a tributary of the Brazos. Overnight facilities include screened shelters, trailer sites with hookups, tent sites with water, and primitive sites with no water that require a hike in; almost all are shaded with massive oaks. In addition to two large fishing piers where you can angle for bass, catfish, or crappie, there are hiking/biking and nature trails, several large playing fields, seven photography platforms for focusing on the park's exceptional wildlife, and an interpretive center. Rangers lead daily programs, so the center should be your first stop to see what's going on. Of interest: Children under seventeen do not need a license to fish in this park. *Caution:* This is alligator country; no one can enter any of the park waters for any reason. All visitors are given a list of alligator etiquette rules when they arrive. A nature trial designed for all, including those with vision, hearing or mobility challenges, now circles the park's Creekfield Lake. Flat and paved, the trial is a half-mile long and has tactile interpretive panels that explain the wetlands ecology. A taped audio tour can be checked out at the park's visitor center. Fee. Park information: (409) 553-5101 or (800) 792-1112.

The George Observatory also is in the park, a satellite facility of the Houston Museum of Natural Science. General public viewing through the large telescope is possible from dusk to 11:00 P.M. on summer Saturdays, dusk to 10:00 P.M. in winter. Passes are given out on a first-come, first-served basis beginning at 5:00 P.M. (arrive about 4:00 P.M. or you won't get a pass). Several smaller telescopes on the top deck of the planetarium are available for those without passes. Fee. (281) 242-3055. Adjacent to the observatory, the Challenger Learning Center offers space lore, including a simulated mission to the moon. For information, call (409) 639-4629.

Christmas Tree Farms. You can cut your own tannenbaum at Houghs Christmas Tree Farm near East Bernard, (409) 335-4301.

Museum of Southern History. 2740 FM-359, approximately 5 miles north of Richmond. The South *may* rise again. This miniature Tara's collection includes muskets, rifles, guns, uniforms, furniture, pictures, money, letters, and other memorabilia relating to both Jane Long and the Civil War. Open Tuesday, Thursday, and Friday from 10:00 A.M. to 3:00 P.M. and on weekend afternoons. Fee. (281) 342-8787.

Decker Park. North of the railroad tracks at Sixth and Preston streets. Three buildings moved here mark the very slow beginning of a living history museum: a 1902 railroad depot, a log cabin replica of the 1822 fort, and the 1850s McNabb House, once owned by Carrie Nation's daughter. The Victorian brick relic across Preston Street was the county jail from 1896 to 1948.

The Fort Bend County Courthouse. Fourth and Jackson streets. This fifth courthouse was built with an air of majesty in 1908 and was so well refurbished in 1981 that it was cited by the Houston chapter of the American Institute of Architects. It also is the only public building in Fort Bend County listed in the National Register of Historic Places. Notable features are the three-story rotunda, the mosaic tile floors, and the rich woodwork on the stairs and in the main courtroom. Free. Open Monday–Friday.

Fort Bend County Museum. Fifth and Houston streets. Just about every aspect of "Life along the Brazos" between 1820 and 1930 is covered here, with displays including items and manuscripts of Mirabeau Lamar, Jane Long, and Austin's first colony. One diorama tells the harrowing tale of early railroad crossings on the Brazos, and special exhibits include the hatchet Carrie Nation used on a Houston saloon in 1905. A clapboard house that stood on property owned by Jane Long from 1837 to 1859 is next to the museum; furnished, it gives an excellent picture of 1840s life.

The museum staff also gives demonstrations of frontier skills and guides historical tours of Richmond for groups by advance notice. Closed Monday. (281) 342-6478.

The George Ranch Historical Park. 10215 FM–762, 8 miles southeast of Richmond. What was life like in rural Texas between 1890 and 1930? This 470-acre living history project (part of a 23,000-acre working ranch) turns back the years and lets you participate as well. Costumed actors re-create Victorian life at the J. H. P. Davis Home (1896) and more modern times at the George ranchhouse (1930s); cowboys rope and ride; ranch hands demonstrate cattle-dipping, blacksmithing, woodworking, and so forth; and tractor-drawn carryalls haul you around the grounds. The 1820s Jones Farmstead, an authentically re-created working farm, includes a furnished dog-trot cabin, a barn, a corn crib, crop lands, an orchard, and a garden.

Nearly every weekend between Memorial Day and Labor Day has a special theme. Don't miss Texian Market Days the fourth weekend of October. Special events such as rodeos and trail rides can be arranged year-round for corporate meetings, conventions, and private groups. Although there's a small eatery on site, picnickers are welcome. Open daily, March through mid-December. Fee. (281) 545–9212 or 343–0218.

Glider Rides. This glorious, silent sport now is available in the Rosenberg area. For information call Thrilling Adventures at (800) 762–7464.

Imperial-Holly Sugar Co. 198 Kempner, Sugar Land. From US-90A turn north on Kempner. On the site of the S. M. Williams cane plantation established in the 1840s, this modern plant gives visitors a look at sugar from the raw product to final packaging. The free one-hour tours (10:00 A.M. and 2:00 P.M.) are interesting, and reservations are not necessary except for groups of ten or more. Note: no sandals, watches, cameras, food, or drink allowed. Open Monday–Friday. (281) 491–9181.

John H. Moore House. Fifth and Liberty streets. Built in 1883 on the present museum grounds, this gracious old home looks as though it will stand for several more centuries. Now used as a gallery by the Fort Bend Museum; call for exhibit schedule. (281) 342–6478.

Morton Cemetery. On Second Street, north of Jackson Street. Used during the 1838–41 period, this is the last resting place of Mirabeau Lamar and the "Mother of Texas," Jane Long.

Rosenberg Opry. The Cole Theatre in downtown Rosenberg swings with traditional C&W and gospel music every Friday night, year-round. There's no drinking or smoking, and children are welcome at this family affair. (281) 342-3827.

Southwest Rifle Range. 16223 Boss Gaston, 1.5 miles west of T-6. Want to shoot a gun without alarming your neighbors? This place has rifle and pistol ranges, trap throwers, supplies, and lessons in safe management of firearms. Open daily except Tuesdays. Fee; (CC). (281) 277-3737.

WHERE TO EAT

Brazos Bottom Inn. 7010 FM-762. This country cafe is an ideal place to stop for tasty vittles en route to either the George Ranch or Brazos Bend State Park. House specialties include seafood and hand-cut steaks, but the luncheon salads and burgers are great also. Save room for the "really homemade" desserts, particularly the Brazos Bottom Pie. They count the calories in this chocolate mousse/cream cheese/whipped cream beauty so you won't have to. Open for lunch and dinner Tuesday-Sunday. $-$$; (CC). (281) 341-5210.

Italian Maid Cafe. 209 South Fourth Street. This tiny eatery is well known locally for its soups, pasta dishes, sandwiches, salads, and fancy coffees. Open Monday-Saturday. $-$$; (CC). (281) 232-6129.

Quail Hollow Inn. 214 Morton Street, Richmond. Long a destination in itself, this outstanding restaurant now has a fresh look and menu with talented 23-year-old Montgomery Staggs as executive chef and his father Alton Staggs as general manager. The menu was still evolving at this writing, but Monty's culinary training is in classical French and innovative Southwestern cuisines, so expect some fabulous choices. Soon to come: hands-on cooking classes on Monday nights, and special Chef-for-the-night opportunities in which you work alongside Monty in the kitchen and then dine on the results. Open for lunch and dinner Tuesday-Friday; dinner only on Saturday; brunch only on Sunday. Reservations suggested. $-$$$; (CC) (281) 341-6733.

Sandy McGee's. 314 Morton in Richmond, 1207 Sixth Street in Rosenberg. If inventive salads, sandwiches, and daily specials sound appealing, don't miss these charming cafes. Save room for dessert. Open for lunch on weekdays. $-$$. (281) 344-9393 in Richmond, (281) 341-9151 in Rosenberg.

WANDERING THE BACKROADS

An alternate route from Houston to Richmond forsakes US-59 and US-90A and instead rambles west out Westheimer (FM-1093) past its intersection with T-6. Turn south on FM-1464 for about 10 miles and then west (right) on US-90A into Richmond. For restaurants on this route, see Day Trip 1, west sector.

To roam among pastures and pecan orchards, go north from Richmond on FM-359 (Skinner Road) and when it curves to the left, stay straight. That puts you on Skinner Lane, one of the prettiest drives around.

Another country ramble takes the long way home. From Richmond turn south on FM-762 (Eleventh Street/Thompson Road) and follow its zigzag southeasterly course through the countryside. Just beyond Crabb, FM-762 turns farther south as the A. P. George Road. Stay on FM-762 as it jogs onto Tadpole Road. At the intersection with FM-1462 at Woodrow, turn east (left) to intersect T-288 and then north (left) toward Houston and home.

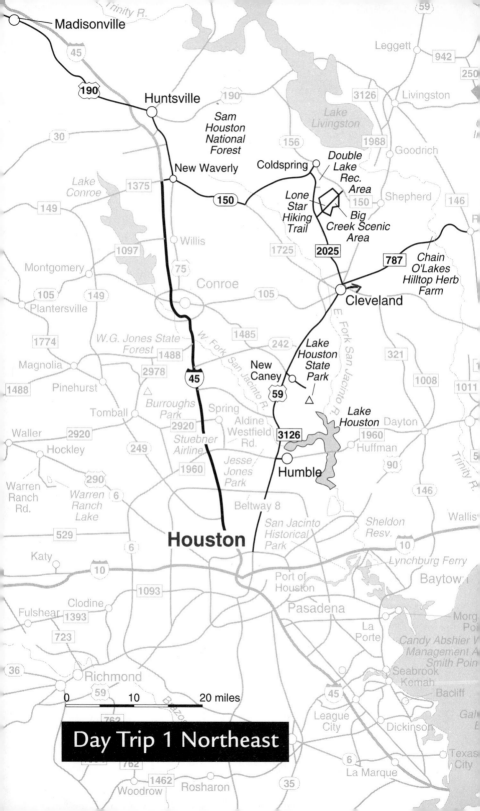

Day Trip 1 Northeast

HUMBLE

As with the small town of Spring in north Harris County, there are two Humbles—old and new. The new is easy to find, a plastic forest of franchise signs and shopping centers around the US-59/FM-1960 interchange. Old Humble lies quietly behind, east of the railroad tracks and south of FM-1960.

Back in 1865 a fisherman named Pleasant Smith Humble established a small ferry across the San Jacinto River near where US-59 crosses it today. Things remained quiet until the railroad arrived in 1878, and Humble became a flag stop on the narrow-gauge HE&WT line, running between Houston and Shepherd. Settlers came, and by 1886 it was officially a town.

Rich with timber, Humble fed a growing logging industry. Back in 1887 a local lumberman, Jim H. Slaughter, rafted logs down the San Jacinto for milling. Pulling into a small backwater to make an overnight camp, he noticed bubbles seeping along the riverbank. When his match brought a flame, he recognized the presence of natural gas and subsequently bought sixty acres of land in the area. Although he personally didn't profit greatly, this was the beginning of the oil fields in Humble and Harris County.

The first wells came into production in 1904, and by mid-1905 the field was producing more barrels per day than any other in the state. The Moonshine Hill area east of town soon had a population of 25,000, and Humble got busy earning a reputation as one of the toughest towns in Texas. The Texas Rangers often had to be called on to keep some semblance of law and order.

In 1909 the Humble Oil and Refining Company was formed in a small, tin-roofed building on Humble's Main Street, one of its organizers being the local feed store owner, Ross Sterling. The company was successful and ultimately became part of the Exxon we know today. Sterling didn't do badly either. He soon bought the Humble State Bank and carved a niche in the state's history as a newspaper publisher, oilman, and governor of Texas from 1931 to 1933.

As quickly as it had come, the oil boom disappeared—no new wells were coming in—and by 1915 Humble once again was a small, quiet community strongly dependent on lumber and agriculture for its financial base. A second oil strike at greater depth in 1929 brought new life, and Humble was chartered as a city in 1933.

Humble's Main Street is now a stroll through struggling small-town Americana, but things are looking up. Fresh interest in restoring Main Street to its original appearance has resulted in a charming restaurant (see Humble City Cafe and Bakery, below), several antiques shops, and a pocket park in the 300 block. Drop in at Especially Yours, a Texas gift shop packed with Humble souvenirs. Owner Wilcene Brisben knows just about everything there is to know about Humble, so stop and chat. The small cottages that line nearby First Street also offer unusual shopping. Stop too at the corner of First Street and North Houston Avenue to see the oldest artesian well in the area, drilled as a wildcat oil venture in 1912. For additional information on the area, contact the Humble Chamber of Commerce, P.O. Box 3337, Humble 77347, (281) 446–2128.

WHAT TO DO

Freestyle Canoeing Instruction. Many times the national champions in tandem interpretive freestyle canoeing, Tryon and Anne Lindabury offer three six-hour lessons focused on boat control, layboating in quiet water, and canoe ballet. Classes generally operate out of Forest Cove Marina near Kingwood. Fee. (281) 820–6319.

Humble Historical Museum. 219 Main Street. A grassroots result of America's bicentennial, this small museum is bursting with a collection of interesting old things donated by local residents. Open Tuesday–Saturday. Free; donations appreciated. (281) 446–2130.

Jesse H. Jones Park. 20634 Kenswick Drive. From US-59 North go west 1.7 miles on FM-1960 and turn right on Kenswick Drive; the park is at the end of the road. This large wilderness preserve on Cypress Creek has ten hiking trails, a playground and picnic area, a pioneer homestead, and a three-acre beach on the creek for fishing (no swimming); with a Texas fishing license, you can angle for white bass, crappie, catfish, and alligator gar. Nature photography is popular here, as are birding and canoeing. About 85 percent of the trails are black-topped for use by the handicapped. Birders can pick up a list at the Nature Center Building, which also has wildlife exhibits, including common poisonous snakes and a cutaway look at a working beehive. This park is the take-out for an 8-mile, five-hour canoe float from Mercer Arboretum upstream. Open daily. (281) 446-8588.

Lake Houston. The best play places (picnicking, swimming, boating) are Dwight D. Eisenhower Park and Alexander Duessen Park, both near the dam. Take the Duessen Drive exit from the Sam Houston tollway, and follow signs.

Lake Houston State Park. Take New Caney exit from US-59, go east approximately two miles on FM-1485, then turn right on Baptist Encampment Road; the park entrance will be 1.5 miles down on your left. Don't rev your boat motors or load your fishing gear; in spite of its name, this 4,913-acre park has no accessible lake frontage. However, it's an outstanding spot for birding, hiking and biking (12 miles of trails), and—thanks to hot showers—tent camping. A small white sand beach on Peach Creek offers shallow water play for children. There also are eight miles of separate equestrian trails, but so far it's BYO horse. Open daily. Fee. (281) 354-6881.

Old McDonald's Farm. 3203 FM-1960 East, 2.5 miles east of Deerbrook Mall. When the pint-size natives get restless, spend the day in this kiddie paradise. The admission price (currently $5.75 for adults, $4.75 for children) includes pony and train rides, petting and feeding animals in twelve barns, playing in a mountain of sand, jigging for crawfish in a pond, swimming, hayrides, milking the cow, and gathering eggs. In addition to food concessions, there's also a shady picnic area to use if you bring food from home. Open weekends November–February, daily March–October. (281) 446-4001.

Southwest Paddle Sports. 1101 Hamblen Road, Kingwood. This firm operates inexpensive quiet water kayaking out of Forest Cove Marina near Kingwood which accesses an oxbow of the San Jacinto River as well as the river itself. They also teach basic canoeing and kayaking skills and organize very affordable canoe and kayaking trips within the greater Houston area throughout the year. Want to go birding by kayak in Christmas Bay (near Freeport) or sea kayaking offshore from Matagorda Island? Canoe on Spring Creek from Jesse Jones Park to the Forest Cove Marina? Go paddling under a full moon? These are the folks to call. Forest Cove Marina (rentals) is open weekdays from 3:00 to 6:00 P.M. and all day on weekends. The store at 1101 Hamblen Road is open Tuesday–Sunday. (281) 359-3474 or (800) We Paddle.

Tour 18. 3102 FM-1960, 2 miles east of US-59. There are hundreds of golf courses in the greater Houston area, but none other like this $5 million layout. In toto it re-creates eighteen of the greatest holes in the nation, a par-72, 6,807-yard challenge engineered across 200 acres. Want to test your skills against the pros on the 17th at Sawgrass? No. 14 at Pebble Beach? Nos. 11 and 12 at Augusta? Come try what may be the most difficult course in the country. Tee times can be arranged up to seven days in advance. Open daily. Cost inclusive of green fees, carts, and range balls is $65 weekdays, $75 weekends at last notice. (CC). (281) 540-1818.

WHERE TO EAT

Chez Nous. 217 South Avenue G. In addition to a menu that features many French classics, chef-owner Gerard Brach and his wife, Sandra, offer outstanding daily specials such as fresh Dover sole or swordfish in an avocado-lime butter or pineapple salsa. French-born and -trained, Gerard also has taught a wine course at the Four Seasons in New York City, expertise that shows on the wine list. This jewel of a restaurant is in an unlikely setting, a hundred-year-old church. You'll want to dress up for this dining experience. As with Quail Hollow Inn in Richmond, this restaurant is worth a trip to Humble if you enjoy fine food prepared with skill and care. Open Monday–Saturday for dinner; reservations strongly advised. Ask for specific directions when you call; it's hard to find. $$–$$$; (CC). (281) 446-6717.

Hasta la Pasta Italian Grill. 202 FM-1960 East bypass, in the Corum Humble Shopping Center. Marvelous aromas from the kitchen start those juices flowing the instant you enter this nicely

styled eatery. In addition to the classic pasta dishes, the emphasis is on marinated chicken, beef, pork, and fish that are then grilled over a combination of oak and pecan. Very popular with Humble's business community. Open daily for lunch and dinner. $-$$; (CC). (281) 446-6414.

Humble City Cafe & Bakery. 200 Main Street, at Avenue A. What was the town's old drugstore (built in 1914) has been restored to its original porch-and-balcony appearance to house this pleasant cafe. Food is Texas home-style stuff, and the portions exceed generous; come hungry. Open daily for lunch and dinner, breakfast also on weekends. $-$$; (CC). (281) 319-0200.

Mardi Gras Restaurant. 113 South Avenue A, Humble. When you need a touch of New Orleans cum Cajun seafood, come to this tiny eatery. From po'boys, jambalaya, and étouffées to seafood plates and platters, it's here (including soft shell crab). Open daily for lunch and dinner. $-$$; (CC). (281) 548-3663.

Menciu's Gourmet Hunan. 1379 Kingwood Drive in the Kingwood development north of Humble via US-59. Popular with local residents, this family-run place uses only fresh foods to prepare its tasty dishes. The lunch specials are excellent values. Open for lunch and dinner daily, and Sunday brunch. $-$$; (CC). (281) 359-8489.

A Taste of Germany. 51 West Main. This combination delicatessen and restaurant is a great introduction to the classics of German cuisine. Good bets include the delicious red cabbage, the rouladen, the kassler rippchen, and the outstanding calf's liver, which comes grilled with onions and apple slices. Potato pancakes or dumplings top off many of the entrees, and owner Heinz Behrend imports many beers from his native Germany. Open for lunch Monday–Saturday, dinner Tuesday–Saturday. $-$$; (CC). (281) 540-7500.

Trigg's Cafe. 1712 First Street at Wilson Road. A bright spot in an otherwise undistinguished shopping center east of the business district, this family-run place offers an all-you-can-eat buffet on Sunday (11:00 A.M. to 3:00 P.M.; $7.50) that draws diners from miles away. The menu also offers steaks, barbecue plates, and assorted fried fish, all in abundant portions for the price. Open for breakfast, lunch, and dinner daily. $-$$; (CC). (281) 540-2700.

Two Cooks. 502 Staitti at the corner of D Street. The catering ladies at this serve-yourself eatery fix one entree, complete with green salad, fruit, roll, and your choice of dessert and beverage. The porch of this eighty-year-old home is delightful in nice weather. Open Monday–Friday, lunch only. $. (281) 446-1005.

The Veranda. 2820 Chestnut Ridge, Kingwood. From Kingwood Drive turn left at the first light and go three blocks. When cost is no object and exceptional food is your desire, try this small treasure of a restaurant. Chef Ben Schulman graduated from the Culinary Institute of America and formerly was sous chef at Tony's, and both high credentials show. House specialties range from tempters such as Redfish Tiara (with mango salsa) to Tournedos Veranda (beef filet topped with shiitake mushrooms, crabmeat, and a Gorgonzola gratinée). Finish with a crusty-topped crème brûlée, made with fresh vanilla beans daily. Open for dinner only, Tuesday–Sunday. $$$+; (CC). (281) 358-2820.

CONTINUING ON

From Humble it's approximately 28 miles north via US-59 to Cleveland.

CLEVELAND

Back in the 1880s this railroad town on US-59 north of Houston thrived with lumber shipping. Now it is better known as the main gateway to the forest and water wonderland that covers most of San Jacinto County. Entrances to the Lone Star Hiking Trail are marked on FM-1725 and FM-945 near Cleveland, and the local chamber of commerce has a brochure listing activities in the area: Box 1733, Cleveland 77328-1733, (281) 592-8786.

WHAT TO DO

Albert Sallas County Park. From Cleveland go north on US-59 to the FM-1485 exit in New Caney; go west to the southbound feeder and continue south to McClesley Road; turn right; the park entrance will be on your right. The five-acre pond in this park usually is stocked with trout in December and January. To check on the stocking schedule, call (409) 822-5067.

Berry Picking. If you come in early summer, consider picking a year's supply of blueberries at Clearwater Blueberry Farm, inside the gates of Chain-O-Lakes Resort (see below). (281) 592-2150.

Big Thicket Downs. From US-59 in Cleveland, go east on T-105, turn right at the second red light (FM-321), then left at the second light (FM-787); go 15.2 miles; the track will be on your right. No longer a brush track with a set schedule of races (although they occasionally host match races), this 105-acre, family-owned place now is a busy training facility for thoroughbreds and quarter horses. Visitors who call ahead are welcome, even during the February-April foaling season. Owner Rich Mock particularly enjoys explaining horsecraft to children and families. (281) 592-8661.

Blooming Haus Herb Farm. On south side of T-321, two miles east of Cleveland; watch for signs. Visitors are welcome to wander amid large herb beds on this pesticide-free farm, and either spring or fall is the best time to come. In addition to herbs, owners Harry and Linda Blumenthal also sell homemade teas and vinegars as well as assorted tropical plants. The Saturday prior to Mother's Day this herb farm hosts a free, mini-renaissance festival featuring local arts and crafts, food samples, and so on. Open seasonal hours Tuesday-Saturday; call for information. (281) 592-4219.

Chain-O-Lakes Resort and Conference Center. Eighteen miles east of Cleveland. From Cleveland go 18 miles east on FM-787; after passing the Trinity River Bridge turn right on CR-2132 (Daniel Ranch Road). Adjacent to the Daniel Ranch—which, colonized in 1818, may have been the first Anglo settlement in Texas—this long-time campground has grown into a quality family resort strongly oriented toward day visitors. There are 130 acres of lakes, all stocked and interconnected, and no fishing license is required. Come ready for some serious angling; eight-pound bass are caught every summer. You can either bring your own boat or rent one, and the bank fishing is good also, particularly if you angle with purple plastic worms. You are welcome to bring bicycles and ride on the roads through the woods, and there's a two-and-a-half-acre artesian-fed swimming lake. There are horse-drawn carriage rides, horseback trail rides, and hayrides. The outdoor ROPES course provides a team-building experience for corporate types on executive retreat. In addition to standard hookup and wilderness campsites and some rustic cottages, owners Jim and Beverly Smith have built 27 well-designed B&B log cabins that are furnished with antiques and sleep two to ten people. Open daily, year-round. Fee. *Bonus:* Both the Clearwater Berry Farm and the Hilltop Herb Farm are adjacent and operated by the Smiths; see "Where to Eat" listings. (281) 592-2150.

Christmas Tree Farms. Call for directions to the following: D Bar B Christmas Tree Farm, (409) 628-3114; and The Prairie Merry Tree Farm, (281) 592-1935.

WHERE TO EAT

Hilltop Herb Farm At Chain-O-Lakes Resort. Delicious food based on the creative use of herbs is the rule here, along with tours of the herb garden, cooking classes, and so on. Call to get on their special events mailing list. The gift shop sells homemade jams, jellies, chutneys, and herbal teas—you'll want to buy some mint-touched Tranquilitea mix for home. Open only by reservation for breakfast (weekends year-round, daily in summer); and for Saturday night dinner (ask about menu when you reserve). *Note:* Drop-ins generally cannot be served. $-$$$; (CC). (281) 592-5859.

Jo Anna's Italian Restaurant. 211 North College. Many locals think this is the best Italian restaurant in the region because everything, from the lasagna and Italian salad to the heavily loaded pizzas, is made on site with fresh ingredients, using ninety-year-old recipes. Open for lunch and dinner, Monday–Saturday. $-$$; (CC). (281) 592-4587.

Yesterday. 106 North Travis, Cleveland. Decorated to a 1950s theme, this spot serves up 45 rpm records on its vintage juke box as well as hamburgers, chicken-fried steak, and other American cafe standards from its kitchen. All the old-time soda fountain treats are here as well, including phosphates and banana splits. Open daily for lunch, Wednesday–Sunday for dinner. $-$$; (CC). (281) 592-2777.

CONTINUING ON

The drive to Coldspring is a day-tripper's delight. From Cleveland take FM-2025 north for 17 miles, then turn east on T-150 and go another 2 miles. This takes you through a major portion of the Sam Houston National Forest. An alternate route leaves US-59 North at Shepherd and follows T-150 West 11 miles to Coldspring.

COLDSPRING

This old community (population 569) was called Coonskin when it was founded in 1847. Now the San Jacinto County seat, it is showing signs of life as a budding tourist center. Most of the structures on Main Street were built between 1916 and 1923, the courthouse in 1918. Many of those vintage structures now house antiques and gift shops. There are numerous historical markers in Coldspring, including one on the United Methodist Church (1848), one of the oldest Methodist churches in Texas. Good times to come: on Friday and Saturday, when most of the shops are open, and on Trades Day (arts, crafts, antiques), the fourth Saturday of every month, March–November. On those rare "Fifth Saturdays," the entire town puts on a humdinger of a garage sale. (409) 653-2184.

WHAT TO DO

Big Creek Scenic Area. From Cleveland continue on US-59 North 12 miles to Shepherd, then west on T-150 for 6 miles to Forest Service Road 217. Part of the 350,000-acre Big Thicket that spatters across vast sections of Southeast Texas, this 1,130-acre preserve has numerous hiking trails, wild and varied topography, spring-fed creeks, and abundant wildlife. One segment of the 140-mile-long Lone Star Hiking Trail (foot traffic only) begins near Montague Church on FM-1725 and loops through the scenic area on a 25-mile jaunt to a trailhead on FM-945. Information: Sam Houston Ranger District, P.O. Box 1000, New Waverly 77358, (409) 344-6205.

Christmas Tree Farms. This is good tree-cutting country in November and December; call the following for directions: Iron Creek Christmas Tree Farm, (409) 767-4541; or Skyvara Family Christmas Trees, (409) 767-4468.

Double Lake Recreation Area. On FM-2025, 15 miles north of Cleveland. This twenty-five-acre lake is edged by picnic and camping areas and has boat rentals, a beach, and a bathhouse with showers. No large motorboats are allowed, but canoeing is popular. Stocked with bass, bream, and catfish, this also is a great place to take kids fishing. One 5-mile path through the woods links Double Lake with the Big Creek Scenic Area and the Lone Star Hiking Trail. (409) 344-6205.

Old Town Heritage Center. Coldspring's original Courthouse Square is now home to a small but interesting museum in the old 1880s jail (open Thursday–Saturday or by appointment, 409-653-2009) and the transplanted Waverly schoolhouse, circa 1926; the latter now houses an antiques co-op. Other memorabilia are scattered around the grounds, including an old Ford fire engine and the replica of a blacksmith shop.

WHERE TO EAT

The Hop. On T–150 West. Good spot for hamburgers, shakes, and pizza. Open for lunch and dinner daily. $. (409) 653-4889.

Kimon's Restaurant. On T–150 west in downtown Coldspring. One of the main nerve centers for this small town, this family-run place cuts its own steaks and also puts on a good lunch buffet and salad bar. Open daily for breakfast, lunch, and dinner. $-$$; (CC). (409) 653-4929.

Sharon's Cafe. On T–150 west, Coldspring. Expect the East Texas cafe basics here: oilcloth on the tables, plastic-coated menus, and a friendly staff. Specialties include chicken-fried steak and fried catfish. Open for breakfast, lunch, and dinner, Monday–Saturday. $. (409) 653-3777.

WANDERING THE BACKROADS

From Coldspring you can continue west on T–150 and connect with I–45 at New Waverly (Trip 2, Northwest Sector). From there continue your travels by turning north (right) on I–45 to Huntsville and Madisonville. If it's time to go home, head south on I–45; from New Waverly it's 55 miles to the Houston city limits.

An alternative: If you want to visit the Lake Livingston area (Trip 2, this sector) from Coldspring, take T–156 north to its intersection with US–190 and turn east. From Livingston take US–59 south to home.

LIVINGSTON

A fire wiped out three downtown blocks around the turn of the century, so little is left of Livingston's beginnings back in 1846. Today this timber town is 76 miles north of the heart of Houston via US-59. The seat of Polk County, it is important to day-trippers in several ways.

Every fall the forest around Livingston resembles the rolling hills of western Massachusetts when the frosts bring up the color in the maple, sassafras, oak, sweet gum, sumac, and hickory trees. One of the town's biggest attractions is 90,000-acre Lake Livingston, 15 miles west of downtown. The lake primarily is an impoundment of the Trinity River, and there are three short but beautiful river float trips possible below the dam. Put-ins for canoes are at the dam, at the US-59 crossing south of Livingston, and at FM-105 near Romayor. The final take-out is at the FM-162 crossing east of Cleveland.

All of Polk County is crossed with old Indian traces, the remains of which are indicated by highway signs. For information on Lake Livingston or the general area, contact the Polk County Chamber of Commerce, 516 West Church, Livingston 77351, (409) 327-4929.

WHAT TO DO 4/19/98 SUNDAY

Alabama-Coushatta Indian Reservation. On US-190, 17 miles east of Livingston. Established by Sam Houston in 1854, this 4,600-acre

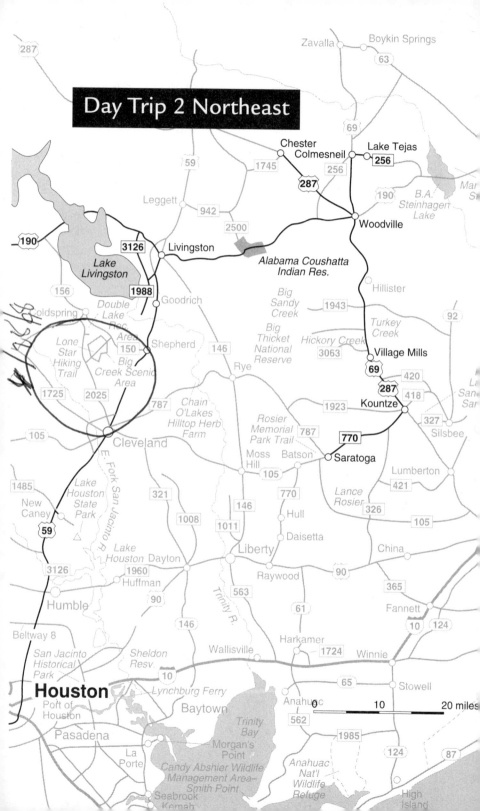

Day Trip 2 Northeast

reservation in the Big Thicket offers a well-executed camping/recreation/tourist complex that's just beginning to achieve its potential. Start at the museum for some historical background, and then tour the Big Thicket forest by either the Indian Chief train or open bus. Except for a trail this is the only public access to the Big Sandy Creek unit of the Big Thicket National Preserve. More than a hundred species of trees are native to this reservation, including eight varieties of oak, the state champion water hickory and laurel oak trees, and a huge 200-year-old magnolia. The tours go through virgin forest, and you may surprise an alligator or two in the swamp regions. Fee.

There are also a historical museum, the Inn of the Twelve Clans Restaurant (see "Where to Eat"), and an Indian village replica where tribal members demonstrate early housing, crafts, and foods. Tribal dances representing war, courtship, harvest, and tribute are performed daily in summer, on weekends the rest of the year. Fee.

One place the Alabama-Coushatta truly shine is in their beautiful baskets, woven from needles of the rare long-leaf pine. Many have lids and are shaped like animals, and all are considered collector's items. A few usually are for sale in the village store, and some rare oldies are displayed in the Polk County Museum in Livingston.

Slightly removed from the central complex is twenty-six-acre Lake Tombigbee, nice for quiet camping, picnicking, and swimming. Canoeing and fishing for bass, perch, and catfish also are popular. The reservation is open daily in summer and Friday–Sunday in spring and fall; closed December–February. Information: Route 3, Box 640, Livingston 77351, (409) 563-4391 or (800) 444-3507.

Blueberry Farms. You can pick a year's supply at reasonable cost at Sandy Foot Farm, (409) 327-2744. Hamilton's Berry Farm has blackberries and raspberries as well, (409) 563-4910.

Christmas Tree Farms. Call the following for directions: Goosby's Christmas Tree Farm, (409) 646-3450.

Johnson's Rock Shop. Ten miles east of Livingston off US-190 in the Indian Springs Lakes Estates; call for directions. You'll see more than 1.5 million pounds of rock, and just about that many varieties, as well as the equipment used to cut, polish, and finish same. Visitors are welcome, and there's no fee for a personal tour. Open daily. (409) 563-4438.

Lake Livingston. From Livingston take US-59 south 2.5 miles and turn west on FM-1988, then north on FM-3126 to Park Road 65. There is good public access through 640-acre Lake Livingston State Park, open daily (fee). Facilities include a swimming pool, paddle and boat rental, an activity center, hiking and biking trails, horseback riding, picnic areas, campsites, and screened shelters. Private resorts, marinas, and campgrounds along this route offer fishing guides or rent boats. Information: Route 9, Box 1300, Livingston 77351, (409) 365-2201; or call the Lake Livingston Area Tourism Council, (800) 766-LAKE.

Polk County Museum. 601 West Church in the Murphy Memorial Library. Exhibits focus on the early days of Polk County, and there are some interesting Indian artifacts. Note the old Jonas Davis log cabin across the street. Donation. Open Monday-Friday. (409) 327-8192.

WHERE TO EAT

Florida's Kitchen. From US-59 in Livingston go west one mile on US-90, then turn left on FM-350 south for .7 mile; cafe will be on your right. Hard to find but worth the hunt, this simple place serves plentiful and delicious ribs, barbecue, catfish, hamburgers, chicken-fried steak and other standards. Thursday night is all you can eat ribs; Friday night is all you can eat catfish. Open 11:00 A.M. to 7:00 P.M. Tuesday and Wednesday, 11;00 A.M. to 10:00 P.M. Thursday-Saturday. $-$$. (409) 967-4216.

Inn of the Twelve Clans Restaurant. Inside the Alabama-Coushatta Indian Reservation, 17 miles east of Livingston on US-190. Recently spiffed up, this place is known for its buffalo burgers, tasty Indian fry bread, and Sunday buffet. Open daily in summer, Friday-Sunday in spring and fall; closed December-February. $; (CC). (409) 563-4391.

Lone Star Charlie's Family Restaurant. One mile south of Livingston on the east side of US-59. A favorite with truckers, this clean and homey spot serves the usual road food standards, along with homemade cobblers. Good place if you're on a budget and traveling with children. Open for breakfast, lunch, and dinner daily. $-$$; (CC). (409) 365-3017.

Shrimp Boat Manny's. 1324 West Church, 1 block east of the US-59 bypass, Livingston. This eatery specializes in seafood prepared Cajun-style. Manny and Nancy Rachal are from Lafayette in "Luziana" and serve a mean étouffée, boiled and fried shrimp, raw and fried oysters, and seafood gumbo. Open for lunch and dinner, Monday–Saturday, and for Sunday lunch. $–$$$. (409) 327-0100.

The Texas Pepper. 930 Highway (US) 59 North Loop. One of the most popular and pleasant eateries in the region, this spacious place serves choice steaks cut on the premises—they hand-bread the CFS as it is ordered and then cook it in peanut oil. They also smoke their own barbeque meats and prepare their Mexican dishes from scratch. Open Monday–Saturday for lunch and dinner, Sunday from 11:00 A.M. to 2:00 P.M. $–$$; (CC). (409) 327-2794.

CONTINUING ON

This day trip now follows US-190 due east for 33 miles through the forest to Woodville.

WOODVILLE

Although history has been relatively quiet here, the town has some surprises in store for those who take the time to poke around. Not only are there twenty-one historical markers in the area, but the entire town also is a bird sanctuary and serves as the northern gateway to the Big Thicket.

Founded in 1846-47 as the county seat for the newly created Tyler County, Woodville is aptly named because it is surrounded by miles of rolling forest. The prettiest times to visit here are in late March, when the Tyler County Dogwood Festival stirs things up a bit, and again in the fall, after the first cold snap coats the woods with color. Brochures, maps, and updates on the current status of spring or fall scenery are available from the Tyler County Chamber of Commerce, 201 North Magnolia, Woodville 75979, (409) 283-2632. That office is inside the Woodville Inn, and brochures about area attractions are available after hours. Weekday mornings are the best times to call. The courthouse in the heart of town no longer is the distinctive architectural showplace it was when built in 1891 for the grand sum of $21,609. An ill-advised 1930s remodeling stole its baroque charm and reduced it to mundane and functional. Visitors today find the antiques shops and tearoom across the street far more interesting.

Should you linger too long in Woodville to safely drive home, you may be interested in knowing that the Antique Rose, 612 Nellius Street, offers comfortable B&B in an 1862 Plantation/Federal-style home, (409) 283-8926.

WHAT TO DO

Allan Shivers Library and Museum. 302 North Charlton, 2 blocks north of the courthouse. The late Governor Allan Shivers had his roots in Woodville, and this restored Victorian showplace houses his papers as well as memorabilia of the Shivers family and the town. Fee. Open Monday–Saturday, Sunday by appointment. (409) 283-3709.

Big Thicket Information. The north district office of the Big Thicket National Preserve is at 507 Pine in Woodville. Open Monday–Friday, when staff is available. (409) 283-5824.

Blueberry Farms. June and July are prime picking months at Ling's Farm, (409) 837-2263 or 283-2664, and Mott's Blueberry Farm, (409) 429-3196.

Boykin Springs Recreation Area. From Zavalla, go southeast 11 miles on T-63, then south (right) 2.5 miles on FSR-313. Some 30 miles northeast of Woodville and pushing the limits of "Day Trips" territory, this pretty nine-acre lake is cold enough in winter (January/February) to nourish stocked trout. Come summer, it offers great swimming, as well as prime birding, hiking, and camping (no hookups; fee). Lovely in itself, this long-leaf pine forest also is extremely rich in wildlife. Hikers should investigate the 5.5-mile-long Sawmill Trail that links Boykin Springs Recreation Area with Bouton Lake Recreation Area. Adventures along the way include an old sawmill site, explorations of the Neches River bottomlands, and crossing a long swinging bridge over Big Creek. For trail information, contact the Texas Forestry Association, (409) 632-TREE. Open daily. Parking fee. (409) 639-8620.

Christmas Tree Farms. Call for directions to the following choose-and-cut operations: Currie's Christmas Tree Farm, (409) 283-2422; Tom and Ruth Drawhorn, (409) 429-3277; Gunter Tree Farm, (409) 429-5323; and Twin Lake Estate, (409) 429-3406.

Dogwood Trail. This 1.5-mile walking trail along Theuvenins Creek is maintained by the International Paper Company. Watch for its sign 3 miles east of Woodville on US-190.

Heritage Village Museum. One mile west of Woodville on US-190. Never underestimate the power of people with a mission. When it looked like Woodville's best-known tourist attraction might either close or move in 1987, the Tyler County Heritage Society turned local pockets inside out to buy the property and its restaurant.

Now what was a weathering conglomeration of early Americana is an outstanding outdoor museum devoted to Texas history in general, Tyler County and Big Thicket territory in particular. Visitors tour a charming replica of a small town, composed of a number of homely historic structures filled with artifacts of early pioneer life (barbershop, blacksmith shop, syrup mill, whiskey still, pawnshop, apothecary, newspaper, etc.). Docents in historical dress provide commentary, a smithy once again works the forge, and artists demonstrate their skills among the refurbished buildings.

A well-done historical musical, *Whispers in the Wind,* turns the village green and surrounding buildings into an open-air stage the last two weekends in June. Costumed to the changing periods, this locally written and produced play follows three generations of a family from the time they settle in East Texas in the 1830s to the coming of the railroad in the early 1900s. Music is live, the horses and old covered wagons are real, and the audience almost becomes part of the show. Tickets ($) can be charged. (409) 283-2272.

Another "don't miss" event, the Harvest Festival and East Texas Folklife Festival on the third weekend of October, fills the village with costumed craftspeople demonstrating all the old-time skills. Although smaller in scale, the quality equals that of the Texas Folklife Festival in San Antonio.

Walkers note: Eleven and a half acres of neighboring woodlands are threaded with trails. The Heritage Society also owns and operates the Pickett House restaurant (see "Where to Eat" listings), and the gift shop specializes in East Texas handcrafts and art. Want a quilt or pine-needle basket? How about an inlaid domino set? This is the place. Open daily. Fee. (409) 283-2272, (800) 323-0389.

James Edward Wheat House. At the corner of Charlton and Wheat streets. One portion of this house was built in 1848. It is a private residence, but you are welcome to enjoy it from the street.

Lake Tejas. Eleven miles north of Woodville via US-69, then east 1 mile on FM-256. When summer's heat hits our neck of the woods, this super swimming hole is the place to be. Operated by the local school district, the lake is open on May weekends and daily from June to Labor Day. The sand-bottom lake has a two-level dive platform, sundecks over the water, lifeguards, bathhouse, concession stand, tubes, and paddle boats. *Note:* Picnicking and camping are available year-round. Fee. (409) 837-5757 weekdays.

Martin Dies Jr. State Park. On the eastern shore of the B. A. Steinhagen Lake, 14 miles east of Woodville on US-190. This 705-acre retreat offers camping (with and without hookups); screened shelters; hiking trails; swimming in two designated areas; fishing for crappie, bass, and catfish; two lighted fishing piers; five boat ramps; and numerous opportunities for wildlife observation and photography. Visitors also find an interpretive nature center, amphitheatre, and canoe/boat rentals; for information on the latter, call H&H Boat Dock, (409) 283-3257. Conservation specialists often guide canoe field trips along the Angelina-Neches River. Fee. For information contact Route 4, Box 274, Jasper 75951, (409) 384-5231 or (800) 792-1112.

River Floating. B. A. Steinhagen Lake, east of Woodville on US-190, also is known as Dam B, an impounding of the Neches River. If you are interested in floating on the Neches below the dam, call the U.S. Army Corps of Engineers at Steinhagen Lake, (409) 429-3491, for a report on conditions.

WHERE TO EAT

The Highlander. 708 South Magnolia (US-69), Woodville. Ever had Snicker pie? Sweet potato pie with pecan liquor? A roast turkey sandwich with cheese and guacamole? Those are just a few of the highly original offerings on the 15-item menu created by chef-owner Martha Stark. She also makes a memorable New Orleans-style bread pudding with whiskey sauce that will bring you back to Woodville again and again. No fried foods here, and no smoking. Open for lunch Monday-Saturday, dinner Friday-Saturday. $-$$. (409) 283-7572.

The Homestead Restaurant. In Hillister; take US-69/287 south 8 miles from Woodville, turn east for 1 block on FM-1013, and then turn right just before the railroad tracks. Don't worry—there are signs, and this restaurant is worth searching for. Two refugees from

Houston, Emily and Otho Sumner, offer country dining with a gourmet touch in a spacious old home they have restored. Built around 1912 in nearby Hillister, the house was moved by the Sumners to its present thirteen-acre shady site and fixed up with charm, including rockers and a swing on the porch. In addition to some nice touches on the standard fish/steak/chicken offerings (the broiled catfish is outstanding), most of the veggies are grown out back, and the Sumners make their own salad dressings. Every entree is prepared to order, and it's all-you-can-eat homemade chicken and dumplings on the first Sunday of the month, ditto boneless skinless chicken breasts (batter dipped and fried) on the second Sunday. Because Emily Sumner is a pie lover, she produces an ever changing selection of unusual pies, such as Toll House, coconut cream, buttermilk pecan, chocolate gold brick, double fudge, and lemon ice box.

While reservations are not essential, they are strongly advised, particularly if you want to sit in a room cleverly adorned with vintage clothing. No liquor is served, but glasses and ice buckets are provided for those who wish to bring their own wine. Open for dinner Friday and Saturday, lunch only on Sunday. $-$$. (409) 283-7324. The Sumners also operate The Getaway, a fully equipped guest retreat on the banks of Theuvinens Creek, 6 miles from their restaurant. Available to nonsmoking adults only, this two-bedroom house has a fireplace, a screened porch, and a great fishing hole in bass territory. Don't count on just dropping in; these digs often are booked months in advance. (409) 283-7324 (restaurant); 283-7244 (cottage).

Pickett House. Two miles west on US-190, behind Heritage Village. This old schoolhouse has been converted into an all-you-can-stuff-in kind of place, with bright circus posters on the walls and family-style service. Authentically replicating an East Texas boardinghouse experience during the 1840-1900 period, this eatery serves huge bowls of food family-style (fried chicken, chicken and dumplings, and three veggies) and your choice of fresh buttermilk or made-from-scratch ice tea, watermelon rind preserves, cornbread, hot biscuits, fruit cobbler, and bread pudding. It's fetch your own drinks and then take your dirty dishes to the kitchen, just like home. September–March hours are 11:00 A.M. to 2:00 P.M., Monday–Thursday; 11:00 A.M. to 8:00 P.M., Friday–Saturday; and 11:00 A.M. to

6:00 P.M. on Sunday. April–Labor Day hours are 11:00 A.M. to 8:00 P.M. daily. $-$$; (CC). (409) 283-3371.

Texas Best. On the south side of US-190, one-half mile west of Woodville. Loaded with country atmosphere, this small spot offers barbecue, steaks, sandwiches, salad bar, as well as all-you-can-eat spreads of fish and shrimp on Friday and Saturday. Open for lunch and dinner Monday–Saturday. $-$$; (CC). (409) 283-5249.

WANDERING THE BACKROADS

If you need a swift return home from Woodville, retrace your route back to Livingston via US-190 and turn south on US-59.

However, from Woodville you can drive northwest on US-287 to the small community of Chester and make a 1.6-mile jog north on FM-2097 East to see Peach Tree Village, composed of lumber tycoon John Henry Kirby's mansion (now a museum) and the community meeting house/chapel, built in 1912. Although drop-in visitors are welcome, advance notice helps ensure that both buildings will be open when you visit. The site is an old Alabama Indian headquarters camp called Ta Ku La, and two trails blazed by pioneers crossed here. Recently refurbished as a retreat and summer youth camp, Ta Ku La makes a pleasant picnic destination. For information or to arrange a tour or group retreat, call (409) 969-2455.

Another scenic drive takes you from Woodville to Saratoga and Big Thicket National Preserve (Trip 3, this sector). Take US-69/287 South from Woodville to Kountze, swing southwest on T-326, and turn right on FM-770 to Saratoga, in the heart of the Big Thicket. To continue home to Houston, follow FM-770 South to US-90 and turn west.

Although the wild azalea canyons near Newton are beyond the geographic scope of this book, they are well worth viewing during their pink and white blooming season, which usually falls in late March. Tip your hat to the Temple Eastex Lumber Industries for preserving these beauties, and tread carefully; bird's-foot violets, cinnamon fern, and jack-in-the-pulpit wildflowers may be underfoot. Newton is 48 miles east-northeast from Woodville via US-190. For information contact the Newton Chamber of Commerce, Drawer 66, Newton 75966, (409) 379-5527.

LIBERTY AND DAYTON

Although this area, east of Houston on US-90, is rich with history, much of what survives remains privately owned, and the towns have little to illustrate their heritages to the general public. Take away the historical markers, and the casual tourist might conclude that nothing much has happened here—which is far from the truth.

Originally this entire corner of southeast Texas was called the Atascosito District, a municipality first of Spain and then of Mexico. Now broken into ten counties, the district was built around the outpost of Atascosito, shown as a freshwater spring on maps as early as 1757. To reach the original site of Atascosito today, take T-146 northeast from Liberty approximately 4 miles and turn west (left) on FM-1011. A marker is just beyond the intersection, and the spring still flows nearby.

After 1821 this wilderness was controlled by Mexico, and Anglo settlers were welcome. For the most part early settlers were independent individuals who came here because they could not gain grants through Austin's colonization farther to the west. They formed settlements like Liberty and Dayton as well as many other places whose names have faded from map and memory.

The Atascosito Road crossed the district, running from Goliad and Refugio to Opelousas, Louisiana. Today its route is roughly paralleled by US-90, and the town of Dayton straddles the historic path.

In 1831 the Villa de la Santissima Trinidad de la Libertad was established slightly south of the spring and officially laid out with six

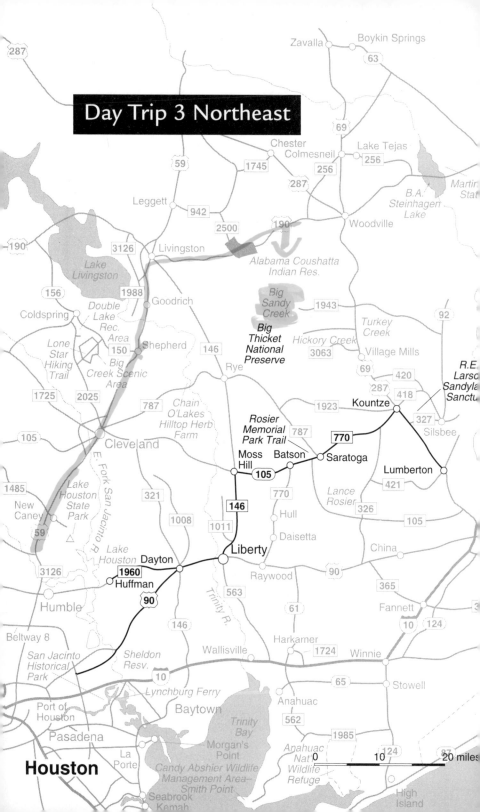

public squares. Now called Liberty, it traditionally is considered to be the third oldest town in Texas.

A map available from the chamber of commerce will direct you to most of the sites of interest, including the Cleveland-Partlow House (1860), 2131 Grand (private); and the T. J. Chambers Home (1861), 624 Milam (private). Graveyard historians love Liberty—there are at least four historic cemeteries in the area. For information contact the Liberty-Dayton Chamber of Commerce, Box 1270, Liberty 77575, (409) 336-5736.

Six miles west on US-90 and across the Trinity River is Dayton. It was first called West Liberty and then Day's Town in honor of an early settler, I. C. Day. Originally a lumber and agricultural community, Dayton got financial boosts with the coming of the railroad in the 1870s and oil strikes in the early 1920s. Today visitors find some vintage buildings slowly being filled with interesting shops. As you pass through, take time to read the historical marker concerning the Runaway Scrape (Trip 3, west sector). This marker is on the eastern outskirts of Dayton on US-90 East.

Day-trippers living north or east of Houston can now access this area by taking the Sam Houston Parkway (Beltway 8) to US-90 East.

WHAT TO DO

Blueberry Farms. Liberty County is prime blueberry territory. You can pick your own at Tanner's Blueberry Farm, (409) 298-2382.

Christmas Tree Farms. If you are en route to Dayton or Liberty in the late fall, you can pick out your Christmas tree at Londa's Christmas Tree Farm in Crosby, (281) 328-1156. Other options include Hatcher's Christmas Tree Farm (near Liberty), (409) 389-2387, and Keiths Christmas Trees (Dayton), (281) 592-5032.

Cleveland-Partlow House. 2131 Grand, Liberty. Built around 1860 and curated by the Sam Houston Regional Library and Research Center, this vintage home is open to visitors on Tuesday from 9:00 to 10:00 A.M. or by appointment. Fee. (409) 336-5488.

Geraldine Humphreys Cultural Center. 1710 Sam Houston Street, Liberty. An active little theater, the Valley Players, puts on plays and musicals here. For the current playbill call (409) 336-5887. A contemporary bell tower houses an exact replica of the famous Liberty Bell, cast in 1960 by a London foundry from the original pattern and mold. The bell rings twice a year—on New Year's Day and again on the Fourth of July during an old-fashioned Independence Day celebration on the center grounds. Free. Open Monday–Thursday and on Saturday. (409) 336-8901 (Liberty Library).

Huffman Horse Auction. On FM-1960 East, 7 miles east of Lake Houston (via Humble), 4 miles east of Huffman, and 7 miles west of Dayton. When you see a big red barn and a large parking lot, you've found a piece of pure redneck Texana. Open all day on Saturday, but the real action starts at 7:00 P.M. with the auction of tack, then used saddles, then trailers, mules, horses, and ponies. (409) 258-3093.

Liberty Opry on the Square. 1816 Sam Houston Avenue. If you enjoy live country and western music laced with liberal servings of gospel, don't miss this family-oriented, three-hour show featuring musicians from throughout the state. The venue is Liberty's former movie theater (circa 1935), complete with plush red velvet seats, and the curtain goes up on Friday and Saturday evenings year-round. Call for reservations. $. (800) 248-8918.

Old French Cemetery. Approximately 3 miles east of Dayton on FM-1008. Established in 1830, this is the burial place of some of the early settlers of the Atascosito District. One grave notes an 1821 death; others are enclosed inside antique iron fences.

Ostrich of Texas International Co., Inc. Near Liberty. This large place specializes in breeding ostrich, emu, rhea, and exotic deer, and it also has some miniature kangaroos called wallabies and a pair of miniature horses. Visitors with advance appointments are very welcome; no children under five. (409) 298-2020.

Sam Houston Regional Library and Research Center. Four miles north of Liberty via T-146 and a turn northwest (left) on FM-1011. Appropriately sited near the original settlement of Atascosito on a high knoll shaded by mature pecan trees, this massive repository is owned by the state and operated free of charge to the public by the Texas State Library. Within its fireproof vaults are valuable historical records, documents, portraits, and other artifacts of the original Atascosito District, most of which can be accessed by special request.

This also is one of the state's least-known and most interesting museums. There are three public display rooms full of goodies like Jean Lafitte's personal diary and other remnants of the days when Liberty was a major steamboat port on the Trinity River. Genealogists note: This library has reprints of the Atascosito census of 1826, valuable because it lists the maiden names of wives.

Several interesting structures dot the museum's grounds: the historic Gillard-Duncan Home (1848), restored and furnished to its period; the Norman House (circa 1883), with changing exhibits drawn from the library's vaults; St. Stephen's Episcopal Church (1898), used for meetings; and the Price Daniel family home, filled with antiques and mementos of former Texas Governor Price Daniel's political years. Tours of the latter require two weeks' advance notice. Free. Open Monday–Saturday. (409) 336-8821.

Sheldon Lake State Park/Wildlife Management Area. 14320 Garrett Road, Houston (via Sam Houston Parkway/Beltway 8). Only 13 miles from downtown Houston's skyscrapers and currently improving as a state park, this public preserve covers 1,200 acres of water, 400 acres of marsh and swampland, and slightly more than 600 acres of rice/milo/soybean farmland. The latter is food for an estimated 10,000 ducks and geese that winter at this refuge; huge flocks often are easily viewed from Garrett Road.

Although you can fish from the banks and five fishing piers daily year-round, the lake is open for boat and wade fishing only from March 1 through October (no motors over 10 hp), so as not to disturb the migrating birds. Catches include bass, crappie, sunfish, and three species of catfish. Additionally, two small ponds at the above address are stocked specifically for groups (limited access; call). A new environmental education center is under construction for the southern end of the park, but for now activities are limited to fishing, walking nature trails, birding, and viewing wildlife. Several heron/egret rookeries exist on barrier islands along the lake's western edge. *Note:* This is alligator territory—no swimming. Park rangers are available weekdays at the above address. (281) 456-9350.

WHERE TO EAT

Ducky's & Purple Duck Tea Room. On the north side of FM-1960, one mile west of Dayton. Filled with antiques and collectibles (for sale), this eatery offers a table d'hô°te menu—whatever the cook feels like fixing that day. For less than $6 you get a hot entree such as lasagne or King Ranch chicken, salad, dessert, and drink. Open Tuesday–Friday for lunch. $; (CC). (409) 258-3509.

Liberty Bell Antique Country Kitchen and Tea Room. 2040 Trinity, Liberty. A touch of the French Quarter where you least expect it, this charming eatery also has a nice patio for alfresco dining when weather permits. A single, health-conscious main dish with fixings is offered daily, but the choice of desserts ($ extra) is dazzling. Open for lunch Monday–Friday. $; (CC). (409) 336-5222.

Nina's Diner. 710 US-90 West, Dayton. Breakfast all day is the specialty at this simple place, and lunch specials run to homemade chicken and dumplings, meat loaf, hamburgers, and other Texas standards. Open for breakfast, lunch, and dinner on weekdays, breakfast and lunch on Saturday. $-$$. (409) 258-2998.

Sunny Acres Herb Farm and Restaurant. On the south side of US-90, one mile west of Dayton. A "must stop" for both gardeners and cooks, this nursery has three greenhouses, several display gardens, and five acres filled with herbs under cultivation. Brochures lead visitors on self-guided tours. There's also an excellent bookshop focused on gardening, herbs, and natural living subjects, as well as occasional classes in soap-making, cooking with herbs, primitive rug hooking and dyeing, and so on. As of spring 1997, the farm's tearoom was open only for groups with advance reservations. However, owner Paula Adlers expects to offer herb-based lunches (also by reservation only) to the general public by fall. $$; (CC). (409) 258-5129, (800) 971-HERB.

The Texas Kountry Kitchen and the Main Street Soda Fountain. 309–313 North Main Street, Dayton. These neighboring spots complement each other so well that the owners have cut a passage through their common wall. The Kountry Kitchen specializes in fresh chicken-fried steak, hand-patted hamburger steak, and catfish fillets, as well as sandwiches, soups, and a large salad bar; the daily lunch special may be the most food for the least money in the area. Open for breakfast, lunch, and dinner Monday–Saturday. $; (CC). (409) 258-4882.

Surrounded by antiques and collectibles (for sale), the Main Street Soda Fountain recalls the 1950s when this spot was the teenage hangout for the town—same counter, same stools, and same menu of classic malts, shakes, floats, and sundaes. The jukebox still plays oldies, and owners Kleve and Liz Kirby keep nonviolent comic books around for kids to read while they "hang out." Open Tuesday–Saturday. $. (409) 258-3553.

CONTINUING ON

This day trip moseys on to the Big Thicket via Moss Hill, Batson, Saratoga, Kountze, and Silsbee. From Liberty take T-146 north 15 miles to Moss Hill, turn east (right on FM-162) to Batson, and then northeast (left) on FM-770 to Saratoga and Kountze.

Moss Hill is a farming and ranch area, named for the Spanish moss draped in the surrounding woods. Batson was a small village called Otto prior to the discovery of the Batson Oil Field in 1903 and was the scene of the Batson Round-Up, in which all the unmarried women were gathered up and auctioned to prospective husbands. It's a bit of a racy story—ask locally or check out the faded pictures of the event at Heritage Village in Woodville (Trip 2, this sector).

SARATOGA, KOUNTZE, AND SILSBEE

Saratoga was named for the famous New York spa because it had several medicinal hot springs. A hotel catering to the health seekers burned decades ago, but some of the old foundation still can be found. No word on the fate of the hot springs. Saratoga today is one of the gateways to the Big Thicket.

Kountze got its start with the railroad's arrival in 1881 and owes its continued existence to the lumber industry. The county seat, it's also the humor center for the region as the home of Hoover and Starr, the world's only legally married live armadillos; their license is recorded in the Hardin County Courthouse. The entire area celebrates their anniversary annually on April Fools' Day with a full program of fun and entertainment. To plug into what's going on and visit the happy couple in their honeymoon haven, stop at Buddy Moore's Big Thicket Museum and Armadillo Mini-Museum, 1020 US-60 North in Kountze (across from city hall), (409) 246-3056. Kountze soon will be home to the headquarters of the Big Thicket National Preserve.

Silsbee sprang to life when lumber baron John Henry Kirby established a sawmill here in 1894. For comprehensive information on the entire Big Thicket area, contact the Hardin County Tourist Bureau, P.O. Box 8801, Lumberton 77757, (800) 835-0343.

WHAT TO DO

Big Thicket Visitor Information Center. On FM-420, off US-69/287, 7 miles north of Kountze. If you don't know the Big Thicket, start with this facility's slide show, and then study the exhibits that detail the plant and animal life that makes this 96,000-plus-acre national preserve so special. Ask specifically about ranger-led activities, hikes, walks, floats, canoe routes, and so forth. Open daily. (409) 246-2337.

    Blueberry Farms. You can pick your own in May and June at the following Hardin County patches: Blueberry Basket (Kountze), (409) 755-6006; Lack's Blueberry Farm (Kountze), (409) 246-2193 or 246-3770; Lee's Berry Haven (Silsbee), (409) 385-5179; Lynch Blueberry Patch (between Silsbee and Kountze), (409) 385-1200; Paradise Patch (Silsbee), (409) 385-0804; and A Patch of Blues in Lumberton, (409) 755-1879.

    Christmas Tree Farms. Get in the holiday spirit with an excursion to the following: Bozeman Family Christmas Tree Farm (near Lumberton), (409) 755-4062 or 755-2706; Double S Christmas Tree Farm (near Buna), (409) 994-3395; Yule Cut Tree Farm (north of Kountze), (409) 246-3711.

    Kirby-Hill Home. 201 Main Street, Kountze. This 1902 Victorian mansion is under restoration and open for tours on Sunday and Tuesday afternoons or by appointment. Donation. (409) 246-3107 or 246-5184.

    Pelt Pond Rural Life Museum. On FM-421, 1 mile west of T-326, between Sour Lake and Kountze. In 1926 Charlie and Mirtie Pelt began to farm ten acres in the Big Thicket woods, little dreaming that their place ultimately would become an open-air museum devoted to telling the story of rural life in early East Texas and South Louisiana. The fourth Pelt home on the property, built in 1959, now houses an extensive collection of folk art, including paintings by Clementine Hunter of Melrose Plantation (Louisiana) and Pauline "Old Lady" Parker of Houston. Elsewhere on five acres barns house animals typical to the region, including Piney Woods rooter hogs and Piney Woods range cattle, both of which are endangered species. Pelt Pond Farm also is the site of the Annual Texas Great Crackling Cookout on the second weekend of November, which includes a $5.00 all-you-can-eat barbecue plate, professional country entertainment, and crafts demonstrations (pottery, smithing, grist-milling, spinning, basket weaving, stained glass, etc.). Open Saturdays from Easter through the Crackling Cookout weekend. Fee. (409) 287-3300 or 287-3516.

Silsbee Ice House Museum. Ernest and Fourth streets, Silsbee. Housed in the community's old ice house, this cultural center displays the work of local artists (new shows monthly) and includes a small museum focused on Hardin County history. Open weekdays and on weekend afternoons. (409) 385-2444.

Timber Ridge Tours. This company specializes in comprehensive guided trips on the lands and waters of East Texas, from Woodville to Beaumont, including the Big Thicket National Preserve and Village Creek State Park. Call for a list of adventures and customized packages; they also rent a cabin in the woods 35 miles from Beaumont. (409) 246-3107.

Village Creek State Park. On Alma Drive, off US-96 in Lumberton. This 942-acre facility has more than 1 mile of frontage on Village Creek and is densely forested, an excellent example of Big Thicket terrain. Facilities and activities include camping (some hookups for RVs), picnic areas, hiking, canoeing, birding, fishing, and swimming; several sandbars along the creek make ideal beaches. Floods are common here, which means there are baygalls (small swamps) within the park boundaries. Wildlife is abundant—expect a multilevel frog chorus at night—and more than sixty species of birds have been seen in a single day. This park is a good put-in or take-out on a Village Creek float; if you don't have your own canoe, contact official park concessionaire Timber Ridge Tours (above) or one of the outfitters listed in the Big Thicket "What to Do" section. P.O. Box 8575, Lumberton 77711, (409) 755-7322.

WHERE TO EAT

See restaurant listings following the next section, The Big Thicket.

THE BIG THICKET

The Big Thicket National Preserve is often described as the biological crossroads of North America. It is a unique place, eight major ecosystems where the flora and fauna mix from all points of the compass. Ferns, orchids, giant palmettos, mushrooms, several types of pine, four types of insect-eating plants—the abundance and variety is unequaled anywhere else on our globe.

Unfortunately, many folks visit what they think is the Big Thicket and go home wondering what all the shouting is about. The problem is that there are twelve Big Thickets in all, and you have to know where to look to find them. The preserve is composed of eight land sections and four river/stream corridors and spreads out over 97,000 acres and seven counties. The beautiful, biologically unique portions lie well away from the highways. Just driving through won't do.

The above statistics refer to acreage already within the national preserve. In general terms the Big Thicket covers 3.5 million acres of Southeast Texas, including portions of Harris County.

All Texans love a tall tale, and the Big Thicket has its share. One concerns the Kaiser Burn-out at Honey Island near Kountze. Local residents called Jayhawkers who had no sympathy for the Confederate side of the Civil War hid out in the woods to escape conscription. Charged with capturing them, Confederate captain James Kaiser set a fire to flush them out. Two were killed, a few captured, and the rest vanished once again. Some claim the descendants of those Jayhawkers still live in the depths of the Big Thicket. As more people explore this wilderness, there may be an update on the story.

Then there's the mysterious light that spooks travelers on the Bragg Road, a pencil-straight graded lane that follows the old railroad right-of-way between Saratoga and Bragg. Sometimes called a ghost or the "Saratoga light," it appears as a pulsating phenomenon and has been seen by enough people to warrant serious investigation. Some say it is the ghost lantern of a railway worker killed on the old line; other, less imaginative types claim it's just swamp gas or the reflected lights of cars on a nearby highway. Whatever, it adds to the Big Thicket mystique.

In addition to the backroads route to Saratoga listed in the preceding day trip, Houstonians have several other ways of getting to the Big Thicket. The most direct route follows US-90 East to a left turn onto FM-770 North at Raywood, continuing to Saratoga. An alternative is to take I-10 East to Hankamer, then go north on T-61 to US-90; turn west and go 4 miles to FM-770, then north to Raywood.

Depending on what unit of the Big Thicket you want to visit, there also is access from Woodville, Kountze, Cleveland, and Beaumont. A good state map is indispensable as are maps and guides of the area itself. Pick up the latter at the Big Thicket Information Center (previously mentioned) north of Kountze or request in advance by contacting Big Thicket National Preserve, 3785 Milam Street, Beaumont 77701, (409) 839-2689. Do remember that this is a young park, developing slowly on limited funds, and that many of the areas are recovering still from people's earlier abuse. *Note:* There are no accommodations within the preserve.

WHERE TO GO

The Turkey Creek, Beech Creek, Hickory Creek Savannah, and Big Sandy Creek units as well as Rosier Memorial Park in Saratoga are operated by the National Park Service. For information, maps, and trails listing, stop at the Big Thicket National Preserve Visitor Information Center on FM-420, 2.5 miles east of US-69/287 between Warren and Kountze (open daily, except Christmas), (409) 246-2337.

The Nature Conservancy operates the Roy E. Larsen Sandylands Sanctuary near Kountze. Guided hikes for groups can be arranged by contacting P.O. Box 909, Silsbee 77656, (409) 385-4135.

Turkey Creek is noted for changing habitats and carnivorous plants and is best accessed from the visitor information center on FM-420, mentioned above. The Kirby Nature Trail loops out from the visitor center, primarily a 1.7- or 2.4-mile walk to Village Creek. Those interested in insect-devouring carnivorous plants should ask directions to the Pitcher Plant Trail, and those seeking a longer hike should ask how to connect with the 15-mile Turkey Creek Trail, which rambles nearly the length of the unit.

Beech Creek, off FM-2992 southeast of Woodville, is a 4,856-acre beech-magnolia-loblolly pine plant community. Unfortunately, a 1975 beetle epidemic killed almost all of the loblolly pines, so the forest is not as pretty as it was. The Beech Woods Trail, a 1-mile loop, passes through a mature stand of hardwoods.

The **Hickory Creek Savannah** unit, 0.5 mile west of US-69/287 via FM-2827 and a dirt road, combines the long-leaf pine forest and wetlands with the dry, sandy soil found in the uplands. This is great wildflower territory in spring. The Sundew Trail (1 mile) is open to the public, and there also is a 0.25-mile trail designed for the handicapped and the elderly.

The **Big Sandy Creek** unit includes a rich diversity of plant and animal life. The 5.4-mile Woodland Trail, at the northwestern edge of the unit (near the Alabama-Coushatta Indian reservation), covers a floodplain, dense mature mixed forest, and upland pine stands. The trail entrance is not well marked, 3.3 miles south of US-190 on FM-1276. The trail also offers two shorter loops and is one of the closest to Houston. Equestrians and all-terrain bikers, *take note:* This unit also offers an 18-mile trail designed specifically for horseback riding, hiking, and all-terrain bicycling.

The **Roy E. Larsen Sandylands Sanctuary** is on T-327, 3 miles east of Kountze. Although it is considered an excellent example of the arid sandylands, it has 9 miles of frontage along Village Creek. The canoe float from FM-418 to FM-327 has some good swimming holes and white sandbars; about three hours long in paddling time, it is one of the most popular outings in the park (see Boating section under "What to Do" for canoe livery services). If you prefer to walk, a 6-mile trail is open daily, and interpretive brochures are available at the trailhead. Guided tours for groups can be arranged by writing to P.O. Box 909, Silsbee 77656, or calling (409) 385-4135.

The **Rosier Memorial Park Trail** is a 0.5-mile loop through a palmetto-hardwoods plant community on the western outskirts of Saratoga near the intersection of FM-770 and FM-787.

WHAT TO DO

Birding. Excellent, particularly from late March through early May, when hundreds of species pass on their way north up the Mississippi flyway. The Big Thicket is the first stop on the upper Texas coast section of the Great Texas Coastal Birding Trail.

Boating. Guided fishing and sightseeing trips on the Neches River can be arranged through Timber Ridge Tours, (409) 246-3107. Small watercraft can be launched at several places on the Trinity River, Neches River, Pine Island Bayou, and both Village and Turkey creeks; road crossings generally provide access. Water levels fluctuate; check before you make firm plans. The national preserve often organizes free trips with a naturalist guide; you must bring your own canoe, life jacket, paddles, and the like. The preserve provides shuttle service at the end of the trip back to the starting point. Reservations required. (409) 246-2337 or 839-2689.

Exploring Big Thicket waterways on your own can be difficult. There are few take-outs, and much of the land bordering on the creeks is privately owned, which makes visitors subject to trespass charges. Seek advice and equipment from one of the following canoe livery services: Canoe Rentals in Silsbee, (409) 385-6241; Eastex Canoe Rentals in Beaumont, (409) 892-3600; H&H Boat Dock and Marina at B. A. Steinhagen Lake, (409) 283-3257; Piney Woods Canoe Co. in Saratoga, (409) 274-5892; Timber Ridge Tours in Kountze, (409) 246-3107; Village Creek Canoe Rentals in Kountze, (409) 246-4481; or Whitewater Experience in Houston, (713) 522-2848.

Camping. Primitive backpacking is allowed by free permit from the National Park Service in the Jack Gore Baygall, Beech Creek, Big Sandy, Neches Bottom, and Lance Rosier units, as well as the Upper and Lower Neches River corridors; (409) 246-2337.

Fishing. Allowed in all waters. A license is required, and state regulations apply.

Guided Trips. Timber Ridge Tours operates a variety of customized guided trips and canoe shuttles within the Big Thicket National Preserve and Village Creek State Park. For information contact the tour company at P.O. Box 115, Kountze 77625, (409) 246-3107.

Hunting and Trapping. Allowed in specific areas. Permit required. For information and season details, write to the National Park Service, 3785 Milam, Beaumont 77701, or call (409) 839-2689.

Hiking. Wear sturdy, water-repellent boots. This is rain country at certain times of the year, and the shady trails often have standing water. Mosquito repellent is an absolute necessity. Pets and vehicles are not permitted on any of the trails, and you must register your hike at the trailhead. *Absolutely do not wander on your own, off-trail.* The Big Thicket has earned its name, and it is easy to get lost. Request in advance a list of hiking trails from the visitor center listed previously.

Naturalist Activities. National Park rangers offer an extensive program that includes talks and guided hikes, boat tours, and canoe trips. Reservations are required. (409) 246-2337.

Picnicking. Many sites throughout the park, some with grills; all are shown on the park map available at the Visitor Center. Open fires and wood collecting are prohibited, and bringing your own water is strongly advised.

Photography. There is a great range of natural subjects, particularly if you use macro or long lenses. Most of the beautiful things are found in deep shade, so bring a tripod and high ISO film. Several outstanding photographic books on the Big Thicket are available at Houston libraries and bookstores to start your creative juices flowing.

Swimming. Although there are no designated swimming areas within the Big Thicket, many people enjoy a dip from the Lakeview sandbar area of the Neches River in the Beaumont unit and from numerous sandbars along the Neches River and Village Creek.

WHERE TO EAT

Big Thicket Bar-B-Que and Smokehouse. 735 Pine (US-69/287), Kountze. This comfortable spot smokes its own meats and has bountiful lunch and dinner buffets on Sunday, Wednesday, and Friday. Meat prices per pound are reasonable, so consider hauling some home. Open for lunch and dinner Tuesday–Sunday. $–$$. (409) 246-4007.

Homestead Restaurant. Hillister. (Trip 2, this sector.)

Red Onion Restaurant. 120 Candlestick, Lumberton. Tucked away behind Wal-Mart, this popular eatery dishes up homecooked specialties such as chicken and dumplings, grilled pork chops, pot roast, veggie soup, and so on. There's a huge all-you-can-eat buffet, with many fish entrees featured on Fridays. On a low-fat diet? Look for the green spoons on the buffet. Tiny appetite? Check out the "Remember When" specials (smaller portions) for $4.25. No surprise that local folks voted this the best restaurant in the area in 1992. Open daily for lunch and dinner. $–$$; (CC). (409) 755-7422.

Stinger's Restaurant. 235 Library Drive (business US-96), Silsbee. Love model trains? Come here; they're part of the fun. House specials range from hamburgers and po'boys to steak, with charbroiled catfish and chicken filling in the menu. Open for lunch and dinner Monday–Saturday. $–$$; (CC). (409) 385-4994.

Wildwood Cafe. Inside the Wildwood Resort development. Entrance is on the west side of US-69/287, midway between Warren and Kountze; ask for specific directions at the entrance gate. This clean, tiny place on the edge of Wildwood Lake makes a great hamburger stop when you're roaming around the Big Thicket. Owner

Hal Dawson also serves tasty chicken-fried steak, catfish, and fried shrimp. Open for lunch and dinner Tuesday–Saturday. $–$$. (409) 834–6251.

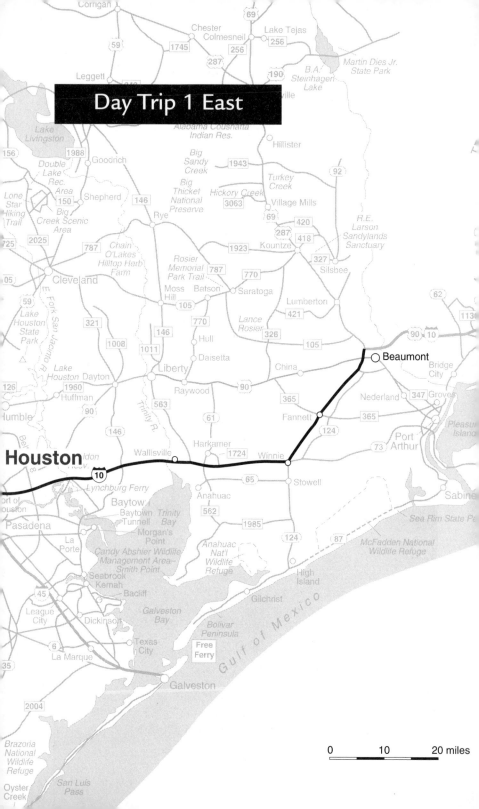

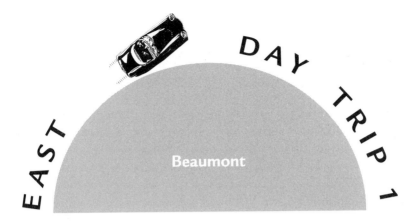

BEAUMONT

The prospect of a day trip to Beaumont may evoke all the wild enthusiasm usually reserved for kissing your sister. But a little exploration in and around this river city may change your mind. There are a surprising number of things to do, not only in Beaumont proper but in the surrounding Golden Triangle area (Beaumont/Orange/ Port Arthur). From Houston there's only one way to get there—due east on I-10.

Although history hasn't painted the town with the color found in Austin's cradle country west of Houston, Beaumont is equally old. The first land grant by Mexico to an Anglo in Texas was issued to Noah Tevis and covered 2,214 acres of richly forested area along the Neches River. Today that is downtown Beaumont. By 1825 there was an active trading post here, and Jefferson County, of which Beaumont is the county seat, is one of the original counties formed by the Texas Republic in 1836. Since that time Beaumont has made its own brand of history in several ways.

Most vivid and important to modern America was the Lucas gusher at the Spindletop oil field in January 1901, the greatest oil well in history. Almost overnight Beaumont grew from 8,500 souls to 30,000 folks with advanced cases of oil fever, and a wooden shantytown called Gladys City was hammered into instant life on Spindletop Hill. By the end of that decade, the oil was gone, and Gladys City was a ghost town of wooden shacks. Th/ose glory days live again in the re-creation of Gladys City, 0.5 mile north of its actual site, at Beaumont's successful bicentennial project.

Economically linked with the volatile oil and petrochemical industry, Beaumont has had its ups and downs in recent years. By the
late 1960s shifting financial fortunes had created another ghost
town of sorts in the downtown area. But that scene slowly is
changing, thanks to major commitments from public and private
sectors. During the past decade more than $120 million worth of
capital improvements have been made downtown, including new
municipal and county government complexes. Work remains under
way on multimillion-dollar hotel and office projects, and the $5 mil-
lion Art Museum of Southeast Texas regularly draws raves. Other
commercial projects involve the restoration of classic buildings
listed in the National Register of Historic Places.

For free maps, brochures, and advice, stop at the Visitor Information Center in the Babe Didrikson Zaharias Memorial (MLK exit 854
from I-10). Open daily, (409) 833-4622. The Beaumont Convention
and Visitors Bureau is another good source, 801 Main Street, City
Hall, Suite 100, Beaumont 77701, (409) 880-3749 or (800)
392-4401.

For a prerecorded weekly calendar of events, call (409) 833-3638,
ext. 1620.

WHAT TO DO

Agricultural and Industrial Tours. Several companies welcome
visitors, among them: American Rice Growers Association (thirty-
minute free tour), (409) 842-1620; Douget's Rice Milling (free
tours on weekdays by appointment), (409) 866-2297; and E. I. du
Pont de Nemours & Co. (one-hour free tours on weekdays), (800)
392-4401.

Art Museum of Southeast Texas. 500 Main Street. This handsome, $5 million museum showcases a wide variety of nineteenth-
and twentieth-century American art. Exhibits change every six
weeks. Open daily. Free. Also here: Cafe Arts (see "Where to Eat" listings). (409) 832-3432.

Babe Didrikson Zaharias Museum and Visitor Center. MLK
exit 854 from I-10. In her time this outstanding woman athlete put
Beaumont on the map, and the town repaid her with a love and ad-
miration that live on beyond her death from cancer in 1956. This
memorial museum chronicles a life and career that saw her six times

named Woman Athlete of the Year by the Associated Press. Free. Open daily. (409) 833-4622.

Beaumont Police Department Museum. 255 College Street (downtown). This unique collection of weaponry and other law enforcement paraphernalia dates from the turn of the century. Open weekdays. Free. (409) 880-3825.

Blueberry Farms. Call the following for directions to pick-your-own berry patches: Dishman Brothers Berry Farm, (409) 752-2161; Griffin's Farm, (409) 753-2247; Lazy D Berry Farm, (409) 296-2882; and Texas Blueberry Plantation, (409) 753-2890.

Christmas Tree Farms. There are numerous places to cut your own tree in Chambers, Jasper, and Jefferson counties: B's Christmas Tree Plantation, (409) 794-1593; Beavers Christmas Tree Farm, (409) 253-2372; Dennis Dugat Farms, (409) 296-4716; Double S Christmas Tree Farm, (409) 994-3395; Ferguson's Christmas Tree Farm, (409) 374-2365; Five "O" Evergreens, (409) 994-3686; Hubert's Christmas Tree Farm, (409) 796-1516; Huckleberry Hollow Farm, (409) 994-2134; Rudolph's Pasture, (409) 423-5961; or F & W Enterprises, (409) 983-1271 or 837-5642.

Clifton Steamboat Museum. South of Beaumont on T-124; call for directions. Opened in 1995, this new attraction honors military and civilian heroes with exhibits relating to the Republic of Texas, the Civil War in Southeast Texas and Southwest Louisiana, the steamboat era, and World War II. Visitors also tour a 1938 tugboat, the *Hercules,* and a replica of the Sabine Pass lighthouse and keeper's dwelling. The latter includes a restaurant. Call for information and hours of operation. (409) 842-4543.

Crawfish Farms. Crawfish ranching is big business in the greater Beaumont area, particularly around the small town of China on US-90. The following offer free tours January-June: Doguet's Crawfish Farm, (409) 752-5105, and H&L Crawfish Farms, (409) 752-5514 or 835-1017.

Eastex Canoes. 5865 Cole. Why not take a paddle on the Neches or Sabine river? This rental and livery service provides paddles, life jackets, maps, and basic instruction. Open daily. (409) 892-3600.

The Edison Plaza Museum. 350 Pine. What was the old Travis Street substation of Gulf State Utilities now houses various adventures in electricity, including inventions of Thomas A. Edison. Open weekday afternoons and by appointment. (409) 981-3089.

The Fire Museum of Texas. 400 Walnut (at Mulberry). This 1927 fire hall now contains a good collection of old fire equipment and memorabilia, including seven major fire-fighting units used from 1779 to the present. A Learn-by-Doing exhibit teaches thirty fire and home safety facts to children ages six to twelve; there's also a child-size safety house, a fire safety theater, displays of toy fire trucks, and a life-size Smokey the Bear. Open weekdays. (409) 880-3927.

Spindletop/Gladys City Boomtown Museum. At the intersection of University Drive and US-69/96/287. Although it lacks the grime of the original, this reconstruction is a good look at 1910 America as well as life in an oil field boomtown. A rickety boardwalk connects most of the structures, just as it did eight decades ago.

The furnished replicas include a surveying and engineering office, the pharmacy and doctor's office, a photographer's studio, a general store, and more. Vintage oil field equipment is scattered around, and the Lucas Gusher Monument is out back on its own site. From I-10 take the US-69/96/287 turnoff to Port Arthur and then the Highland Avenue/Sulphur Drive exit. Signs guide you from there. Open Tuesday–Sunday afternoons. Fee. (409) 835-0823.

John Jay French Museum. 2985 French Road (Delaware exit from US-69/96/287 North; turn west and watch for signs). This substantial museum was John J. French's trading post and home back in 1845, now restored and operated by the Beaumont Heritage Society in a beautiful wooded setting north of town. Open Tuesday–Saturday. Fee. (409) 898-3267.

McFaddin-Ward House. 1906 McFaddin. Don't leave Beaumont without touring this impressive home; it is one of the few restored Beaux Arts-Colonial houses in the United States. Built in 1906 on land granted by the Mexican government to earlier generations of the McFaddin family, it was occupied by that oil-wealthy and socially prominent family until 1982. Tours begin every thirty minutes with an excellent slide show and continue through numerous rooms, a kaleidoscope of family life and American decor styles from the 1907 period on. Most of the furniture is American, most of the accessories are European, and the 1908 Pink Parlor is particularly grand. Open Tuesday–Saturday and on Sunday afternoons; no children under eight are allowed. The last tours begin at 3:00 P.M. Fee. (409) 832-2134.

Old Time Trade Days. I-10 and T-124 in Winnie. This buy-and-sell trade market has more than 400 exhibitors on the weekend that follows the first Monday of each month. Fee. (409) 296–3300 or 892–4000.

Old Town. East of Calder and Eleventh streets. When the first Gladys City was in its heyday, this portion of Beaumont was a highly desirable, tree-lined residential neighborhood. Today it still is. Some of the homes remain impressive, and many now house galleries, restaurants, and specialty shops. A free map helps you find out what's what in this thirty-block area. Pick one up at the Tourist Information Center or order it in advance from the convention & visitors bureau, Box 3827, Beaumont 77704, (409) 880–3749 or (800) 392–4401.

Port of Beaumont. 1255 Main Street. You'll have a bird's-eye view of the busy port from an observation deck on top of the Harbor Island Transit Warehouse; ask the security guard at the Main Street entrance for directions. This modern port handles more than thirty million tons of cargo annually and is one of the four largest ports in the United States in terms of tonnage. The far banks of the Neches River, on the other hand, remain richly forested and undeveloped, just as they were when clipper ships stopped here a century ago. Open daily; guided tours by appointment. (409) 832–1546.

Riverfront Park. On the Neches River behind City Hall at Main and College streets. "Sunday in the Park" is the big event here from April through November. Civic groups host fun and games almost every Sunday from 2:00 to 4:00 P.M., and the activities are different every week. Great for kids, so bring a picnic and spend the afternoon. Free.

Texas Energy Museum. 600 Main at Forsyth, across from the civic center complex. Exhibits about Beaumont before and after Spindletop are featured in this $5 million showcase, along with the entire collection of oil patch artifacts of the Western Company Museum of Fort Worth. Exhibits animated with cine-robots show how oil is created, found, pumped, and refined. Open Tuesday–Sunday. Fee. (409) 833–5100.

Tyrrell Historical Library. 695 Pearl. People come from all parts of the world to research their roots at this genealogical library; the building was built in 1906 as a Baptist church. Open Tuesday–Saturday. (409) 833–2759.

WHERE TO EAT

Al-T's Seafood & Steakhouse. 244 Spur 5 (T–124) in Winnie; take exit 829 from I–10 and go 1 block south; the restaurant will be on your left. A welcome stopping spot between Houston and Beaumont, this is where the locals go when they want great regional and Cajun food. House specialties include chicken sausage gumbo, fried 'gator balls, alligator appetizers, and a rib-eye steak topped with a spicy crawfish étouffée. The breakfasts also win raves. Open daily for breakfast, lunch, and dinner. $–$$; (CC). (409) 296–9818.

Bando's. 745 North Eleventh Street. Owner-chef Debbie Bando has created one of Beaumont's favorite bistros, similar in many ways to the Cafe Express in Houston. The smell of freshly baked bread brings your taste buds to attention first. Then you have to decide between dining inside or on the patio. Next comes the hard stuff: which of the four major entrees, twenty salads, twenty kinds of coffee, fifteen to twenty wines (by the glass), or uncountable sandwiches to order at the counter? Nor do you have to stand around clutching a number; your order is brought to your table. There are super desserts and a wide variety of cheeses, pâtés, and other gourmet goodies, because this is also a retail food and gift shop. Unless you pull up at the drive-in and order snacks or a picnic to go, real china and linen napery are the rule. Bando's is one of the few places in Beaumont serving authentic espresso and cappuccino. Open for lunch Monday–Friday. $–$$; (CC). (409) 898–8638.

Cafe Arts. 500 Main in the Art Museum of Southeast Texas. Another venture by Debbie Bando. (see previous listing), this pleasant spot not only serves in the museum's foyer, but also outside when weather permits. Offerings include creative salads, soups, and sandwiches, as well as a quiche of the day. If you're feeling sinful, you can feast just on the desserts. $–$$. Open for lunch Monday–Friday. (409) 838–2530.

Carlo's. 2570 Calder. If you want Italian and your spouse wants Greek, this is the place; it specializes in both. Paintings by local artists and live entertainment provide a pleasant ambience. Open for lunch and dinner Tuesday–Friday, dinner only on Saturday. $$–$$$; (CC). (409) 833–0108.

David's Upstairs. 745 North Eleventh Street. Can't make it to New Orleans? This classy Continental restaurant brings the French

Quarter to Beaumont, right down to the live jazz and rhythm-and-blues music nightly. Chef Alex Pickens adds his own flair to classics like beef Wellington and steak Diane, and his oysters stuffed with crabmeat entree and Bailey's Irish Cream cake are favorites. Popular with Beaumont's young professional crowds, this dining club has an à la carte menu and an "adults only" policy after 8:00 P.M. Open for dinner Monday–Saturday. $$–$$$; (CC). (409) 898-0214.

Elena's. 1801 College (downtown). In addition to the Mexican standards, this place also serves menudo and chorizo. Open daily for lunch and dinner. $–$$; (CC). (409) 832-1203.

The Green Beanery Cafe. 2121 McFaddin, at Sixth Street in Old Town. This chef-owned restaurant offers tasty, unusual twists on classic American and Continental dishes, and all the veggies are fresh and crisp. Several interesting shops share this old home complex. Open Tuesday–Saturday for lunch, Friday and Saturday for dinner; reservations are required. $$; (CC). (409) 833-5913.

J&J Steakhouse. 6685 Eastex Freeway. Although many locals come to this family-owned place for affordable steaks and seafood, the big draw for visitors is the unique "Eye of the World" museum in the back room. Hand-carved by the late John Gavrelos, this large display of folk art covers many biblical and patriotic themes. Open for breakfast, lunch, and dinner Monday–Saturday. $–$$; (CC). (409) 898-0801.

Patrizi's Other Place. 2050 I-10 south, between Washington and College streets. This family-owned restaurant features more than thirty entrees, homemade soups, and freshly baked breads, all from the owner's own recipes. Open for lunch and dinner, Sunday–Friday, dinner only on Saturday. $–$$$; (CC). (409) 842-5151.

Pig Stand. Two locations: 1595 Calder, (409) 835-9702, and 3695 College, (409) 835-9394. A local favorite since 1921, this nostalgic place serves "pig" sandwiches and old-fashioned malts. The College Street location is open around the clock. $.

Quality Cafe. 730 Liberty. These folks must be doing something right; they've been in the same location since 1930, and the menu has hardly changed. From buttermilk biscuits and gumbo (Fridays only) to plate lunch specials it's just good southern homestyle cooking. Their Italian salad dressing is so good it's become a satellite business; buy a bottle to take home. Watching your weight or cholesterol? Their shrimp pasta salad, fresh fruit bowl, and Dagwood veggie sandwich highlight a heart healthy menu. Open Monday–Friday for breakfast and lunch. $. (409) 835-9652.

Sartin's Seafood. 6725 Eastex Freeway (I-10). This latest venture of the Sartin family brings back the barbecued crab and shrimp that made the first Sartin's in Sabine Pass the seafood dining destination in Southeast Texas for years. Open daily for lunch and dinner. $$; (CC). (409) 892-6771.

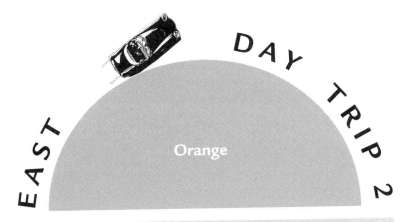

ORANGE

Some 32 miles east of Beaumont and the last gasp of Texas on I–10 before you find yourself in Louisiana, Orange has some interesting places to visit.

Officially founded in 1836, Orange has a traceable history that begins about 1600, when the Attacapas Indians settled here. French fur traders came a century later, followed by the Spanish, and the city's name comes from this latter period—early French and Spanish boatmen looked for the wild oranges that grew along the banks of the Sabine River. Anglo settlers ventured west across the Sabine in the early 1800s, but little is left in Orange to mark those times. Most of the city's tourist attractions date from the prosperous lumber and ranching days of 1880 to 1920.

Local information, including a list of antiques stores, can be had from the Orange Chamber of Commerce, 1012 Green Avenue, Orange 77630, (409) 883–3536 or (800) 528–4906. Do cross the Sabine when you come on this day trip; the Louisiana State Information Center combined with the Sabine National Wildlife Refuge is on the right immediately beyond the bridge. It has an outstanding picnic area and boardwalk through the marshes where you may see numerous water birds, nutria, and so on, so bring your camera, preferably one with a long lens. You also may want to play the ponies at Delta Downs racetrack, just over the bridge in Vinton, Louisiana.

Anyone who thinks chili is the definitive Texas dish hasn't been in Orange for the International Gumbo Cook-off on the first Saturday

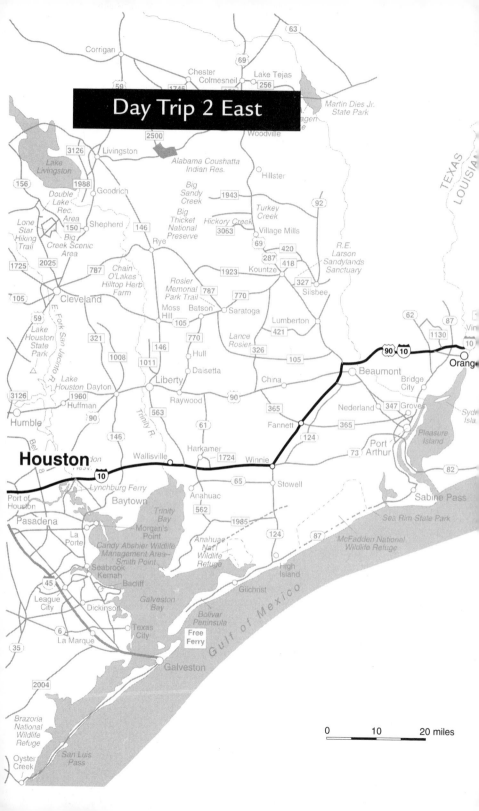

in May. More than 20,000 folks mob this annual event, proving that the Cajun heritage thrives in this part of the state.

WHAT TO DO

Blueberry Farms. Pick to your heart's content at Buna Blueberry Ranch, (409) 994-5427, or Clegg Blueberry Farm, (409) 994-2549 or 994-3425.

Christmas Tree Farms. Orange County may be the Virginia pine capital of Texas. Call any of the following for directions: K&K Evergreen Christmas Tree Farm, (409) 746-2412 or 746-3268; Nichols Christmas Trees, (409) 746-2276; Reaves Christmas Tree Farm, (409) 746-2522; or Spell's Golden Triangle Trees, (409) 746-3615.

Country Cottage Emu. This Orange-area breeding and training ranch welcomes visitors by appointment. (409) 886-0919.

Delta Downs. Twenty miles east via I-10, then north on L-109. Slightly beyond the two-hour, 110-mile limit of this book, this track is still a good reason to visit the Beaumont/Orange/Port Arthur area. September–March is for thoroughbreds only, and April–Labor Day is strictly for quarter horses. Open daily for video poker (free admission) and off-track betting; races Thursday–Sunday. Fee. For information contact P.O. Box 175, Vinton, LA 70668, (800) 737-3358 (reservations) or (318) 589-7441.

Farmer's Mercantile. Corner of Sixth and Division streets, just where it's been since 1928. Saddles rest next to bins of nuts and bolts, onion sets are offered just below packets of bluebonnet seeds, and horse collars line the high walls. Whatever you might need, it's here—somewhere. People have been known to dawdle here for hours, remarking on the old wood stoves, bottle cappers, and such. You can't miss the place—just look for hay bales on the sidewalk. Open Monday–Saturday. (409) 883-2941.

First Presbyterian Church. 902 Green Avenue. One wonders what there would be to see or do in Orange without the Lutcher and Stark families (see entries on Stark House and Stark Museum that follow). This impressive domed building is a Lutcher/Stark contribution to the city and is thought to be the first public building to be air-conditioned in the world. The power plant with the air-conditioning unit was installed during the church's construction in 1908. The handmade stained glass windows are impressive, as is the entire interior of the church. Tours are available for six or more by advance reservation. If you can't fit those tour requirements, stop in for Sunday services. (409) 883-2097 or 883-4116.

Heritage House. 905 West Division Street. While not as elegant as the Stark House (below), this turn-of-the-century home is worth a stop. Not only is it furnished as an upper-middle-class home would have been in those times; there are several "see-and-touch" exhibits for children, as well as historical items of interest. Fee. Closed Saturday and Monday. (409) 886-5385.

Linden of Pinehurst (Brown Center of Lamar University). US-90 (business route), just off I-10 on the western outskirts of Orange. When Mrs. Gladys Brown saw a famous Natchez antebellum home called Linden, she ordered its duplicate built in 1956 at Pinehurst, the Browns' ranch in Orange. With its furnishings and forty-eight acres of parklike grounds, it was donated in 1976 to Lamar University by the Brown estate and is open to the public unless a special conference is being held on the premises. *Note:* The gate sign says PINEHURST RANCH, and a nearby gate says LINDENWOOD, which leads to a subdivision. Go past Lindenwood and a cemetery; this home will be on your right. Tours may be arranged through Brown Center of Lamar University, 4205 Park Avenue, Orange 77630, (409) 883-2939.

Lutcher Theater for the Performing Arts. 707 West Main, in the Orange Civic Plaza. If you are coming over for the weekend anytime during the September–May season, call to see who and what is playing. Recent offerings have ranged from road shows such as *Cats* and the *Will Rogers Follies* to Trisha Yearwood. Tours available weekdays; advance reservations required. (409) 886-5535 or (800) 828-5535.

Piney Woods Country Wines. 3408 Willow Drive. This small vineyard produces some tasty fruit wines—drop in for a sample of Texas-grown sunset muscadine or peach. The tasting room is open daily, except for some weekends and vacation periods; call ahead, (409) 883-5408.

Stark Museum of Western Art. 712 Green Avenue, across from the Stark House. William H. Stark was a prominent financial and industrial leader in Orange, who married Miriam Lutcher in 1881. She began collecting European art in the 1890s, and her son Lutcher and daughter-in-law Nelda continued the family tradition with further emphasis on art of the American West and the Taos school of New

Mexico. The Audubon print and Steuben glass collections also are particularly worth seeing. This contemporary museum was completed by the Starks in 1976 and houses the varied and impressive collections. Free. Open Wednesday–Saturday and on Sunday afternoon. (409) 883-6661.

Super Gator Tours. 108 East Lutcher Drive, on the westbound side of I-10 (exit 878). Few thrills compare to skimming over water aboard an airboat. This firm welcomes families for hour-long explorations of the bayous and cypress swamplands that make up the Sabine River. Reservations suggested. Open daily except Monday year-round, weather permitting. Fee. (409) 883-7725.

W. H. Stark House. In the Stark Civic Center complex at Green Avenue and Sixth Street. Built in 1894, this massive Victorian home with its gables and turrets is a visual delight, inside and out. A ten-year restoration project and now on the National Register of Historic Places, this fifteen-room structure can be toured only by advance reservation. No children under fourteen are allowed. Tours start in the carriage house, where an excellent glass collection is on display. Open Tuesday–Saturday. Fee. (409) 883-0871.

WHERE TO EAT

Cajun Cookery. 2308 I-10. Although the regular menu is good, nearly everyone comes here for the Cajun seafood buffet. Open daily for lunch and dinner. $-$$; (CC). (409) 886-0990.

Cody's. 3130 North Sixteenth Street (at I-10). Stop here for charcoal-broiled hamburgers, steaks, seafood, and salads. The burgers were rated best in Southeast Texas some years back by *Texas Monthly*. Open for lunch and dinner Monday–Friday, dinner only on Saturday and Sunday. $-$$; (CC). (409) 883-2267.

Crawfish Capitol. At the intersection of T-12 and T-62 in Mauriceville, 8 miles north of Orange. This is a good place to get crawfish, live or boiled. Bill Harris purges the little devils and sells them live or cooks them up into tasty Cajun-style étouffée, gumbo, and jambalaya. Barbecued crab in season is another treat, as is the seafood buffet. Save time for a tour of the vats of crawfish outside. Open daily for sales; restaurant is open December through July and sometimes well into August if the crawfish supply holds out. $-$$. (409) 745-3022.

Old Orange Cafe. 914 West Division. In addition to savory lunch plates daily, these inventive folks serve some super salads, sandwiches, spuds, soups, and desserts. They also have special pre-theater dinners prior to certain performances at the Lutcher Theater for the Performing Arts; call for schedule and reservations. Open from 8:00 A.M. to 2:00 P.M. weekdays. $-$$; (CC). (409) 883-2233.

Ramada Inn. 2600 I-10 West. If you are eastbound, exit at Sixteenth Street; if westbound, exit at Adams Bayou. Folks come from as far away as Beaumont for the Friday and Saturday night seafood buffets—mountains of fresh shrimp or crawfish, depending on the season. Open daily for standard meals also. $$; (CC). (409) 886-0570.

Someplace Special. 6521 I-10. Overlooking a pond, this quiet spot serves a variety of tasty country vittles. If the weather's nice, eat outside. Open only for weekday lunch. $-$$; (CC). (409) 883-8605.

Tuffy's Eatery. Intersection of T-12 and T-62 in Mauriceville. Memorable pastries and biscuits keep the locals coming back to this unusual spot. Surrounding log structures house tiny shops. Open for breakfast, lunch, and dinner daily. $-$$; (CC). (409) 745-3170.

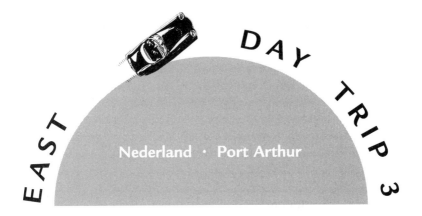

NEDERLAND

When you want to fish or hunt in Southeast Texas, you well could be headed for the Port Arthur area. From Houston the most direct route is I-10 East to Beaumont, followed by a swing southeast on US-69/96/287. For the day-tripper there are several activity options in the area, but first let's take a look at one of the smaller towns you will pass on the way—Nederland.

You'll think you are in Cajun country when you first drive up the main street of this small community—the local market usually is advertising fresh boudin (sausage). Confusion may set in when you see Dutch names on some stores and a windmill at the end of the street. Established as a railroad town in 1897, Nederland first was settled by Dutch immigrants, who were soon followed by French settlers from the Acadiana area of southwestern Louisiana, and both ethnic groups make Nederland what it is today. For information contact the Nederland Chamber of Commerce, 1515 Boston Avenue, Nederland 77626, (409) 722-0279.

WHAT TO DO

La Maison Beausoleil. 701 Rue Beausoleil off Grigsby Avenue, in Port Neches Park, Port Neches. This fully furnished 1810 Acadian home was barged in from Vermilion Parish, Louisiana. Notable for its mud and moss walls that are mortised and pegged with square nails, this "House of Beautiful Sunshine" is fully furnished and open

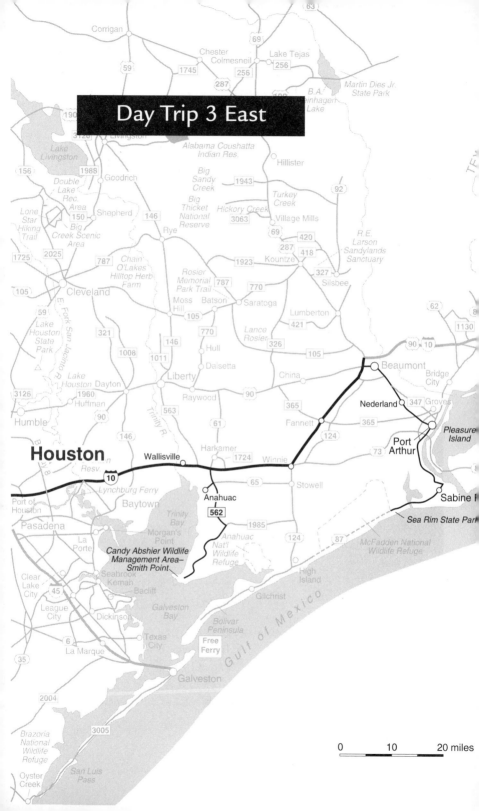

weekend afternoons; weekdays by appointment. (409) 722-1688 or 832-6733.

Windmill Museum and La Maison des Acadian Museum. 1528 Boston Avenue in Tex Ritter Park, Nederland. These adjacent museums keep the dual heritage of Nederland alive. The first floor of the authentic Dutch windmill is devoted to mementos of a local boy who made the big time in country-and-western music—Tex Ritter. The remaining two floors have a sparse but interesting collection of assorted cultural treasures. Best is the old pirogue, hollowed out of a cypress log prior to 1845 and in use until bought and donated to the museum in 1969.

La Maison des Acadian Museum honors the French Cajun culture. A bicentennial project by local volunteers, this authentic replica of a French Acadian cottage has furniture to match. Both museums are open Tuesday–Sunday afternoon March through Labor Day, and Thursday–Sunday afternoon thereafter through February. (409) 722-0279.

WHERE TO EAT

Dorothy's Front Porch. 1000 Smith Road. This family-owned lakefront restaurant is known for steaks and seafood. Open for lunch and dinner daily. $$; (CC). (409) 722-1472.

Eellee's. 4748 Main, Groves. Don't ask for Mr. Eellee here—this eatery's name is Lee spelled backward and forward, which gives you an idea of chef-owner J. L. Lee's sense of humor. Known primarily for its seafood, this place was suggested by a Day Trips reader who recommends "Ron's Special," one of Lee's unique recipes. Lee also has won national recognition for his St. James sauce, particularly memorable over fresh grilled tuna or fettucine. As for ambience, this old house was an antiques shop when Lee bought it, and it shows. Open for lunch and dinner Tuesday–Friday, dinner only on Saturday. $-$$$; (CC). (409) 962-9585.

The Schooner. US-69/96/287 at FM-365. Famous for stuffed flounder and stuffed red snapper steak, this restaurant goes all the way with a few stuffed fish and game trophies for decor as well. Open daily for lunch and dinner. $$; (CC). (409) 722-2323.

PORT ARTHUR

From Nederland continue southeast on US-69/96/287 to Port Arthur. The Sabine and Neches rivers form a large lake that empties into the Gulf of Mexico 8 miles south of Port Arthur; the town sits on the northwest edge of Sabine Lake.

Settled as Aurora about 1840, the town became Port Arthur in 1897 as the terminus of the Kansas City-Pittsburgh and Gulf Railroad, and the ensuing oil strike in nearby Beaumont ushered in Port Arthur's golden age of growth. Today the city is primarily a large industrial and refining center with a growing number of things of interest to visitors; you can survey the scene on weekdays from an observation balcony on the fifth floor of City Hall, 444 Fourth Street, (409) 983-8100. Guided tours to the port of Port Arthur can be arranged, (409) 983-2029. The Port Arthur Convention and Visitors Bureau is a good source of specific information, maps, discount coupons, and so on: 3401 Cultural Center Drive, Port Arthur 77642, (409) 985-5583 or (800) 235-7822.

Planning to drive to Port Arthur from Galveston via T-87? Be aware that, at this writing, that road remains washed out 5 miles south of Sea Rim State Park. From High Island (on Bolivar Peninsula), go north 29 miles on T-124 to Winnie, then east 30 miles on T-73 to Port Arthur.

WHAT TO DO

Airboat Rides. This activity comes and goes in Port Arthur. At this writing Sea Rim State Park is operating airboat and outboard marsh tours (see park entry below), but check either with the park (409-971-2559) or with the visitors bureau (800-235-7822) for an update before you come.

Birding. This is a growing sport here, particularly at Sabine Woods, an Audubon society-owned preserve on T-87 south of Port Arthur and five miles west of Sabine Pass. Like High Island on the Bolivar Peninsula, this is a major "fall out" zone for migratory birds in spring and fall. A complete list of birding sites is available from the Port Arthur Convention & Visitors Bureau (previously mentioned).

Fishing. You can fish in the lake, the freshwater bayous that feed it, or the Gulf of Mexico via Sabine Pass. Top game fish are speckled trout, red snapper, mackerel, billfish, and tarpon. A license is required except for party-boat excursions. For information on party boats, marinas, guides, and so forth, contact the visitors bureau, above. Fishing charters currently are available through Sabine Lake Guide Service, (409) 736-3023.

Hunting. To see vast flocks of birds on the wing in sunrise light is unforgettable. Even seasoned hunters have been known to put down their guns in awe, though you rarely find one who will admit it. You can have that experience in the Port Arthur area; it's prime territory for duck and goose hunting, with four areas open to the public at various times during the November–January season. For overall information contact Sea Rim State Park, P.O. Box 1066, Sabine Pass 77655, (409) 971-2559, or the J. D. Murphree Wildlife Management Area, (409) 736-2550. Other areas open for public hunting include the Texas Point and McFaddin Beach national wildlife refuges, (409) 971-2909.

La Rue Des Soldats. This one-way drive tops Port Arthur's $89 million hurricane protection system, which forms a dike around the city. Open weekdays to vehicular traffic and accessed via the first drive to the left just past Gates Library on Lakeshore Drive.

Museum of the Gulf Coast. 700 Procter Street, on the ship channel in downtown Port Arthur. Before the construction of the Intracoastal Canal, there were beautiful sand beaches on Lake Sabine. Several sprouted luxury hotels that live on only in the photographs displayed with other area memorabilia in this interesting museum. The Port Arthur area also has spawned a number of noted musical artists, among them Janis Joplin, Harry James, Aubrey "Moon" Mullican, Johnny Preston, and Ivory Joe Hunter. Their legacies, complete with gold records and a replica of Janis Joplin's wildly painted convertible, are celebrated in the museum's outstanding Southeast Musical Heritage exhibit and Music Hall of Fame. *Also here:* extensive works depicting Gulf Coast life over the centuries, the Robert Rauschenberg Art Gallery, the Snell Decorative Arts Collection, a maritime and petroleum hall, and a mammoth mural by Kerrville artist Travis Keese. Open daily. Fee. (409) 982-7000.

Oriental Village. 801 Ninth Avenue. More than 8,000 Vietnamese settled in the Port Arthur area in the early 1970s, 95 percent of whom were Roman Catholics and 5 percent of whom were Buddhists. Their culture and expressions of religion have changed the face of this town.

Hoa-Binh (Area of Peace) shrine has a triple life-size statue of the Virgin Mary, surrounded by ornamental gardens. A block of Vietnamese shops is adjacent. The Buddhists bought an old Baptist church at 2701 Proctor Street and turned it into Buu Mon Buddhist Temple, complete with a lighted, four-tiered pagoda tower that is open for guided tours, (409) 982-9319. Their dragon dances for Buddha's birthday and the Tet (New Year's) celebration every year.

Pleasure Island. In Sabine Lake, across the Sabine-Neches ship channel and south from metro Port Arthur. Follow signs to the Martin Luther King bridge and Pleasure Island. This multimillion-dollar development is stirring things up, and there's more to come. For now, there are miles of free levees for fishing and crabbing; a marina, restaurant, and golf course; a hotel and resort; spots for picnicking and RV camping; an airfield for ultralights; boat ramps; and a ten-acre concert park that hosts musicals and festivals late spring through fall. Part of the lake around the island is reserved exclusively for sailboarders. (800) 235-7822 weekdays.

Pompeiian Villa. 1953 Lakeshore Drive. Believe it or not, this is a billion-dollar house. Built in 1900 by Isaac Ellwood, the "Barbed Wire King," it later was sold to the president of Diamond Match Co. He in turn traded it for $10,000 worth of Texaco stock worth $1 billion on today's market—or so the story goes in Port Arthur. Whichever, this pink stucco villa is listed in the National Register of Historic Places and is now owned by the Port Arthur Historical Society. Open Monday–Friday. Fee. (409) 983-5977.

Sea Rim State Park. About 23 miles south of metropolitan Port Arthur on T-87. Thanks to enlightened management, the sea rim marshlands between Port Arthur and Galveston are treated as the fragile natural resource they are. Important to the seafood industry as nursery grounds for shrimp and fish, they also provide a unique experience for the visitor.

Sea Rim State Park is a perfect example; it is far more than the usual seaside camping and sunning spot. With more than 15,000 acres, this is the third largest state park in Texas. Also the only marshland park, it is divided into two distinct areas. The beach unit has camping with and without hookups, 3 miles of sand; a main headquarters with restrooms; hot showers; and concessions; an outstanding interpretive center; and the Gambusia Trail, a 3,640-foot boardwalk through the wetlands behind the dunes.

The second unit is a pristine marsh, easily explored on your own via a small powerboat or canoe. Be aware, however, that you must file a float plan with the rangers and that marsh maps are essential to safely navigate this wilderness. Inquire also about the airboat and outboard tours operated by park rangers on Wednesday, Saturday, and Sunday year-round (fee). You may surprise a flock of herons or egrets or see an alligator or two—unless they see you first. There are four camping platforms and observation blinds within the marsh, reservations required. Fee. Information: P.O. Box 1066, Sabine Pass 77655, (409) 971-2559.

Snooper's Paradise. 5509 East Parkway, at the northwest corner of Thirty-ninth Street and T-73 in Groves. For thirty-four years these folks have been importing antiques from Europe, and their 50,000-plus-square-foot facility bulges with beautiful things, primarily from the 1860–1900 period. Delivery to Houston is all in a day's work. Open Monday–Saturday. (CC). (409) 962-8427.

Vuylsteke Dutch Home. 1831 Lakeshore. This home was built in 1905 for the first Dutch consul to Port Arthur and contains its original furniture. Tours by appointment. Fee. (409) 983-4921.

White Haven. 2545 Lakeshore. Now owned by the DAR, this 1915 Greek Revival mansion is open for tours on Monday, Wednesday, and Friday or by appointment. Fee. (409) 982-3068.

WHERE TO EAT

Channel Inn Seafood Restaurant. 5157 South Gulfway (T-87), Sabine Pass. How does an all-you-can-eat serving of barbecued crab sound? Or a brimming-with-seafood platter? Come here, and bring a bib. This is a real "down-home" place, right down to the rolls of paper towels on the tables. Do bring family or a friend, though. The seafood platters are served only to two or more. Better yet, bring five friends, because reservations are accepted only for six or more; that will get you past the usual thirty-minute wait. Open for lunch and dinner daily. $-$$$; (CC). (409) 971-2400 or (800) 544-7939.

Domingue's on the Neches. 9999 Gulfway Drive, under the Rainbow Bridge on the Port Arthur side; watch for signs on the west side of the road. This family-owned place offers good seafood and great views of both the Veterans and Rainbow bridges. Open for lunch and dinner Monday–Saturday, until 3:00 P.M. on Sunday. $$; (CC). (409) 962–5470.

Esther's Seafood and Oyster Bar. 99021⁄2 Gulfway Drive, Groves. If you're hungry for spicy Cajun seafood and steaks, search out this barge eatery at the foot of the Rainbow Bridge. Open for lunch and dinner Sunday through Friday, dinner only on Saturday. $$–$$$; (CC). (409) 962–6268.

Golden Gate Restaurant. 3444 Gulfway Drive, Port Arthur. You'll find authentic Vietnamese food here, as well as a Chinese food buffet. Open daily for lunch and dinner. $–$$; (CC). (409) 982–3100.

The Lighthouse. 600 Pleasure Pier Boulevard, overlooking Lake Sabine on Pleasure Island. This is a good place for seafood and steaks. Open for dinner Tuesday–Friday, lunch and dinner on Saturday and Sunday. $$; (CC). (409) 985–3535.

Parrot Head. At the marina on Pleasure Island. The deck of this laid-back pub/snackery is the place to be when the roseate spoonbills fly over around 6:00 P.M. on a fair-weather summer evenings. Families love this low-key place, particularly when the end-of-the-day singing and dancing music starts. Open Wednesday–Sunday from 7:00 A.M. $; (CC). (409) 982–2811.

WANDERING THE BACKROADS

The most logical and swift access from Houston to the entire Golden Triangle area is via I-10 East. But if time is no problem and you prefer quiet country roads, detour south from the interstate just past the Trinity River Bridge and explore Wallisville and Anahuac, Day Trip 4, this sector.

Interested in rice farming? Plan a stop at the Agricultural Historical Museum in Winnie, open weekdays during business hours or by appointment, (409) 296–2231. From I-10, take exit 829, turning south on T-124; turn east (left) at the third signal; the museum will be one block down on the left. Winnie also hosts Old Time Trade Days on the first Friday-Sunday after the first Monday of the month. This event draws many of the dealers from First Monday at Canton and is of major interest to hunters of antiques and general junk. Exit off I-10 and go north. For trade days information, call (409) 892–4000 or 296–3300. The event is free, but parking is $2.00 per car.

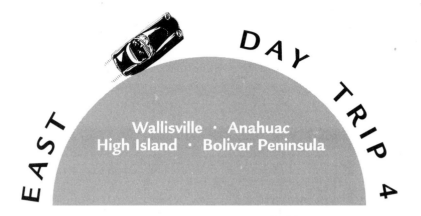

WALLISVILLE

One of the oldest towns in Chambers County, Wallisville was torn down in 1966 by the U.S. Army Corps of Engineers in preparation for a large flood control dam that then remained stalled in controversy for many years. The project's scope has been scaled back, construction is under way, and the result should be new recreation opportunities near Houston's eastern boundaries by the end of the century. In the meantime, what was the Wallisville townsite remains green, rolling, and open.

In 1979 the nonprofit Wallisville Heritage Park Foundation was created to restore the old town and preserve the adjacent El Orcoquisac Archaeological District. So far only the old post office and school are back in business, and visitors are welcome at the small but interesting Wallisville Heritage Museum, open Monday–Saturday; (409) 389-2252. Take the Wallisville exit from I-10; the museum and heritage park are on the eastbound feeder road. This facility also includes an extensive genealogical library focused on America's eastern coast, the ancestral home of many Chambers County pioneers.

CONTINUING ON

From Wallisville take the Old Wallisville Road to its intersection with FM-563 and continue south to Anahuac. The road itself is a delight—no center stripe or traffic—and it's easy to imagine how things were when this was a horse and buggy route.

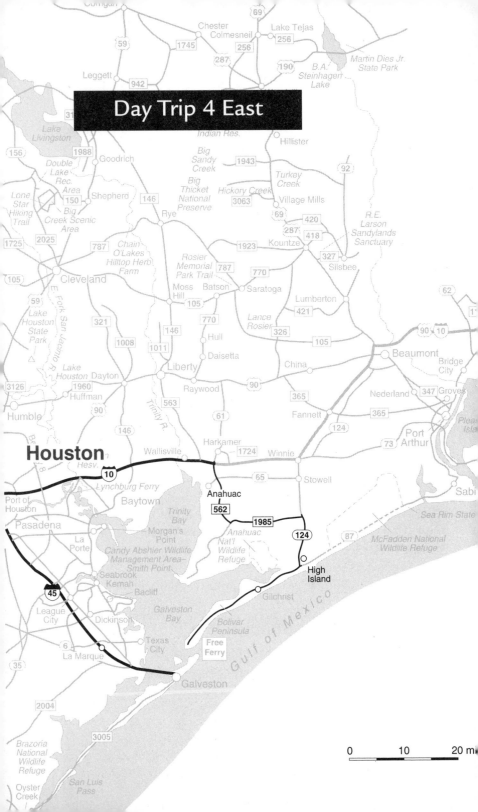

ANAHUAC

Founded as a Spanish fortress in 1821, Anahuac (pronounced "Ana-whack") was the site of a fort and customs house constructed in 1831 by prisoners of the Mexican government. Built where the Trinity River empties into Galveston Bay, the fort was captured the following year by Texian forces under the command of William B. Travis, who subsequently met his doom at the Alamo. The site now is a large city park south of town (see below). Today Anahuac is both the Chambers County seat and the official alligator capital of Texas, a fact the town celebrates with Gatorfest every September.

WHAT TO SEE

Anahuac National Wildlife Refuge. On East Galveston Bay, 18 miles southeast of town via FM–562 and FM–1985 (signs). This 35,000-acre wildlife refuge hosts more than 270 species of birds (40 of which nest here), 30 to 50 species of mammals, an extensive number of reptiles, and uncountable mosquitoes; wear industrial strength repellent. In addition to 20 miles of all-season road, there are 12 miles of foot access in dry weather. A major stop on the Great Texas Coastal Birding Trail, this refuge offers birders a short board-walk with observation platform along Shoveler Pond and a footpath to The Willows, a major "fallout" area during the spring and fall tropical migrations; the rare palm warbler often is sighted here during spring migration. There also are two boat ramps if you want to explore on your own by shallow draft boat. Hunting is allowed on three tracts in season; request information on times, restrictions, and required permits. Other activities include photography, fishing, and crabbing. Apart from restrooms, there are no amenities, conces-sions, or picnic facilities; bring drinking water. Maps and leaflets are available at the visitor contact station. For advance information and a birding list, contact P.O. Box 278, Anahuac 77514, (409) 267–3337.

Candy Abshier Wildlife Management Area. At Smith Point on east Galveston Bay, 23 miles south of Anahuac via FM–562. Also a major "fallout" area for migrating birds in spring and fall, these 207 acres of oak-studded coastal prairie provide welcome roosts and cover for orioles, buntings, warblers, swallows, pelicans, storks, frigates, and raptors. Some 20 species of the latter have been sighted here during the fall migration (late August to early October; third week of September is prime). Apart from a 30-foot-tall viewing tower on the shore of East Bay, there are no other public facilities or water. Insect repellent strongly advised. Open daily. Guided tours can be arranged through the Texas Conservation Passport Program. (409) 736-2540.

Chambers County Library. 202 Cummings Street, Anahuac. What were the contents of the Chambers County Museum now are housed here. Open Monday–Friday, Saturday until 1:00 P.M. (409) 267-8261.

East Bay Bayou Tract. On FM-1985, seven miles east of the entrance to Anahuac National Wildlife Refuge. A new birding and fishing area scheduled to open in 1998, this spot will have a 1.5 mile wooded trail along East Bay Bayou, an area managed specifically to host shorebird migrations, and sites where you can freshwater fish from the bank. To check on progress, call (409) 267-3337.

Fort Anahuac Park. Main Street at Trinity Bay. Diligent researchers here find traces of Fort Anahuac (circa 1831), built as a combination fort and customs house by prisoners of the Mexican government. This also was the site of a skirmish between Texian and Mexican forces prior to the Texas Revolution.

Historic Buildings. Chambersea, built in 1845 and an early doctor's office, floated in from its original site in Cedar Bayou, stand on the courthouse lawn. For access to either, call the historical commission in advance, (409) 267-8225.

Picnic and Play places. Two pretty parks make enjoyable stops in the Anahuac area. Double Bayou Park, on Eagle Ferry Road between FM-563 and FM-562, offers day use areas, covered pavilion, boat ramps, and other amenities. White's Park, on T-61 south of I-10, has a rodeo area, bayou access for fishing and crabbing, picnic area, and camping. Insect repellent is advised at both parks.

WHERE TO EAT

DJ's. At the intersection of I-10 and US-61. This unfancy grocery store serves some of the best barbecue in the region which you can eat at picnic tables under the trees. Open daily for lunch and dinner. $. (409) 374-2144.

The Chaparral Restaurant. Main and Park streets, Anahuac. In addition to a daily steam table meal, the menu here ranges from hamburgers and sandwiches to seafood, steaks, chicken, and quail.

Open weekdays for breakfast, lunch, and dinner (closed 2:00 to 5:00 P.M.); weekends for breakfast and lunch. $-$$; (CC). (409) 267-4000.

CONTINUING ON

To continue this day from Anahuac to High Island and the Bolivar penisula follow FM-562 south to FM-1985, then turn east (left) and go 15 miles to a south (right) turn on T-124 to High Island. From that tiny community continue south on T-124 to its intersection with T-87 at the coast. *Warning:* The washed-out sections of T-87 to the left of that intersection are no longer passable, even with four-wheel drive.

After touring Bolivar you have two options in returning to Houston. The first is to ride the free car ferry that connects Bolivar's southwestern tip with Galveston and then take Broadway down-island to I-45 north. Or just park your car at the Bolivar ferry dock, walk aboard (no waiting) for a round-trip ferry ride, and then return home the way you came: T-87 back up the Bolivar peninsula to T-124 and High Island, then 20 miles north on T-124 to I-10 west at Winnie. From there, it's 63 freeway miles west to Houston.

HIGH ISLAND

Another major stop on the Great Texas Coastal Birding Trail, this tiny community, just one mile inland from the Gulf of Mexico, is particularly rewarding to birders from mid-March through mid-May. Following instinctive migration patterns, as many as 25,000 exhausted songbirds (wood warblers, tanagers, orioles, catbirds, buntings, and so on) make their first landfall here after flying 600-700 miles across the Gulf from winter homes in Mexico and Central America. Many carry colorful plumage in preparation for breeding and nesting farther north. Their favored landing trees are the 100-year-old live oaks that shade two High Island sites, a total of 24 acres now protected as Boy Scout Woods and Smith Oaks. Both are operated by the Houston Area Audubon Society, (713) 932-1392 or 932-1639. Bring binoculars, insect repellent, and your best manners; the birds must not be disturbed. Donations requested. For accommodations, contact the Birder's Haven Resort, 2081 Winnie, High Island 77623, (409) 286-5362.

BOLIVAR PENINSULA

In contrast to Galveston's burgeoning commercial development, this 32-mile-long stretch of unrestricted sand flexes with the whims of Mother Nature, changing with every storm. However, as a laid-back, low cost, somewhat funky getaway, Bolivar can't be beat.

Once on Bolivar you won't find much, which is its biggest attraction—just some fishing camps and stilt-legged residential developments, a seemingly endless beach, a few small communities, and an abandoned lighthouse built in 1872 and currently closed to the public. The latter was used some years ago as the set for the film *My Sweet Charlie*.

The beaches are open—you can drive, ride horses, or just walk for miles. There are waves to play in, sand to loll in, and enormous numbers of shorebirds to keep you entertained. *Two warnings:* Apart from an occasional portable toilet, there are no public facilities on Bolivar's beaches, and the strand opposite the blinking light in Crystal Beach is locally known as "the Zoo," a mecca for unsupervised teenagers, particularly during Spring Break.

Love seashells? Time your visit to catch either an outgoing high tide or a minus tide. The beaches around High Island usually have the most abundant shells as well as an occasional fossil liberated from the prehistoric clay deposits that line much of the Gulf bottom. The flats at the southwestern tip of the peninsula also are good for shelling; wear repellent.

Tip to oyster lovers: Locals consider those harvested from beds in Bolivar's East Bay to be among the best in the world. Local oysters are big deals on Bolivar menus, they're also sold by the pints and quarts at several local markets. For a vacation packet and tourist information on Bolivar, call (409) 684-5940.

WHAT TO DO

Fishing. Rollover Pass is the favored spot because strong currents bring large numbers of flounder, redfish, croakers, speckled trout, sand trout, and other game fish close to shore. This narrowest part of the peninsula got its name during Prohibition when bootleggers would take delivery of barrels of hooch from ships on the Gulf side of the peninsula and then roll those barrels overland to local boats waiting in East Bay.

Fort Travis Seashore Park. South end of the peninsula, near the ferry. Noted as the spot where Jane Long, "the Mother of Texas," gave birth to the first Anglo child on Texas soil, it also has the remains of a fort built before the turn of the century. Now partially renovated, the fortifications provide stairs to a long beach and rocks for fishing. (409) 766-2411.

Horseback riding. You can rent a steed at the Crystal Beach Riding Stables, (409) 684-0773.

WHERE TO EAT

De Coux's Pub & Restaurant. 3150 T-87, Crystal Beach. A good Sunday drive destination in itself, this clean and classy eatery offers the chef's creations on a blackboard menu in addition to burgers, sandwiches, crabmeat nachos, crawfish in season, and so on. If the weather turns chilly, come enjoy their fireplace. Open for dinner daily year-round, lunch also on weekends. $-$$; (CC). (409) 684-0177.

Little Chihuahua. On ground level of Stingaree (see below), 1295 Stingaree Road, Crystal Beach. Looking for Mexican food minus the usual Tex-Mex twist? Try the seafood enchiladas and quesadillas here. Open for lunch and dinner Wednesday–Sunday in winter, Tuesday–Sunday in summer. $-$$; (CC). (409) 684-2731.

Outrigger Grill. 1035 T-87, Crystal Beach. This family-oriented restaurant even has toys to keep the kiddies happy while you wait for a delicious oyster po'boy, giant burrito, Mexican plate, burger, steak, or whatever else takes your fancy on their long menu. Owner Skip Rohacek buys her fish fresh off local boats, and while she won't take credit cards, she says deadbeats can do the dishes. Open daily for breakfast, lunch, and dinner. $-$$. (409) 684-6212.

Stingaree. 1295 Stingaree Road, Crystal Beach. Considered by many to be Bolivar's premier eatery, this spot's specialties include barbecued crab, charbroiled snapper, honey jalapeno shrimp, and snapper throats (when available). Save room for the bread pudding with bourbon sauce. For drinks and appetizers, the second floor deck with its view of East Bay and the Intracoastal Canal is the place to be on Bolivar. Open for lunch and dinner Thursday–Sunday in winter; Wednesday–Sunday during Spring Break; daily during summer. $-$$; (CC). (409) 684-2731.

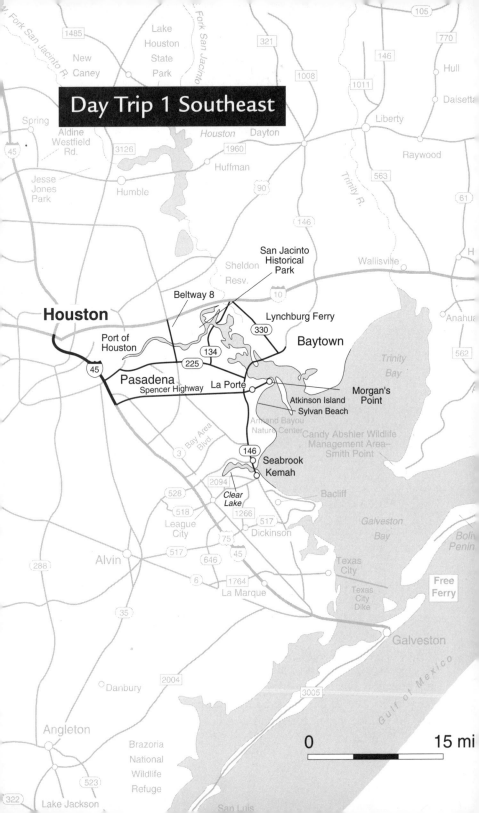

Day Trip 1 Southeast

Houston

1485

Fork San Jacinto R.

Lake Houston State Park

New Caney

Fork San Jacinto

321

105

770

Hull

Daisetta

Spring

Aldine Westfield Rd.

45

3126

1008

1011

146

Liberty

Jesse Jones Park

Humble

Houston Dayton

1960

Raywood

Huffman

90

146

563

61

Trinity R.

Sheldon Resv.

San Jacinto Historical Park

Wallisville

H

Beltway 8

10

Lynchburg Ferry

Anahua

Port of Houston

330

Baytown

Trinity Bay

562

134

45

225

Pasadena

Spencer Highway La Porte

Atkinson Island

Sylvan Beach

Morgan's Point

Armand Bayou Nature Center

Candy Abshier Wildlife Management Area–Smith Point

3

Bay Area Blvd.

146

Seabrook

Kemah

2094

Clear Lake

Bacliff

528

Galveston Bay

518

1266

517

Boli Penin

League City

75

Dickinson

Alvin

517

646

45

Texas City

288

6

1764

La Marque

35

Texas City Dike

Free Ferry

Galveston

Danbury

2004

3005

Gulf of Mexico

Angleton

Brazoria National Wildlife Refuge

523

322

Lake Jackson

San Luis

0   15 mi

Pasadena · La Porte
Baytown · Morgan's Point

PASADENA

As you drive southeast from Houston on I-45 and look east to the vast industrial-chemical complex that is Pasadena today, it's hard to believe that this once was projected to be Houston's garden. Its bucolic future was altered permanently by two events: the completion of the Houston Ship Channel as a deep-water port in 1915 and the discovery of oil in nearby Baytown the following year.

Slightly off the usual Sunday drive itinerary, this upper bay region has several things to see and do. Start with a tour of the Port of Houston and the ship channel, and then head east on T-225 to digest some history at San Jacinto Battleground State Historical Park in La Porte. From there ride the free Lynchburg Ferry to Baytown and return to the Morgan's Point/La Porte area via the Fred Hartman Bridge. En route you'll find crabbing, swimming, and bird-watching—all at a laid-back pace.

WHAT TO DO

The Beltway 8 Bridge. Accessible from either I-10 on the north or T-225 on the south. No reservations needed here, just some toll change for a fantastic bird's-eye view of the port from atop the bridge.

Our Family's Herbs and Such. 702 Llano, Pasadena. If you're interested in starting an herb garden, stop here. Lana and Bob Sims offer a garden full of herbs acclimated to our Gulf Coast climate, as

219

well as numerous "Taste of Texas" jellies, vinegars, salsa mixes, and so on. They also make herb-based toys and flea-repelling collars for domestic pets. Open Saturday or by appointment. (281) 943-1937, (800) 441-1230.

The Pasadena Historical Museum and the Strawberry House. 201 Vince Street in Memorial Park. The museum's well-done displays include an authentic doctor's office, and an early kitchen, complete with water pump, is one of the features of the adjacent Strawberry House. That structure originally stood on a nearby Mexican land grant and is furnished to illustrate three periods: the early 1880s when it was new, the 1920s, and the 1940s. The museum is open Wednesday–Sunday; Strawberry House is open those same days by request. (713) 477-7237.

Port of Houston. 7300 Clinton Drive (Clinton exit from Loop 610 East). The observation deck on the northwest side of the turning basin is open daily, but a boat tour is better. The free ninety-minute trip aboard the M-V *Sam Houston* takes you close to huge ships from around the world, grain elevators, refineries, docks—the heart of the second largest port in America. This is an official inspection vessel, and reservations are required. Make them two to three months in advance. Closed on Monday, holidays, and for the month of September. (713) 670-2416.

LA PORTE

Founded by French settlers in 1889, this modest community now stretches north to include one of the state's most significant historical sites. See that portion of La Porte now, en route to the Lynchburg Ferry, and the Sylvan Beach area on the final leg of this trip.

WHAT TO DO

Jim Watson Texas History Museum. 826 San Jacinto, La Porte. Now owned by the La Porte School District, this former home houses an outstanding review of Texas history from the 1820s through the Vietnam War. Each of six rooms covers a different era and is staffed with well-informed docents, antiques, and hands-on exhibits specifically designed for children. The fifty-cent admission fee includes refreshments. By appointment only. (281) 471-3010.

Little Cedar Bayou Park. From T-146 in La Porte, turn east onto Fairmont Parkway, right on Eighth Street, and left on M Street. This pleasant city park has play and picnic areas, a mile-long nature trail that ends at Galveston Bay, and a WaterWorld-type wave pool that operates during the summer. (281) 471-5020.

Lynchburg Ferry. From the cemetery and picnic area of the battleground park (see below), continue northeast on T-134 to this free ferry, a relic from pre-freeway days. You are welcome to park your car and take the fifteen-minute round-trip as a passenger, or you can drive aboard and then continue to Baytown. The ferry operates twenty-four hours a day, year-round. (281) 424-3521 or 755-5000.

San Jacinto Battleground State Historical Park. From Pasadena continue east on T-225 to T-134, and turn north to Park Road 1836. Here, in just eighteen minutes, Sam Houston and his ragged Texian Army defeated the Mexican Army in 1836. This event changed not only the future of Texas but that of the western half of continental America. The dramatic story is chiseled in granite and unfolds as you walk around the base of the 570-foot-tall San Jacinto Monument. There is no better capsule lesson in Texas history.

Inside, the interesting **San Jacinto Museum of History** has artifacts from the Spanish-Mexican period (1519-1835) and the Anglo-American settlement years (1835-81). A documentary film, *Texas Forever! The Battle of San Jacinto,* brings history to life in the museum's Jesse H. Jones Theatre for Texas Studies. The museum is free, but there are charges to see the film and to ride the elevator to the top of the monument. Open daily.

The battlefield flanks the monument, and a free map available at the museum will guide you to markers and various positions of the Texas and Mexican armies. This oak-studded parkland also has numerous picnic sites along one arm of the bay and on the ship channel, so bring your lunch and crabbing gear.

The **Battleship *Texas*** is nearby. Moored here since 1948 and recently restored, it is billed as the only surviving heavily armed dreadnought-class battleship, a relic of both world wars. Open daily. Fee. (281) 479-4414.

Sylvan Beach. On Bayshore Drive (Spur-410), La Porte. This pleasant, thirty-two-acre county park has a playground, picnic areas, a bait and tackle shop, restrooms, and a free boat launch but no swimming. There also is good crabbing here. Park information: (281) 326-6539. The old train depot at the park's entrance now serves as a historical museum for La Porte and is open by appointment. (281) 471-3961.

WHERE TO EAT

Candy Garden Tea Room & Gift Shop. 710 Park, La Porte. Specialties here include soups, salads, sandwiches, and homemade desserts. Open Monday–Saturday for lunch. $. (409) 471-3560.

Monument Inn Restaurant. 4406 Battleground Road, La Porte. This long-standing favorite place still serves up whopping portions of seafood, chicken, and steak. House specialties include the Mojo Basket (a variety of their finest seafood, highly recommended), the "Monumental" salad, and key lime pie for dessert. A scrumptious cinnamon roll comes in your bread basket, just right for breakfast the next day. Open for lunch and dinner daily. $-$$$; (CC). (281) 479-1521.

Sodaro's Tea Room Eatery. 319 West Main, La Porte. A handy spot for a soup/salad/sandwich lunch while shopping for antiques along West Main. Open Tuesday–Saturday for lunch. $. (409) 471-9064.

CONTINUING ON

From the San Jacinto Monument area and La Porte, the Lynchburg Ferry takes you across the ship channel to Baytown, where you continue on T-134 to Decker Drive (T-330). Turn southeast (right) and drive into Baytown. At the intersection with T-201, a turn southwest (right) will take you back to La Porte via the Fred Hartman Bridge.

BAYTOWN

Both Lynchburg and Baytown were early Anglo settlements, the former an important trading post and the latter originally a sawmill and a store on Goose Creek near the junction of the San Jacinto River and Buffalo Bayou. What was then known as Bay Town boomed after the Civil War and again with the discovery of oil nearby in 1916. When Humble Oil and Refining Co. bought 2200 acres for a refinery in 1919, today's Baytown began to evolve. Antiques hounds may enjoy a stroll through the Goose Creek historic district (Texas Avenue and Defee Street between Pruett and Commerce).

WHAT TO DO

Baytown Historical Museum. 220 West Defee. This interesting look at the area's past is housed in a 1936 post office. Note the fresco on the lobby wall, painted by noted artist Barse Miller as part of a WPA project during the Great Depression. Other major exhibits include replicas of an Indian hut and midden; the poetry of the Sage of Cedar Bayou, John P. Sjolander; and Humble/Exxon memorabilia from the early days in the oil patch. The Texas Room has artifacts relevant to David Burnet, Sam Houston, and Lorenzo de Zavalla, all of whom lived in the area. Open Tuesday–Saturday; call for hours. Donation. (281) 427-8768.

Fred Hartman Bridge. Glorious double diamond-shaped towers mark this soaring structure over the waters between La Porte and Baytown. Total length of this portion of T–146 equals eight football fields. Drive slowly and enjoy the views.

Houston Raceway Park. 2525 FM–565 South. Take exit 798 from I–10 east of downtown, go south to T–146, then right to FM–565. Billed as the world's fastest drag-racing track, this quarter-mile strip hosts the NHRA Slick 50 Nationals annually in late February/early March and the Jet Car Nationals in June. Want to test your wheels in pro territory? Come Wednesday night and bring $12. Some type of racing or special event is on every Wednesday and weekend, year-round. Fee. (281) 383-2666.

WHERE TO EAT

Cafe on Texas Avenue. 214 West Texas Avenue, Baytown. You can survey work by local artists while filling up on unusual salads, sandwiches, and desserts. Open for breakfast and lunch Tuesday through Saturday. $. (409) 837-6117.

Going's Barbeque Company. 1007 North Main, Baytown. The name says it all at this locally popular spot. In addition to the usual meats/plates/sandwiches, there's an all-you-can-eat evening buffet Monday through Wednesday. Open daily for lunch and dinner. $-$$; (CC). (281) 422-4600.

Ninfa's Seafood Cantina. At Bayland Park Marina south of the Fred Hartman Bridge (T-146). Great views come with your snapper, swordfish, or seafood quesadillas and enchiladas here. There's also outside dining in nice weather. Open daily for lunch and dinner. $-$$$; (CC). (281) 837-9100.

MORGAN'S POINT

Back in those good old days, Morgan's Point combined with La Porte to provide a beach and bay playground for Houstonians. Big-name bands brought crowds to the dance pavilion at Sylvan Beach, and folks drove around Morgan's Point just to see the handsome homes on the "Gold Coast."

A drive along Bayridge Road still takes you past some of those places, among them a grand replica of the White House, built by former Texas Governor Ross Sterling. It has been a landmark on the Houston Ship Channel for nearly three generations. At the end of Morgan's Point is an undeveloped beach area well known to birders. With binoculars you can watch roseate spoonbills and other species on Atkinson Island, a sanctuary in this upper portion of Galveston Bay.

WANDERING THE BACKROADS

From the San Jacinto Monument, you easily can skip tours of Baytown, La Porte, and Morgan's Point in favor of a jaunt to Clear Lake and Kemah (Trip 2, this sector). Just retrace your route to T-225 and turn east (left) to its intersection with T-146. Turn south (right) and go approximately 10 miles to Clear Lake and Kemah.

CLEAR LAKE

A drive south from Houston on I-45 brings you to NASA Road 1. Turn east to explore Clear Lake and the laid-back towns of Seabrook and Kemah.

The launching of *Sputnik* also launched America's space program and triggered the construction of the NASA/Lyndon B. Johnson Space Center. Visitors now access some portions of that facility via Space Center Houston, a neighboring $70 million educational/ entertainment project designed in part by Walt Disney Imagineering (See "What to Do" section). This is one of the biggest visitor attractions in the state.

After investigating the exploration of space, you can challenge some new frontiers on your own. A few miles away is nature at its most primitive, a wilderness bayou seemingly untouched by civilization, and almost across the road you'll find the boating and water fun capital of Texas, Clear Lake. That 2,418-acre water playground sports more marinas, boat slips, and boats than any other Lone Star lake. Less adventurous folk enjoy the shops and docks in Seabrook and Kemah, a day's outing in themselves. Toss a cooler in the car to haul home some fresh fish. You'll also enjoy exploring the oak-shaded shops and tearooms in League City.

For information on the area, contact the Clear Lake-NASA Area Convention and Visitors Bureau, 1201 NASA Road 1, Houston 77058, (281) 488-7676 or (800) 844-LAKE (5253).

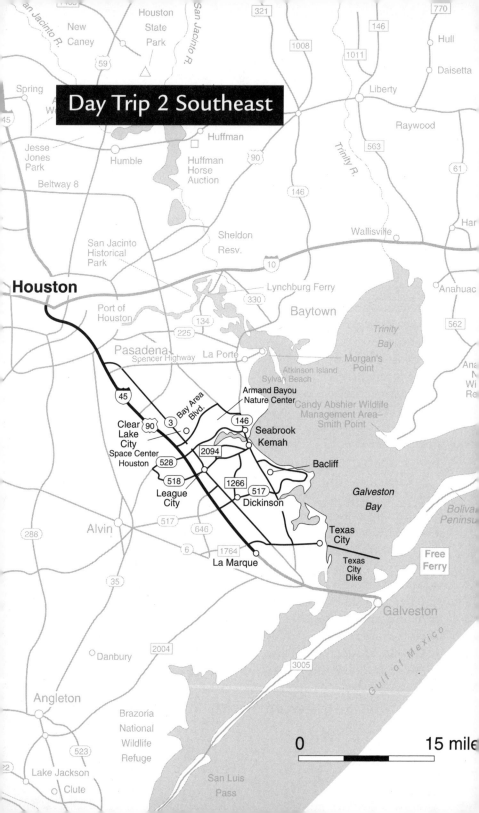

WHAT TO DO

Armand Bayou Nature Center. 8500 Bay Area Boulevard. One of the largest urban wilderness and wildlife refuges in America, this 2,500-acre haven is home to more than 370 species of wildlife. This refuge hits its birding peak during March and April as a major stopover for migrating flocks. A covered bird blind with interpretive materials allows an educated look.

A 500-foot-long teaching boardwalk leads from the parking lot to the nature center, and additional walking trails thread woods, prairie, and the bayou's edge. Also on the grounds are an observatory and a three-acre exhibit farm focused on the 1890s–1900s, complete with a restored and furnished farmhouse (live demonstrations on weekends), a barn, outbuildings, and a vegetable garden. There's also a children's day camp program here in June and July.

The water portions of this wilderness park are best explored by canoe (bring your own and put in at Bay Area Park); groups of ten to twelve can reserve naturalist-led trips via pontoon boats. (Fee.) Consider buying a family membership ($45) while you're at the nature center to help preserve this wilderness. Open Wednesday–Sunday. Fee. (281) 474-2551.

Boating and Other Water Sports on Clear Lake and Galveston Bay. At this writing at least twenty sources provide charters, rentals, lessons, or excursions. The following are of particular interest to casual day visitors:

Clear Lake Charter Boats and Clear Lake Powerboat Rentals, based at South Shore Harbor in League City, offer sail- and powerboat rentals, bay and gulf fishing trips, and parasailing. (281) 334-4858.

Houston Barge and Rowing Club at Watergate Yachting Center offers free introductory rowing excursions on Saturday mornings as well as affordable membership which allows you use of club craft. (281) 334-3101.

Houston/Bay Area Rowing Centers, based at Watergate Marina in Kemah and at Clear Lake Shores Marina, teaches the fundamentals of rowing and sculling and rents equipment. (281) 334-3101.

Jim's Water Sports Center of Clear Lake, based in Clear Lake Park, is a great source for hourly rentals of sailboats, wave runners, sailboards, canoes, pontoon boats, ski boats and equipment, and kayaks. (281) 326-2724.

The Lake Rose taxi boat offers private charters ($50 per hour); one hour voyages on Clear Lake ($7 per person); and taxi runs anywhere on the lake, including service to waterfront restaurants ($5 per person each way). Operates Wednesday–Sunday from 2:00 P.M. (281) 538-1771 or 208-5913.

Nassau Bay Watersports, based at the Nassau Bay Hilton Marina, offers parasailing as well as hourly and daily rentals of sailboats, Hobie-Cats, jet skis, wave runners, and jet boats. (281) 333-2816.

Windsurfing Sports, based at 2300 NASA Road 1 in Seabrook, offers sailboard and kayak rentals by the hour or day. (281) 291-9199.

The following offer sailing lessons and/or fishing trips:

At the Helm, based at Lafayette Landing in Kemah, offers sailing and rowing lessons, with an emphasis on instruction for women. Membership in this sailing club ($350–$600) lets you use one of its sleek craft for free on any weekend. Charters also. (281) 334-4101.

Bay Charter, Inc., based at 1900 Shipyard Drive, Seabrook, is an ASA sailing school providing certification through seven levels of instruction. They also offer captained and bareboat charters as well as club memberships. (281) 474-4535.

Blue Marlin Sailing School, based at Portofino Harbour in Clear Lake Shores, offers basic sailing courses, along with brush-up sessions for those who have sailed before. (281) 639-3856.

Blue Water Cruising, based at Portofino Harbour in Clear Lake Shores, teaches basic sailing, celestial navigation, and seamanship. (281) 334-7678.

Windward Seaventure Charters, based at Waterford Harbor in Kemah, offers sailing lessons as well as sail- and powerboat rentals (with or without a captain). (281) 334-5295 or (800) 910-SAIL.

The following offer charters: Gateway Charters, (281) 334-2840; Houston Sailing Association, (281) 334-1856; Interlude Yacht Charters, (281) 952-8984; Sackett's Sailing Center, (281) 334-4179; Sakonnet & Cape Cruises of Seabrook, (281) 474-2026; Star Fleet, (281) 334-4692; and Ultra Sailing Charters, (281) 538-3388.

Canoeing the Bayous. You can float through the Armand Bayou wilderness on your own and not get lost, thanks to a free waterways map available from the Armand Bayou Nature Center.

There is canoe access at Bay Area Park and at the NASA Road 1 bridge at Clear Lake Park, 5001 NASA Road 1. Canoes can be rented by the hour at Cecil's Red Lantern Restaurant, 2908 Red Bluff Road (at the bridge on Taylor Lake), (281) 474-7660, and at Jim's Water Sports Center of Clear Lake (see p. 228). If you don't want to canoe at those specific sites, inquire whether the proprietors provide or rent car-top carriers or racks to transport canoes; you may need to bring your own.

You'll also find pleasant canoeing in Dickinson Bayou, which roughly parallels FM-517, both west and east from I-45. You'll find a good put-in and parking at the T-3 bridge in Dickinson, and then you have your choice of take-outs: a carry either at the FM-646 crossing (3.5 miles) or at Cemetery Road. This last section is the most beautiful and undisturbed. *Note:* Canoeing here is best on weekdays, it's crowded with motor vessels on weekends.

Galveston Bay Foundation. There's no need to go to Galveston to explore and enjoy baywaters. This volunteer nonprofit organization sponsors more than 50 activities and workshops annually, all focused on the natural ecology of Galveston Bay. Recent trips included canoe tours of Armand Bayou, Cedar Bayou, and Double Bayou; inspection by boat of the Houston Ship Channel; and a guided look at Anahuac National Wildlife Refuge. Emphasis always is on responsible ecotourism. Trips fill fast, and preference goes to members. Membership fees start at $15. (281) 332-3381.

Space Center Houston. 1601 NASA Road 1. From I-45 South take the NASA Road 1 exit and go 3 miles east. Billed as "A Magical Place to Discover Space," this new focal point for America's manned space flight program has interactive exhibits that are easy to understand and fun to operate. Care to try your hand at landing the shuttle? Intercepting an errant satellite in space? Performing space chores at zero gravity? You can do all three and more, courtesy of a large bank of computer stations in the "Feel of Space" section, on your left as you enter.

An ideal outing regardless of the season or weather, Space Center Houston has three theaters, a full-size mock-up of portions of the space shuttle, a super display of moon rocks (you can touch one), and tram tours that scoot you around limited portions of Johnson Space Center, next door. Got children under twelve in tow? A $1.2

million Kids' Space Place offers 40 out-of-this world activities designed specifically for that age group. Kids can now create a mock shuttle flight at Mission Kidtrol, experience what it feels like to walk on the moon, and so on. Plan to spend at least four to six hours here, more if you eat at the Zero G Diner, a cafeteria-style food court ($). *Nice to know:* If you just want to visit the gift shop, you have a forty-five-minute free period during which you can get your entrance fee back. There's also a day camp program for children in summer. *Also note:* The NASA–Lyndon B. Johnson Space Center, including Rocket Park, is no longer open to the public except through Space Center Houston. Open daily. Fee. (281) 244-2105 or (800) 972-0369.

WHERE TO EAT

The Cross-Eyed Seagull Restaurant & Bar. 1010 East NASA Road 1 at Egret Bay Boulevard, Webster. Happiness is chowing down on delicious shrimp while sitting on this cafe's over-bayou deck. The burgers, quesadillas, meat loaf, and pizzas are popular as well, and there's live entertainment nightly. Open for lunch and dinner daily. $-$$; (CC). (281) 333-3488.

Frenchie's. 1041 East Nasa Road 1 at El Camino Real, Webster. This small, friendly place has been a local favorite since it was opened fifteen years ago by the Camera family, formerly of the Isle of Capri in Italy. You'll find scads of photographs on the walls, as well as a menu that ranges from family-style Italian to seafood and steaks. Although casual for lunch, it's a bit dressier for dinner. Open for lunch and dinner Monday–Saturday. $$-$$$; (CC). (281) 486-7144.

CONTINUING ON

From Clear Lake this day trip takes NASA Road 1 east to its intersection with T-146 in Seabrook and then turns south. The area on the north side of the bridge is Seabrook. On the south side it is Kemah.

SEABROOK AND KEMAH

Both of these fishing villages are heaven for shrimp lovers and boat watchers. The channel under the bridge is the only passage from Clear Lake into Galveston Bay, and the view of the constant marine traffic is best from the outside dining decks of Kemah's many restaurants, clustered together at the eastern end of the channel. If you want to buy shrimp fresh and relatively cheap, check out the numerous fish markets that line the channel on the Seabrook side of the bridge. The quaint buildings of "Old" Seabrook are blossoming anew with antiques stores, boutiques, and specialty shops. NASA Road 1 becomes Second Street east of the T–146 stoplight; turn right and just mosey along until you see something of interest. If you like bazaars and flea markets, don't miss Seabrook's Back Bay Market on the second weekend of every month. Looking for a getaway? Try one of Seabrook's B&Bs: The Crew's Quarters, (281) 334-4141; High Tide Bed & Breakfast, (281) 474-2042; or The Pelican House Bed & Breakfast Inn, (281) 474-5295.

Much of what was the funky little fishing village of Kemah has been swept away by storms and bulldozers. The swanky new Lafayette Landing Marina complex has gentrified the area at the south end of the bridge, and new galleries and gift shops are popping up like mushrooms around the Bradford–Sixth Street intersection. Things will be changing on Kemah's "Restaurant Row" that lines the channel between Clear Lake and Galveston Bay. In early 1997 the Landry's restaurant folks bought out all the eateries on the Kemah side of the channel. Although the very popular Flying Dutchman will remain unchanged, plans call for closing of several other major establishments in preparation for redevelopment of the entire waterfront into a rustic fishing village. Stay tuned. Meanwhile, to reach Kemah's restaurants, turn east at the Sixth Street stoplight at the southern end of the T–146 bridge, then go north on Bradford.

To overnight here in a high-quality B&B and be within walking distance of nearly everything, call the Captain's Quarters, (281) 334-4141; owner Mary Patterson also puts on an elegant afternoon tea with live entertainment on the first Thursday of every month. $$. Reservations are required. Mary also operates four other B&Bs in the Kemah-Seabrook area.

WHERE TO EAT

Chatchawal's Bay Thai Restaurant. 1101 Second Street, Seabrook. Tucked away in a pink cottage on a back bay residential street, this small, family-owned place has oriented its front door to the west, an omen for success suggested by a Thai fortune-teller. No need. The food at this eatery makes it on its own. Entrees on the à la carte menu range from traditional Thai dishes to specialties such as wild boar curry and emu with Thai seasonings. Owner-chef Gil Lobeck is Bangkok-born, and his love of fine food shows. Open for lunch Wednesday–Friday, dinner Tuesday–Sunday. $$–$$$; (CC). (281) 474-4248.

Claudio's Piano Bar Restaurant. 700 Kipp, Kemah. When a nondescript restaurant prospers off the waterfront and against heavy competition in this small town, you know it has good food. Locals consider this their private retreat from the tourist scene on restaurant row, and the owners welcome everyone as family. Everything on the menu, from steaks and seafood to classic Italian dishes, is delicious and freshly prepared when you order. Come hungry. Open for lunch Tuesday–Friday, dinner Tuesday–Sunday. $–$$; (CC). (281) 334-7378.

Crab House. 317 Todville Road, Seabrook. A local institution, this spot serves a variety of delicious boiled and steamed seafood but the big draw is the crab. It comes cum mallet and is served on newspapers. If that sounds like too much work, order the fried shrimp or oysters, the Cajun fish fillets, or seafood gumbo. Just want a dozen fresh oysters? This is the place. Open for dinner on Thursday, lunch and dinner Friday–Sunday. $–$$; (CC). (281) 474-5836.

The Crazy Cajun. 2825 NASA Road 1, Seabrook. No way can you stay in a bad mood in this relaxed and zany place. The waiters will charm you right out of the blues, a cup of gumbo will rev up your taste buds, and the Cajun Shrimp Combo will satisfy hunger pangs for hours. Open daily for lunch and dinner. $$–$$$; (CC). (281) 326-6055.

Delesandri's. 2513 NASA Road 1, Seabrook. This waterfront eatery (deck and indoors) offers great seafood with an Italian flair along with a full menu. Open for lunch and dinner daily.$–$$; (CC). (281) 326-4221.

The Flying Dutchman Restaurant and Oyster Bar. 505 Second Street, Kemah. Ask local residents where they take visitors for good and inventive seafood, and this place wins by a landslide. It's dressy duds upstairs, cutoffs and casual boating wear down. Unless the weather's at one of its uncomfortable extremes, try for a table on the deck, the better to watch the boat traffic. Open daily for lunch and dinner. $-$$$; (CC). (281) 334-7575.

Frenchie's Villa Capri. 3713 NASA Road 1, Seabrook. Dress up here. This "Cucina d'Italia" is one of the prettiest places on Clear Lake, complete with an outdoor patio and Italian-style gardens stretching to the water's edge. Italian dishes get top billing, along with grilled seafood and steaks. Open for lunch and dinner Tuesday–Sunday. $$-$$$; (CC). (281) 326-2373.

Lakeview Grill. 1002 Aspen, Clear Lake Shores. A great place to get some personal fuel when boating on Clear Lake, this local hangout has its own docks, tables both inside and out, and a menu that runs from sandwiches, salads, and seafood to chicken and steak. Open for lunch and dinner daily in summer; dinner only in winter; breakfast on weekends. Call to re-check hours of operation. $-$$; (CC). (281) 334-7486.

Landry's at Jimmy Walker's. 201 Kipp, Kemah. Seafood with a Continental flair is the rule here, with fine dining on the second floor, a more casual atmosphere and outdoor tables on the first. If there's a see-and-be-seen place in the area, it's this pricey spot. Open daily for lunch and dinner. $$-$$$; (CC). (281) 334-2513.

Seabrook Classic Cafe. 2511A NASA Road 1, Seabrook. This is a great place for weekend breakfasts, particularly if you have a fondness for those nifty little New Orleans doughnuts called beignets. Everything is fresh here and made from scratch. Open for lunch and dinner daily, breakfast on weekends. $-$$; (CC). (281) 326-1512.

Sundance Grill. 222 Jennings Island, Seabrook. Located in the Seabrook Shipyard immediately west of the T-146 bridge, this waterfront eatery specializes in very creative seafood and salads. Try the Sausalito Salmon (topped with an avocado citrus salsa), Cozumel Cyclone (a seafood tamale), Canadian drunken mussels (steamed in beer), or the Hawaiian Island Shrimp Kabob—you'll come back. The menu also includes crab bisque, seafood gumbo, fish sandwiches, hamburgers, and po'boys. Open for lunch and dinner daily; reservations advised. $-$$; (CC). (281) 474-2248.

T-Bone Tom's Meat Market and Steakhouse Restaurant. 707 T-146, Kemah. Why anyone would want a great steak, spicy sausage, ribs, chicken or barbecue in the midst of fresh fish territory is beyond understanding, but if that's your pleasure, this is the place. Open Monday–Saturday for lunch and dinner. $-$$; (CC). (281) 334-2133.

Tookie's. 1202 T-146, Seabrook. When you are hankering for a hamburger, thick and sweet onion rings, and real iced tea (huge and made with freshly brewed hot tea), come here. Open daily for lunch and dinner. $; (CC), (281) 474-3444.

CONTINUING ON

From Kemah, drive south on T-146 to the signal at FM-2094 and turn west (right) to the FM-518 west intersection. That latter road becomes Main Street in this day trip's next stop: League City.

LEAGUE CITY

In pre-Anglo settlement times the site of a Karankawa Indian village, this community at the conjunction of Clear Creek and Sugar Bayou was known as Butler's Ranch and/or Clear Creek when it was first settled by farmers around 1873. Two decades later J.C. League acquired a large amount of local land and laid out his namesake townsite along the right-of-way for the Galveston, Houston & Henderson Railroad. Today's League City melds its Victorian past with current tourism in several pleasant ways. Walking tour maps, available in several shops and cafes, lead you to more than two dozen historic sites, and tearooms as well as antiques shops seem growth industries. For advance information, contact the League City Historical Society, P.O. Box 1642, League City 77574, or the League City Chamber of Commerce, 1201 East NASA Road 1, League City 77058, (281) 488-7676.

WHAT TO SEE

Bayou Wildlife Ranch. Take the Dickinson/FM-517 exit from I-45, then drive west on FM-517 for 6 miles; the entrance will be on your left. From antelopes to a zonky (a cross between a zebra and a donkey), more than 260 animals representing forty-two species roam this eighty-six-acre preserve. Many are either endangered or nearly extinct in their natural habitat. Visitors tour with a guide via an open-air tram, buckets of feed ($2.00) at the ready. This outstanding facility gives you a good look at major zoo-type animals roaming free in a natural environment. If you've never been nuzzled by a camel or scratched a giraffe's neck, this is the place. *Also here:* a children's barnyard (which includes pony rides in spring and summer), an alligator farm, a monkey island, and a feeding barn for young animals who need extra TLC. Although no human food is sold here, picnickers are most welcome. Open daily in summer, Tuesday–Sunday in winter. Fee. (281) 337-6376.

Gulf Breeze Downs. 7602 FM-2004 in Hitchcock; take exit 15 from I-45 and turn west. Visitors are welcome to tour the barns and watch the daily workouts at this training track for Sam Houston Race Park. You may get lucky and catch a pari-mutuel race. Free.

Gulf Greyhound Park. Thirty miles south of Houston via exit 15 from I-45. This 110-acre, $50 million attraction is the world's largest greyhound racing facility—a Cadillac of racetracks—and when it opened in 1992 it offered the first legal pari-mutuel betting in the Houston area in more than fifty-five years. General admission is $1.00, parking is $1.00, and the minimum bet is $2.00. If you want to go first class, choose valet parking ($4.00) and lounge/clubhouse admission ($4.00). Expect numerous well-designed lounge areas, closed-circuit color TV, and plenty of instruction on the various methods of betting. Post times on this quarter-mile track are 7:30 P.M., Tuesday and Thursday–Sunday; 4:00 P.M. and 7:20 P.M. on "Winning" Wednesday; and 1:30 P.M. Friday–Sunday. Families are welcome. (409) 986-9500, (800) ASK-2-WIN.

Stardust Trail Rides. 3001 Calder Drive, League City. This 1,000-acre working ranch attracts would-be cowboys from all over the world with its guided trail rides ($15.00 for one hour). Open daily in summer, Wednesday–Sunday in winter. (281) 332-9370.

West Bay Common School Children's Museum Complex. 210 North Kansas Street (at Second Street), League City. This award-winning, hands-on history experience captivates everyone regardless of age. A costumed "school marm" brings alive the rural education experience typical of Texas at the turn of the century; there's even a 45-star American flag. Sitting at old-fashioned desks in a real one-room school, youngsters use slates to learn the three R's from late 19th century textbooks, practice Spencerian penmanship in old time pen and ink, and so on. The building itself was built in 1898 in west Chambers County and moved to the site of League City's original school in 1992. League City's 1927 ice house and neighboring barber shop (1936) also have been moved here and restored as exhibits. Open Tuesday–Friday from 9:00 A.M. to 1:00 P.M. or by appointment; classes are conducted only for groups with advance reservations. (281) 554-2994 or 480-8404.

WHERE TO EAT

Clifton by the Sea. At bay end of FM-646, Baycliff. Destroyed in early 1997 by a fire of suspicious origin, this great local favorite was scheduled to rebuild at press time. For update, call (281) 339-2933.

Enchanted Garden Tea Room. 501 East Main, League City. This spot is known for tasty soups, sandwiches, salads, and desserts as well as special coffees. Open for lunch Monday–Saturday; afternoon tea and desserts on Saturday from 3:00–5:00 P.M. $; (CC). (281) 338-4472.

Esteban's Cafe and Cantina. 402 West Main, League City. One of the most appealing Mexican eateries in the greater Houston region, this family-owned spot makes its own sauces and tortillas from scratch daily. Don't miss either the spinach or crab enchiladas, just two of the house specialties. Open daily for lunch and dinner. $-$$: (CC). (281) 332-4195.

Truffles-N-Tarts. 815 East Main Street (inside the Main Street Emporium), League City. Good spot for light lunches and desserts. Open Monday–Saturday for lunch, late afternoon snacks, gourmet teas, and designer coffees. $; (CC). (281) 338-4438.

WANDERING THE BACKROADS

To return to Houston, swing west on FM-518 to its intersection with I-45 north. However, if you want to extend this day trip, consider heading east on FM-518 to T-146 and then turning south for a short drive to the Texas City Dike (signs). A five-mile-long strip of road and breakwater jutting into Galveston Bay, the dike is popular with sailboarders and folks with small sailboats and catamarans because the winds are relatively dependable. Fishing and crabbing are wherever you find a spot, and there also are boat-launching facilities, bait and tackle shanties, some cafes, and a lighted fishing pier. The dike is unpleasant with debris, however, and swimming is dangerous. Also there are few amenities such as public restrooms, designated parking areas, and drinking water.

As an alternate to the dike, sailboarders and wade fishers may prefer to turn left at the entrance to the dike onto Skyline Drive. Great kite-flying territory, it also offers a six-mile view and water playground along the bay.

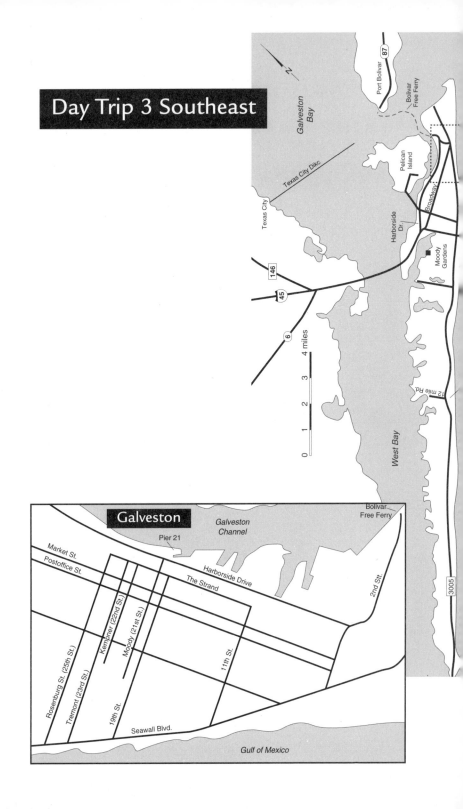

GALVESTON

Cabeza de Vaca found it first. Later a pirate named Jean Lafitte made this sliver of island his base of shady operations in 1817. Legend says his treasure still lies buried in the shifting sands, and hunting for it with metal detectors is a favorite Galveston pastime.

To Houstonians this small city, one hour's drive south via I-45, traditionally has been a relief valve, a place to escape from big-city life for a lazy day or weekend at the beach. But Galveston is far more than surf and sand.

Long before Houston was much more than a landing on Buffalo Bayou, Galveston was a major port and the threshold to Texas for thousands of immigrants. By the 1870s it was the wealthy and thriving "Queen City of the Southwest," and during the golden era of 1875–1900 some of the most remarkable architecture in America lined its streets.

A devastating hurricane in 1900 killed some 6,000 people and swept much of the city out to sea. Vulnerable to every passing storm, Galveston seemed doomed to follow the earlier Texas coast ports of Indianola and Lavaca into oblivion. To save the city and ensure its future security, two major engineering projects were undertaken, both remarkable for their times. The first was the building of a massive seawall, 17 feet tall and 10 miles long. The second was the raising of all the land behind that seawall from 4 to 17 feet.

These projects took seven years and were followed by another economic blow in 1915, when the successful completion of the Houston Ship Channel began to draw off the cream of the port trade. Galve-

239

ston never recovered its prehurricane commercial importance, and gradually it degenerated into one of the wildest gambling towns in the state. The Texas Rangers finally brought down the law in the 1950s, and after that Galveston slumbered along as a rather seedy seaside city for a time.

But all is changing and on the upswing once again. The renovation and restoration of many historic buildings and a growth in the hotel/convention sector has sparked fresh capital investment, and Galveston now is thriving. Don't miss a ride on the $10 million rail trolley system that connects, in 1890s–1920s style, the Strand Historic District with the seawall.

Information on Galveston is available from the Galveston Historical Foundation (GHF), 2016 Strand, Galveston 77550, (409) 765-7834 or (713) 280-3907, and the Galveston Convention & Visitors Bureau, 2106 Seawall Boulevard, Galveston 77550, (409) 763-4311 or (800) 351-4236. The con-vis bureau offers, by mail only, a free discount coupon booklet that gives reduced rates on accommodations, attractions, and restaurants.

EXPLORING THE BEACHES

There are 32 miles of beachfront on the island and a variety of options. The decisions start after you cross the causeway from the mainland on I-45 and see the directional signs for East and West beaches. If you continue east (left lanes), I-45 becomes Broadway Boulevard and runs in an easterly direction the length of the island. If you follow the signs to West Beach from I-45, you will cross the island on Sixty-first Street, which ends at Seawall Boulevard, the island's second east-west main drag. Turn right; West Beach starts where the seawall ends. The road becomes FM-3005 at this point and continues down-island to San Luis Pass. Do note that cars are not allowed on Galveston's beaches at any time of the year, and that alcohol is banned both along the seawall and at Stewart Beach.

Good news: A $4.8 million replenishment program begun in 1995 is piping sand from an offshore reef to increase the width of Galveston's beaches by 50 feet.

Seafood tip: Want to buy fresh from the boats? Bring a cooler and check out the fish markets in the 1700–1900 blocks of Sixty-first Street.

There are three beach pocket-park facilities on FM-3005, operated by Galveston County. Each has changing rooms, showers, food concessions, playgrounds, and picnic areas and is backed by protected natural dunes. Horseback riding, parasailing, sailboarding, and other commercial beach activities often are available nearby during warm-weather months. West Beach offers the best jogging and shelling, particularly near San Luis Pass.

In town you'll find numerous small beaches tucked between the rock jetties along Seawall Boulevard. Stop and watch the dolphins roll in the offshore swells and then walk out onto the jetties and chat with the fishermen. There are several places to rent roller skates, bicycles and pedal surreys, and the wide sidewalk along the top of the seawall is a favorite promenade. The boulevard curves at the east end of the island and intersects Broadway at Stewart Beach. This city-run stretch of sand is popular with families because of its lifeguards, bathhouse, lockers, parking, concessions, and so on.

A short drive farther east brings you to R. A. Apffel Park, a $2 million, 1980s development at the extreme end of East Beach. A favorite with fisherfolk and families as well as teenagers looking for like kind, it has excellent boating and fishing facilities and an 11,000-square-foot recreation center that includes a bathhouse and concessions. *Also here:* the Big Reef Nature Park with observation platforms for birding.

Galveston Island State Park. West of downtown Galveston on FM-3005 at the intersection with Thirteen Mile Road. Another beach facility with picnicking and camping, this 2,000-acre state park also offers birdwatching from observation platforms and nature trails along its north boundary; the latter faces the protected waters of West Galveston Bay. Some seven acres of freshwater ponds within the park often are stocked with trout during the winter months. (409) 737-1222 or (800) 792-1112. The park's Mary Moody Northen Amphitheatre features major musical productions during the summer months, (409) 737-3440.

Palm Beach. West of town in Moody Gardens, 1 Hope Boulevard off Eighty-first Street. This three-acre freshwater swimming complex faces the bay. Facilities include whirlpools, lockers, a boardwalk, concessions, and lifeguards. This is the only beach in Texas with Caribbean-style white sand and palms. Fee. (409) 744-PALM.

EXPLORING HISTORIC GALVESTON

Start at The Strand, once called the "Wall Street of the Southwest" and now the heart of one of the island's three historic districts. In itself The Strand is considered one of the largest and best collections of nineteenth-century iron-front commercial buildings remaining in America.

To reach The Strand area from the I–45 south causeway, take the Harborside Drive exit and turn east (left). To get to The Strand from Broadway, turn north on Twenty-fourth Street and continue 8 blocks. Most of the buildings along The Strand now house shops, galleries, businesses, and restaurants—more than 95 in all. Dickenson-The Strand, a Victorian-themed Christmas festival on the first weekend in December, often draws crowds in excess of 70,000 and is covered by the national press.

Stop first at the Strand Visitors Center, 2016 Strand, operated daily, year-round, by the Galveston Historical Foundation in the restored Hendley Row (1856–60). Brochures outlining walking and biking tours are available here, along with audio-guide equipment (fee) and information on Galveston's many points of interest. The following are among the main stops:

The Bishop's Palace. 1402 Broadway. The only home in the East End Historic District open to the public, this massive place was built between 1887 and 1892 for the Walter Gresham family. Designed by noted Galveston architect Nicholas Clayton, it is considered one of the hundred most outstanding residential structures in America. Even more interesting than its turreted, rococo exterior are the details and furnishings inside. Fee. Guided tours are given year-round (closed on Tuesday, September–June). (409) 762-2475.

The Center for Transportation and Commerce (The Railroad Museum). Strand at Twenty-fifth Street. Top draw here is the original waiting room of Galveston's old train depot, where life-size sculptures of travelers are frozen in a moment of 1932; unusual "hear" phones allow visitors to eavesdrop on their conversations. Out back are forty-seven steam locomotives and assorted railroad cars, a snack bar and picnic gazebo, and exhibits of steam-powered machines. Open daily. Fee. (409) 765-5700.

The East End Historical District. This special area includes 40 blocks of Victoriana bounded by Broadway, Market, Nineteenth, and Eleventh streets. It can be driven or walked, but the best way to see the most is by bicycle or on the historical foundation's Homes Tour in early May. Self-guiding tour brochures as well as audio tours are available at the Strand Visitors Center.

1839 Samuel May Williams Home. 3601 Bernardo de Galvez (Avenue P). One of the two oldest structures in Galveston, this charming restoration now looks as it did in 1854. Open daily. Fee. (409) 765-1839.

1859 Ashton Villa. 2328 Broadway. This Italianate beauty was built in 1859 of bricks made on the island and survived both a disastrous island-wide fire in 1885 and the 1900 storm. It now is restored as the showplace of the Galveston Historical Foundation. An interesting urban archaeological dig exposes a small portion of the home's original raised basement, which was filled in when the level of the island was raised after the 1900 storm. Open daily. Fee. (409) 762-3933.

The 1871 League Building. Strand at Tremont. One of the nicest restorations in the city and home to several interesting shops and The Wentletrap Restaurant (see "Where to Eat" listings).

The 1882 H. M. Trueheart–Adriance Building. 210 Kempner. This Nicholas Clayton-designed building is one of the most ornate and distinctive structures in the area. Its restoration in 1970 sparked The Strand's renaissance.

The Elissa/Texas Seaport Museum. Pier 21, 1 block north of The Strand. An 1877 square-rigged barque called *Elissa* rides at anchor here. One of the oldest vessels in Lloyd's Register of Shipping, she also represents Texas in assorted "tall ship" parades and is open daily for tours. Visitors roam through restored after-cabins, the hold (self-guided), and the decks. In addition to a film detailing *Elissa's* acquisition and restoration, the museum chronicles Galveston's rich maritime heritage through interactive exhibits and a wide-screen multimedia presentation on the age of sail. Open daily. Fee. (409) 763-1877.

Galveston Arts Center. 2127 Strand. If you like mixing art with history, drop in at this eclectic gallery. This is the old First National Bank Building, restored to its 1866 grandeur. Closed Tuesday. (409) 763-2403.

Galveston County Historical Museum. 2219 Market Street. The handsome City National Bank Building, circa 1919, houses more of Galveston's glorious past. Open daily, except major holidays. (409) 766-2340.

Galveston Island Trolley. Styled to resemble the trolleys operating in turn-of-the-century Galveston, this fixed-rail, free streetcar system runs a 4.7-mile route across the island, connecting The Strand with Seawall Boulevard. (409) 763-4311.

The Grand 1894 Opera House. 2020 Postoffice Street. The interior of this interesting building has been restored to its turn-of-the-century grandeur, and the stage once again hosts a variety of performing arts throughout the year. For box office information call (409) 765-1894 or (281) 480-1894.

John Sydnor's 1847 Powhatan House. 3427 Avenue O. Home to the Galveston Garden Club, this handsome mansion with its oak-filled gardens is on the National Register. No high heels, please; they damage the beautiful pine floors. Two public tours on Saturday afternoon. Fee. (409) 763-0077.

The Marx and Kempner Building. 2100 block of The Strand. Can you spot the clever trompe l'oeil mural? The original window detailing of this building was removed decades ago, and what looks like several vintage facades actually is hand-painted artwork.

The Michel Menard Home. 1605 33rd Street. Galveston's oldest home has recently been restored as a private residence. For tour information, call (409) 762-3933.

The Moody Mansion & Museum. 2628 Broadway. This marvelous old home is the Smithsonian of Galveston. The city's grande dame, the late Mary Moody Northen, never threw anything away—archivists even found Christmas presents in their original wrappings, with full notation as to year and giver—and her lifelong home has been restored to the way it looked at her debut in 1911. Open daily. Fee. (409) 762-7668.

Postoffice Street. Four blocks south of The Strand between 20th and 23rd streets, this once busy thoroughfare again bustles with life as the main artery of Galveston's evolving art and entertainment district. A stroll here finds shops, galleries, coffeehouses, antiques stores, and The Grand 1894 Opera House (see above).

The Silk Stocking Historical District. Biking or windshield tours of this 9-block area, loosely bound by Rosenberg, J and N avenues and Tremont Street, are visual fun. Unfortunately, no historic homes here are currently open to the public.

The Tremont House. 2300 Ship's Mechanic Row. This superbly restored 1879 building now houses one of the most elegant small hotels in Texas. (409) 763-0300, (713) 480-8201, or (800) 874-2300 (reservations only).

TODAY'S GALVESTON

If you've had it with history or are burned out with beaches, there is still plenty to do.

Airplane Rides. For bird's-eye sightseeing (fee), call (409) 740-1223.

All About Town. Departing from Twenty-first and Seawall on the hour, this firm's Galveston Flyer Yellow Trolley tour is a one-hour narrated look at the best of Galveston. One ticket is good all day, so you can get on and off as you wish. Operates daily except Wednesday, year-round. Fee. (409) 744-6371.

Bicycle Rentals. Numerous shops along Seawall Boulevard rent almost anything that rolls.

Boat Launching. Free facilities on Teichman Road, Sportsman Road, and at Washington Park on Sixty-first Street.

Carriage Rides. Authentic horse-drawn surreys leave daily from the vicinity of Twenty-first and The Strand on thirty- and sixty-minute tours of the various historic districts. Fee.

David Taylor Classic Car Museum. 1918 Mechanic. This extensive collection of vintage wheels includes a 1955 Thunderbird convertible, a 1929 Chevy roadster, a classy 1931 Caddy roadster with rumble seat, and a 1934 Ford Roadster convertible. Open Tuesday–Sunday afternoons. Fee. (409) 765-6590.

Fishing. In addition to the rock jetties along the seawall, there are commercial fishing piers at Twenty-fifth, Sixty-first, and Ninetieth streets and at Seawolf Park on Pelican Island. Surf fishing is allowed along most of the open beaches; common catches are speckled trout, flounder, catfish, and redfish.

Party boats for fishing in either the bay or the Gulf leave early in the morning from Piers 18 and 19 and from the yacht basin. A Texas fishing license is required for everyone between the ages of seventeen and sixty-five unless you are fishing at least 10.5 miles offshore. Check to see if a license is required when you make your reservations. Common Gulf catches include red snapper, sailfish, pompano, warsaw, marlin, ling, king mackerel, bonito, and dolphin. Take precautions against seasickness before you go—the Gulf can get rough.

For further information, call A-Plus Charters, (409) 740-7467 or (800) 880-7587; Abra-Cadabra, (409) 765-8731; Aqua Safari Charters, (409) 935-4646; Coastal Yacht Brokers, (409) 763-3474; Extra Labor Charters, (409) 765-9700; Galveston Charter Service, Inc., (713) 944-FISH; Galveston Party Boats, (409) 763-5423 or (713) 222-7025; Reel Adventures, (409) 744-5464; Southbound Charters, (409) 762-1601; Williams Party Boats, (409) 762-8808 or (713) 223-4853); or Yellow Fin Charters, (409) 762-8535.

Galveston Harbour Tours. Pier 22 at Fisherman's Wharf. This 45-minute narrated boat tour of Texas's oldest seaport frequently includes dolphin sightings. Fee. (409) 765-1700.

Galveston Sightseeing Train. Hop aboard at Moody Center, Twenty-first and Seawall. You'll get a ninety-minute, 17-mile guided tour of Galveston old and new. Fee. Several tours daily, weather permitting. (409) 765-9564.

Harbor and Gulf Boat Tours. Moody Gardens. *The Colonel,* styled like an old-fashioned sternwheeler, churns its way around Galveston harbor on two-hour narrated cruises daily during the summer and Friday–Sunday in winter. Also offered are dinner/dance/jazz cruises. Call for times. Fee. (409) 740-7797.

Horseback Riding. Weather permitting, you can rent a steed from either Sunshine Stables, 11118 West Beach between Seven and Eight Mile roads, (409) 744-7470, or Gulf Stream Stables, Eight Mile Road, (409) 744-1004.

Kemp's Ridley Sea Turtle Head Start Project. 5000 Avenue U. Operated by the National Oceanic and Atmospheric Administration of the U.S. Department of Commerce and by the Galveston laboratories of the National Marine Fisheries Service, this research facility offers free tours three times a week. By appointment only. (409) 766-3523.

Lone Star Flight Museum. 2002 Terminal Drive, next to Moody Gardens and Galveston Municipal Airport. Aircraft from the 1930s to the 1960s fill this immaculate facility, all restored and in flying condition. In all, this is considered the world's finest (and possibly largest) collection of mint-condition "war birds." Situated on what was a military airfield during World War II, this growing collection includes fighters, bombers, a rare F-7-F Tigercat, and one of only two P-47-G Thunderbolts remaining in the world. The gift shop carries World War II memorabilia, aircraft engines are on display, and the research library is a find for historians. Don't miss the remarkable essay on what World War II was all about, particularly if you have teens in tow. Open daily. Fee. (409) 740-7722.

Mardi Gras Museum. Inside Old Galveston Square, Twenty-third and Strand. If you can't participate in the island's annual festival, a visit here is the next best thing. Fee. Open Tuesday–Sunday. (409) 763-1133.

Mary Moody Northen Amphitheatre. Galveston Island State Park, west on FM-3005 at the intersection with Thirteen Mile Road. Broadway favorites light up this stage Monday–Saturday from Memorial Day through Labor Day. Tickets are available at Houston ticket centers and at the gate. Fee. (409) 737-3440 or (281) 530-3600.

Moody Gardens. 1 Hope Boulevard, near the Galveston Municipal Airport. This $18 million, twenty-year project now sports the Rainforest Pyramid, a ten-story glass biome housing botanical specimens from Asia, Africa, and South America. This 40,000-square-foot conservatory is filled with waterfalls, cliffs, caverns, butterflies, exotic birds, and a replica of a Mayan temple; it is one of the largest single structures under glass in the country. An IMAX Theater showing 3-D, 2-D, and feature films is part of the complex, as are Discovery Pyramid with forty interactive exhibits, the Palm Beach swimming area and the Learning Center. Fee. (409) 744-1745 or (800) 582-4673.

Sailing, Surfing, and Waterskiing. These scenes are ever changing; for a list of operators, contact the Galveston Convention & Visitors Bureau, 2106 Seawall Boulevard, Galveston 77550, (409) 763-4311 or (800) 351-4236 in Texas, (800) 351-4237 elsewhere.

Seawolf Park on Pelican Island. Accessible from either Broadway or Harborside Drive via a turn north on Fifty-first Street. Adults enjoy watching Galveston's busy harbor from this unusual vantage point, and children love scrambling over a series of naval exhibits that include an airplane, a destroyer escort, and a submarine. *Also here:* the *Selma,* one of the ill-fated cement ships built as an experiment during World War II. It ran aground here years ago. Fee. There is no swimming at Seawolf Park, but there are good facilities for fishing and picnics. Open daily. Parking fee.

Strand Harborside. Pier 21. This lodging/restaurant/marina/shopping complex adjacent to the Texas Seaport Museum also houses the

Great Storm Theatre, a multimedia presentation on Galveston's devastating 1900 hurricane. Fee. For information contact Harbor House, (409) 763-3321.

Strand Theatre. 2317 Mechanic. This local variety company has something on the boards almost every weekend, year-round, and children's theater and film series as well. (409) 763-4591.

Summer Band Concerts. If you're planning an August outing to the island, time your trip to take in the free summer band concerts on Tuesday evenings in Sealy Pavilion at the Mary Moody Northen Plaza. The Galveston Beach Band performs patriotic marches, Broadway tunes, polkas, Dixieland, and Big Band music, while you stretch out on a blanket under the stars. Kids love the musical games and flag parade. For a schedule call (409) 762-3988 or 744-2174.

Tennis and Golf. Information on specific locations is available from the Galveston Convention & Visitors Bureau. If you are a hotel guest, ask about membership privileges at private facilities on the island.

Treasure Isle Tour Train. The tram with the fringe on top takes you all over town on a ninety-minute narrated tour. Daily trips, year-round. Fee. (409) 765-9564.

WHERE TO EAT

Benno's on the Beach. 1200 Seawall. This informal eatery features Cajun-flavored crab, shrimp, oysters, and crawfish. $$; (CC). (409) 762-9625.

Charley's 517 at The Wentletrap. 2301 Strand. Many Texans consider this one of the finest restaurants in the state. Housed in the historic League Building, erected in 1871, The Wentletrap boasts an inventive menu and upscale, dressy decor. Open Monday-Saturday for lunch and dinner, Sunday for brunch. $$-$$$; (CC). (409) 765-5545 or (713) 225-6033.

Clary's. 8509 Teichman Road, across from the *Galveston Daily News.* Don't judge this place by its low-key exterior. Locals think it serves some of the best seafood on the island, often with a Creole touch. An off-menu item, spiced shrimp, is a house specialty. Slightly dressy crowd here, so no beach clothes, please. Open Tuesday-Friday and on Sunday for lunch and dinner, Saturday for dinner only. $-$$; (CC). (409) 740-0771.

Fisherman's Wharf Seafood Grill. Pier 22. You'll find indoor and outdoor dining here, with great views of the port and the tall ship *Elissa*. The fresh seafood menu ranges from shrimp and oyster po'boys to full course meals—the Shrimp-T entree is named for Houston Rockets coach Rudy Tomjonovich—and there's also a fresh seafood market with a tank where children can fish for perch. Formerly a shrimp unloading and cold storage facility until its reincarnation as a restaurant in mid-1995, this eatery's hardwood floors came from some of Galveston's old cotton warehouses, and the vintage photographs that line the walls are either family memorabilia or reproductions from the Rosenberg Library collection. Open daily for lunch and dinner. $-$$; (CC). (409) 765-5708.

Gaido's. 3800 Seawall. Whether it's fried, broiled, or boiled, the fresh seafood here is excellent, partly because the dressings and sauces are made from scratch. The menu changes daily to reflect the best from the sea, but you can't go wrong with the grilled red snapper. Open daily for lunch and dinner. $$-$$$; (CC). (409) 762-9625. *Tip:* If Gaido's is crowded, try Casey's next door; they share a kitchen.

Hill's Pier 19. Twentieth and Wharf. Almost always crowded, this is the place for fresh fish, salads, gumbo, and more served cafeteria-style. You can eat inside or up on the top deck overlooking the boat basin. Open daily for lunch and dinner. $-$$; (CC). (409) 763-7087.

Landry's. Two locations: 1502 Seawall, (409) 762-4261, and Fifty-third and Seawall, (409) 744-1010. Excellent steaks and seafood, often with Cajun touches, bring crowds to both eateries. Open daily for lunch and dinner. $$-$$$; (CC).

The Merchant Prince. 2300 Ship's Mechanic Row, inside the Tremont House hotel. This quiet retreat may well be the finest "fine food" restaurant in town, particularly when your psyche begins to respond to the piano music coming from the Tremont's lobby. Inventive food beautifully served is the rule here, but ultrafancy dress is not. Open for breakfast, lunch, and dinner daily. $-$$$; (CC). (409) 763-0300 or (713) 480-8201.

Ocean Grill. 2227 Seawall. If you want to eat alfresco above the waves, this is the place. The gumbo is great, as are the mesquite-smoked fish entrees. Open daily for lunch and dinner (until 2:00 A.M. on weekends). $$-$$$; (CC). (409) 762-7100.

The Phoenix Bakery and Coffee House. Ship's Mechanic Row and Twenty-third Street, 1 block south of The Strand. Although the great sandwiches and salads will tempt, go straight for the New Orleans–style beignets and café au lait, and then head for one of the umbrella tables in the patio. It's not quite like New Orleans's French Quarter, but close. Open daily for all three meals. $-$$; (CC). (409) 763-4611.

Shrimp & Stuff. Thirty-ninth at Avenue O. Beach-weary folks love this simple place for its tasty shrimp and oyster po'boys, homemade gumbo, and ample fish dinners. Open daily for lunch and dinner. $-$$; (CC). (409) 763-2805.

Yaga's Cafe. 2314 Strand. *Tropical* is the working adjective at this casual place, from decor to food to music. Try the spicy shrimp only if you have some very cool liquid to quench mouth fire. This is a good spot also for burgers and sandwiches, and it jumps with reggae at night. Call for hours. $-$$; (CC). (409) 762-6676.

WANDERING THE BACKROADS

Driving southwest on FM-3005 the length of the island brings you to great fishing at San Luis Pass. Go over the causeway, and it's another 38 miles to Surfside Beach and Freeport. For activities there see Trip 1, Southwest Sector.

Heading east from Galveston along the coast is possible. Just take the free Bolivar ferry and continue on T-87 (Day Trip 4, East Sector). In Galveston the Bolivar ferry slip is at the end of Second Street (turn north from Broadway), but don't plan to take it on a prime-time weekend unless you love waiting in long lines.

CELEBRATIONS
AND FESTIVALS

Note: Many of the telephone numbers given are answered on week-days only. For specific event dates consult the current issue of *Texas Highways* magazine. Also note that admission charges may apply.

Baytown's "Goose Creek Texas Chili When It's Chilly" Cook-off. (281) 422-8359.

Festival Hill. Concerts followed by dinner and a classic film lure people to Round Top once a month from August through April—always enjoyable, but most welcome during the quiet days of winter. The dinner includes wine, and overnight accommodations are available in attractive studio residences as well as in historic Menke House. (409) 249-3129.

Go Texan Celebration. Clear Lake swings in late January. (281) 488-7676.

Janis Joplin Birthday Bash. Port Arthur celebrates a native daughter with concerts and special displays. (800) 235-7822.

Bryan–College Station. The Continental Antique Show brings more than ninety dealers to Brazos Center, usually on the first weekend of the month. (409) 260-9898 or (800) 777-8292.

Clear Lake Annual Epicurean Evening. Area restaurateurs show off their best creations via booths at Baybrook Mall. (281) 488-7676.

Clear Lake Gem and Mineral Show. This event is one of the best of its kind in the country. (281) 488-7676.

Galveston Mardi Gras. This reincarnation of a long-gone tradition keeps the island swinging with parades and balls during the two weeks prior to Lent. (409) 763-4311 or (800) 351-4236.

Go Texan Parade in Conroe. Call for specifics of this early February event. (409) 756-6644.

Go Texan Weekend in Navasota. Plenty of good country fun, including boot-scootin', chili cook-offs, and horseshoes. (800) 252-6642.

Mardi Gras Parade and Celebration. Bolivar Peninsula gets in on the pre-Lenten fun, with a parade and dance. (409) 684-3345.

Mardi Gras of Southeast Texas. Port Arthur swings on a long February weekend with a Doo-Dah Parade, the Majestic Krewe of Aurora Grand Parade, fireworks, art and auto shows, a carnival, concerts, and children's activities. (409) 721-8701 or (800) 235-7822.

Texas Independence Day. Washington-on-the-Brazos relives its brief moment in the Lone Star limelight every year on the weekend closest to March 2. (409) 836-3695.

MARCH

Dogwood Festival and Western Weekend. Woodville celebrates the beauty of spring in the East Texas woods with this annual event that spreads over three consecutive weekends into early April. Fun ranges from a parade and historical pageant to a beard contest, rodeo, and trail ride. There's also bluegrass and country music on an outdoor stage. Call for specifics. (409) 283-2632.

Freeport's Joy Ride & Rod Run. This judged show mid-month features custom and classic cars (including pre-1949 street rods), a parade, entertainments, and door prizes. (281) 444-8680.

The Great Exchange. This antiques show brings crowds to Bellville the third weekend in March. (409) 865-3407.

Heritage Day at Jesse Jones Park & Nature Center, near Humble. All the homely arts that ultimately tamed the Texas frontier are demonstrated, and the park's reconstructed homestead is open to the public. (281) 446-8588.

Historical Tour and Downtown Spring Fling. Many of Brenham's surviving antebellum homes can be toured during this event, and there's a festival of fun for the entire family. (409) 836-3695 or 836-1690.

Liberty Jubilee. Lots of fun in Liberty. (409) 336-3684.

Montgomery County Fair & Rodeo. Everything from chicken flying to a barbecue cook-off keeps the fairgrounds jumping for ten days. (409) 760-3631.

Nederland Heritage Festival. Lots to do with a beauty pageant, parade, golf and tennis tournaments, craft market, and fun run. On Boston Avenue, between Fourteenth and Seventeenth streets in front of the city hall. (409) 724-2269.

Renegade Round-Up. Humble hosts fun that includes a livestock show and rodeo. (281) 446-2128.

Round Top Herb Festival. Festival Hill hosts a one-day celebration of herbs that includes lectures, luncheon, and a plant sale. (409) 249-5888.

Winedale Spring Festival and Texas Craft Exhibition. Expect pioneer demonstrations of old-time skills, an outstanding juried craft show with working artists, live musical entertainment, barbecued chicken picnic, and a barn dance. (409) 278-3530.

APRIL

Biathlon. This biking and swimming competition in Bryan-College Station is open to all who preregister. (409) 764-3486.

Big Bird Fly-In. This model airplane jamboree enlivens Crockett. (409) 655-2360.

Blessing of the Fleet(s). Take your pick. Galveston and Freeport both host these festivals annually. Freeport: (409) 265-2508. Galveston: (409) 763-4311 or (800) 351-4236.

Bluebonnet Festival. Chappell Hill shows off its old things early in this best of Texas seasons. Expect cloggers, folk dancers, dulcimer music, hayrides, home tours, and pony and train rides for the children. (409) 836-3695.

Burton Cotton Gin Festival. This tiny town's wonderful old gin hums again in mid-April while locals give tours and explain how it works. Lots of food and entertainment, as well as demonstrations of other old-time skills. (409) 289-5102, or 289-3489, or 836-3695.

Country Livin' Festival. Formerly Bellville's Bluebonnet Festival, this annual event comes when the wildflowers in the fields around town are at their peak. The chamber of commerce has booths around town where you can pick up packets of bluebonnet seeds and maps of driving tours to see the year's best color. At the city square and Austin County Fairgrounds, it's everything from Civil War battles to mock Indian dances, Cajun music and food, folk artists, and buggy rides. (409) 865-3407.

Crazy Cajun Annual Clear Lake Firecrackin' Hot Crawfish Festival. This shindig in Seabrook's Clear Lake Park raises funds for Fourth of July fireworks and celebrations. (281) 488-7676.

Eeyore's Birthday Party. Costumes are a tradition for this annual Winedale event, which also includes music, games, maypoles, a lollipop tree, and birthday cake for everyone. This is an ideal outing for families with small children. There's even Shakespeare in the evening in the old barn. (409) 278-3530.

Folk Weekends at Star of the Republic Museum. There's something going on nearly every April weekend in Washington-on-the-Brazos State Park, from Buffalo Soldiers reenactments to a kids' day of frontier activities. (409) 878-2461.

The General Sam Houston Festival. Sam and his cronies wander around the historic homes in Huntsville's Sam Houston Memorial Park, while citizen-soldiers show off camping techniques and equipment of the 1800s. Lifestyle skills of that period also are demonstrated; local ethnic groups are celebrated with food and music. (800) 289-0389.

Good Oil Days Festival. Humble's streets fill with food, crafts, and entertainment on an early April weekend. (281) 446-2128.

Hoover & Starr's Wedding Anniversary. Kountze and much of the rest of Big Thicket territory celebrate the marriage of the world's only legally hitched armadillos on the weekend closest to April 1. Family activities and entertainment, including the world's biggest fool contest, a giggling contest, and so on. (409) 246-3056.

Migration Celebration. Early in the month, Brazosport offers seminars, keynote speakers, trade show, and field trips of major interest to serious birders. (800) 725-1106.

Montgomery Trek. Many of Montgomery's old homes open their doors to the public on a mid-April weekend. (409) 597-4155 or 597-4899.

Nassau Bay Russian Festival. Full day of Russian dancing, food, and art. (281) 333-4211.

Navasota Nostalgia Days. Family fun on the first Saturday in April includes 10K run, golf tournament, street dance, art show, antique car show, crafts sale, carnival, and professional entertainers. (409) 825-6600 or (800) 252-6642.

Neches River Festival. Beaumont celebrates water for a week with historical pageants, shows, lighted boat flotilla and boat races, a sky diving show, and exhibitions all over town. (409) 880-3749 or (800) 392-4401.

Pioneer Quilt Show. Woodville's open-air historical museum displays some treasures. (409) 283-2632.

Pleasure Island Music Festival. Port Arthur fun features big names in rock, C&W, and nostalgia music, along with folk art, ethnic foods, and a children's play area. (800) 235-7822.

Round Top Antique Fair. Annually on the first weekend in April, Round Top's old Rifle Association Hall and two satellite sites brim wall-to-wall with antiques dealers showing their best. (281) 493-5501.

San Jacinto Festival. East and West Columbia celebrate the early days of the republic in mid-month with entertainment, a barbecue cook-off, a fajita dinner, Plantation Days at Varner-Hogg State Park, arts and crafts show, a pentathlon, a baseball card show, a petting zoo, street dances, and tours of a replica of the first state capitol. (409) 345-3921.

Spring Barbecue and Auction. This annual fund-raiser for Boys and Girls Country includes a country store, Granny's Attic Garage Sale, carnival, and a silent auction as well as bidding on large animals. (281) 351-4976.

Spring Roundup at The George Ranch. This opening weekend event in early April stars pioneers, cowboys, a dutch oven cookoff, as well as all the normal ranch fun. (281) 343-0218.

Sylvan Beach Festival. La Porte revives its heyday with a parade, a chili cook-off, and entertainment. (281) 471-2151.

Texas Trek. Anderson comes to life each spring with a trail ride and dance. (409) 873-2151.

Washington-on-the-Brazos. A bluebonnet festival brings arts, crafts, and entertainments to this historic hamlet. (409) 836-3695.

Wine and Roses Festival at Messina Hof. Grape-stamping, fun runs through the vineyards, the conclusion of the Texas Artist Competition, live music, equestrian shows, and a cook-off keep you busy in Bryan-College Station. (409) 778-9463.

MAY

Clear Lake Greek Festival. Clear Lake Park in Seabrook hosts ethnic dancing, crafts, foods, etc. (281) 326-1740.

Columbus Springtime Fest. Columbus rolls back time the third weekend in May with an opera house performance, a historic homes tour, and antiques/crafts shows. (409) 732-8385.

Czech Fest. Rosenberg celebrates its ethnic heritage every spring at the Fort Bend County Fairgrounds. (281) 342-6171.

Homes Tour. Galveston's annual peek behind historic doors. One of the best in the state. (713) 280-3907 or (409) 765-7834.

International Gumbo Cook-Off. Orange and its Cajun folks relegate chili to the back burner in favor of every sort of gumbo brewed in the South. Other special events include an antique car show, a parade, a carnival, and arts and crafts. (409) 883-3536.

Kaleidoscope. Beaumont spreads out the best in creative arts and crafts on the art museum grounds, the largest such festival in Southeast Texas. (409) 832-3432. This outstanding family event features hands-on activities focused on the arts of various world cultures, as well as ethnic dancing and entertainments.

Maifest. Brenham hosts the oldest spring festival in the state in the heart of the wildflower season. (409) 836-3695.

Memorial Day Celebration at The George Ranch Historical Park. A traditional "Decoration Day" event at the family cemetery as well as dramatic vignettes at the Davis House bring real meaning to the holiday. (281) 343-0218.

Maypole Festival and Homes Tour in Calvert. This old railroad town opens the doors of its vintage homes. If you love Victoriana and antiques, don't miss this. (409) 364-2559 or 364-2020.

Old Town Spring. The Texas Crawfish Festival brews up pots and pots of those tasty little critters, along with all the multistage live entertainment you can handle, on the first weekend in May. (713) 353-9310 or (800) 653-8696.

Oleander City Festival. Any bloomin' excuse for a party in fun-loving Galveston. (409) 763-4311 or (800) 351-4236 in Texas.

Pasadena Strawberry Festival. This mid-May event at the Pasadena Fairgrounds draws an estimated 30,000 people annually. Activities include a historical village with working artisans, helicopter rides, beauty pageant, carnival rides and games, cookoffs (ribs, beans, fajitas, and briskets), a mud volleyball tournament, fireworks, and the world's largest strawberry shortcake (covers more than 600 square feet and requires 2,000+ pounds of fruit!). (281) 910-2232.

Spirit of Flight Air Show and Walkabout. Galveston's Lone Star Flight Museum hosts World War II- era aircraft in reenactments of explosive dogfights. Many of the old "birds" are open for tours. (409) 740-7722.

Taste of the Town. Sample the best dishes from Brazosport's restaurants, at the Armadillo Ballroom. (800) 938-4853.

Texas Crab Festival. Tiny Crystal Beach offers crab races, crab legs contests, and a crab cookoff to all comers. Activities also include live entertainment, a volleyball tournament, sand castle competition, tug-of-war, and treasure hunt in the sands of Bolivar Peninsula. (409) 684-5940.

Winedale's Concert by the Lake. This annual benefit event on the first Saturday afternoon in May features great regional music. (409) 278-3530.

JUNE

Agricultural Society Barbecue. Cat Spring turns out for country-and-western music, cake walks, crafts, and a dance on the first Sunday of the month. (409) 865-9525 or 992-3647.

Alabama-Coushatta Indian Powwow. Our region's only Indian reservation (on US-190, between Livingston and Woodville) is your destination for this ethnic celebration the first weekend of the month. Expect a parade, along with authentic Indian foods, dances, and crafts. (409) 563-4391 or (800) 444-3507.

Brazoria's "No Name" Festival. Want to know what's doing on the second weekend of the month? Give them a call. (409) 798-6100.

Bryan–College Station's Annual Bluegrass Festival. Music, food, and entertainments. (409) 361-3658 or (800) 777-8292.

Festival Hill Concerts. Outstanding classical music by some of the world's best young professionals highlights weekends June through mid-July. (409) 249-3129.

Fiddler's Festival. Some old-time toe-tapping music in Crockett the first weekend in June. (409) 544-2359.

Firemen's Picnic. Frelsburg draws folks into town with music, an auction, and other shenanigans on the second weekend of the month. (409) 732-8385.

Gospel Music Fest. Groups from all over the United States gather in Woodville for this three-day event. (409) 283-2632.

Grimes County Fair. Head for the fairgrounds in Navasota for this one. (409) 825-2508 or (800) 252-6642.

Juneteenth Celebrations. Emancipation is cheered with special events in Beaumont, (800) 392-4401; Brenham, (409) 836-3695; George Ranch, (281) 343-0218; Huntsville, (800) 289-0389; and Port Arthur, (800) 235-7822.

Lobster Fiesta & Golf Tournament. Huntsville hosts a high-stakes golf tournament and a two-plate Maine lobster/steak feed at the Walker County Fairgrounds. Reservations and tickets essential. (800) 289-0389 or (409) 295-8113.

Sandcastle Building Contests. Freeport invites people to try their hand at this timeless childhood art at Surfside Beach the second weekend of the month, (409) 265-2508. Galveston's contest, featuring more than fifty teams of professional architects and designers, usually is the weekend following Memorial Day. (409) 763-4311, (800) 351-4236, or (713) 622-2081.

Summer Band Concerts in Galveston. Every Tuesday night, June through August, the Galveston Beach Band presents free evenings of music at the Sealy Gazebo. Bring a blanket to sit on. (800) 351-4236.

***Whispers in the Wind* in Woodville.** This historical musical plays the last two weekends of the month at Heritage Village. (409) 283-2272.

JULY

Antique Show. In Bryan, at the Brazos Center. (409) 776-8338 or (800) 777-8292.

Crockett's Annual Lion's Youth Rodeo. Call for list of events. (409) 544-2359.

Fireworks. The folks in Humble often can't hire a qualified pyrotechnician on the Fourth of July, so they shoot the works on the third. (281) 446-2128.

Fourth of July Celebrations. The following all have their own versions of an old-fashioned Independence Day: Baytown, (281) 420-6597; Beaumont, (409) 838-3435; Brenham, (409) 836-3695; Bryan-College Station, (409) 260-9898; Chappell Hill, (409) 836-3695; Clear Lake, (281) 488-7676; Columbus, (409) 732-8385; Crockett, (409) 544-2359; Huntsville, (800) 289-0389; Lake Conroe, (409) 756-6644; Lake Jackson, (409) 297-4533; Palacios, (512) 972-2615; Round Top, (409) 249-4042; Seabrook,

(281) 488-7676; Sea Rim State Park, (409) 971-2559; and Woodville, (409) 283-2632.

Freeport Jay-Cee's Fishing Fiesta. Fisherfolk from all over the state compete for prizes. (409) 233-4434.

Great Texas Mosquito Festival. Brazosport celebrates the area's bumper crop of buzzers on the last weekend of the month in Clute Municipal Park. Expect a Miss Mosquito Legs look-alike contest, a mosquito-calling contest, the Ms. Quito pageant, a "skeeter beater" baby crawling contest, C&W headliners, dancing, food, games, and both barbecue and fajita cook-offs. (409) 265-8392 or (800) 938-4853.

Gulf Coast Jam. Port Arthur rocks early in the month with headliner talent in Cajun, C&W, and rock music. (409) 722-3699 or (800) 235-7822.

Harvest Days at Messina Hof Cellars. On Saturday mornings from mid-July through early August, the pickers' training sessions begin at 8:00 A.M., after which you get to stamp the grapes. (409) 778-9463.

Hempstead Watermelon Festival. Here's your chance to test your seed spitting skills for prizes. Other events include a parade, street dance, and professional entertainment. (409) 826-8217.

Lake Conroe Boat Parade and Fireworks. Call for specifics. (409) 756-6644.

Lunar Rendezvous. The Clear Lake area celebrates with art shows, festivals, tournaments, and a decorated boat parade. (281) 532-1254.

Moody Gardens Watermelon Fest and Ice Cream Crank Off. Call for specifics. (409) 762-3933 or (800) 351-4236.

AUGUST

Antiques Celebration. Calvert puts on a show and sale of quality antiques and collectibles on historic Main Street; events also include Civil War reenactments. (409) 364-2559 or 364-2020.

Ballunar Liftoff Festival. Johnson Space Center in Nassau Bay opens its usually closed campus for this three-day event that includes more than 100 hot air balloons in competition flights, team skydiving, live entertainment, arts and crafts, concessions, and aviation exhibitions. Call for schedule; (281) 488-7676 or 483-4241.

Blessing of the Fleet. Kemah invokes heavenly blessings on the shrimp crop with a boat parade, a carnival, crafts, dances, and a cook-off. (281) 334-2322.

Firemen's Fiesta in Brenham. City Park comes alive with dancing, water polo, pumper races, cook-offs, and both horseshoe and washer pitching competitions. (409) 836-1683 or 836-3695.

Prazka Pout. Praha hosts its annual Czechoslovakian homecoming at St. Mary's Catholic Church on August 15. (512) 865-3560.

Schulenburg. This small town welcomes visitors to "A Texas Style Adventure" annually on the first full weekend in August. (409) 743-4514.

Shakespeare at Winedale. The historic old barn at this open-air historical museum rings with the undying words of the Bard Thursday-Sunday evenings through mid-month, with weekend matinees. There's also a hunter's stew dinner before the Saturday evening show. (409) 278-3530.

Shrimporee and Fishfest in Palacios. There's a boat parade and blessing of the fleet, with anglers competing for cash fishing prizes. (512) 972-2615 (Fishfest); 972-2446 (Shrimporee).

SEPTEMBER

Antique Show. Cat Spring gathers the best of treasures in a country setting. (409) 865-3407 or 885-7955.

County Fairs. This is the month, so plan a trip to Brenham, (409) 836-4112; Columbus, (409) 732-8385; Hempstead, (409) 826-8217; or La Grange, (409) 968-5756.

Dick Dowling Days. Port Arthur turns out on the first weekend of September with special events to honor this Irish hero of the Confederacy. (800) 235-7822.

Fiesta Hispano Americana. This Wharton event celebrates Hispanic culture in Southeast Texas with food, music, and dancing. (409) 532-1862.

Heritage Days in Beaumont. Entertainment and activities, including demonstrations of old-fashioned crafts. (409) 880-3749 or (800) 392-4401.

Houston International In-The-Water Boat Show. Four days in late September to see the latest and greatest in power- and sailboats, luxury yachts, fishing boats, and so on, at Watergate Marina in Kemah. (281) 488-7676 or 526-6361.

Mexican Fiesta in Port Arthur. Call for specifics. (800) 235-7822.

Pasadena Stock Show and Rodeo. This weeklong event at the rodeo grounds includes a barbecue cook-off. (281) 487-0240.

Ranching Heritage Weekend at George Ranch Historical Park. Usually held on the first weekend of September, this event combines traditional cowboy ranching activities with a lively evening rodeo. (281) 343-0218.

Shrimpfest. Port Arthur's Pleasure Island comes alive mid-month with a gumbo cooking contest, a shrimp peeling/cooking contest, shrimp food booths, music, arts and crafts, and a carnival. (409) 963-1107.

Texas Gatorfest in Anahuac. The "Alligator Capital of Texas" celebrates the opening of gator season. Come prepared for the Alligator Roundup, carnival rides, live entertainment on dual stages, a 5K run, airboat rides, street dance, petting zoo, arts and crafts, and an exhibit of live gators. Food includes alligator delicacies. (409) 267-4190.

Texas Pecan Festival in Groves. This two-week celebration mid-month includes sporting events, carnival, concessions, arts and crafts, and more. (409) 962-3631.

Texian Days in Anderson. This historic little town celebrates its history with home tours, a Texas Army encampment, a flea market, a beauty contest, and live entertainment. (409) 825-3386.

OCTOBER

Antique Show. Bellville traditionally has one of the most extensive shows in the state on either the third or fourth weekend in October in the city park pavilion. Also on the grounds are a farmer's market, pumpkin-decorating contest, folk art, a quilting bee, rug weaving, pony rides, and country cooking. (409) 865-3407.

Bryan Festifall. This early October event features hands-on activities for children, lots of arts and crafts booths and demos, entertainment, food, and dance. (409) 268-2787.

CAF Wings over Houston. Ellington Field hosts Confederate Air Force air power demonstrations with authentic World War II planes and a flight show. Expect air aerobatics, jet dragster speed demos, flight simulators, and a large military aircraft exhibit. (281) 531-9461 or 488-7676.

CavOilcade Celebration. Port Arthur celebrates its economic base with a street parade, an old-timers' breakfast, boat races, golf and tennis tournaments, Hungry Artists' show, antique automobiles, and a thieves' market. (409) 985-7822 or (800) 235-7822.

Conroe Cajun Catfish Festival. This three-day celebration mid-month is filled with music, food, arts and crafts, children's activities, a parade, and dancing in the streets. (409) 756-6644 or 539-6009.

County and Regional Fairs. Try the Fort Bend County Fair at Rosenberg, (281) 342-6171; the Harris County Fair near Bear Creek, (281) 550-8432; the South Texas State Fair in Beaumont, (409) 832-9991 or (800) 392-4401; or the Tyler County Fair in Woodville, (409) 283-2632. Other possibilities include the Brazoria County Fair, (409) 849-6416, and the Austin County Fair with its PCRA-sanctioned rodeo in Bellville, (409) 865-3407.

Fair-on-the-Square in Huntsville. Downtown's historic heart hosts entertainment, arts and crafts, and so on, on the first Saturday in October. (409) 295-8113 or (800) 289-0389.

Harvest Festival and East Texas Folklife Festival. Woodville's Heritage Village literally comes to life with artists, craftspersons, and demonstrations. (409) 283-2272.

Historic Business Association Pecan Festival in Richmond. Test your pecan eating and shelling talents at this event. Other activities include dancing, fire department demonstrations, and a courthouse fun run. (281) 341-1575.

Jesse H. Jones Rendezvous. This shindig at Jesse H. Jones Park west of Humble takes you back to the days of fur trading with demos, competition, and activities involving blackpowder weaponry, flint knapping, primitive archery, firemaking, period clothing, primitive campsites, and tepees. (281) 446-8588.

Lickskillet Celebration. Fayetteville relives its heritage with crafts, reunions, and a parade on the third weekend of the month. (409) 968-5756 or 378-2231.

Octoberfest. Round Top and Winedale combine efforts for this special celebration. Expect demonstrations of pioneer skills, including horseshoeing, muleskinning, fireplace cooking, soap making, and so forth, following a German heritage theme in Winedale, an antiques show in Round Top. (713) 493-5501 or (409) 278-3530.

Polk County Pinecone Festival. Livingston hosts street dances, trail rides, hot air balloon races, timber exhibits, food, crafts, and more in Petticoat Park on the US-59 bypass. (409) 327-4929.

Renaissance Festival. Sixteenth-century England is re-created every weekend this month in the woods between Magnolia and Plantersville. Amid parades, jousting, races, and games of skill, you'll chat with Robin Hood, assorted wenches, minstrels, comics, jugglers, knights and their elegant ladies, and other anachronistic characters. Dress to the theme and join in the fun. (281) 356-2178 or (409) 894-2516.

Rice Festival in Bay City. Parades, concerts, carnival, and other events fill a full week. Call for specifics. (409) 245-8333.

Round Top Antiques Fair. Always held on the first full weekend in both April and October, this event draws dealers and buyers from all over the country. Main venues are Round Top's venerable Rifle Hall and Carmine's Dance Hall. A third site on SH-237 is devoted primarily to folk art. (281) 493-5501.

Scarecrow Festival. Chappell Hill's biggest event of the year includes arts and crafts booths, continuous entertainment, historical home tours, hayrides, a quilt raffle, and a scarecrow contest. (409) 836-3695.

Seabrook Celebration Festival. A carnival, arts and crafts, live music, a silent auction, assorted cook-offs, and so on, at Rex Meador Park. (281) 488-7676 or 334-3253.

Splendora's Pumpkin Patch. Throughout the month more than 40,000 pounds of pumpkins greet visitors to Splendora Gardens. Bring your camera and a picnic. (281) 689-2823.

Texas Rice Festival. The small town of Winnie (west of Beaumont on I-10) celebrates its prime crop with a carnival, parades, art and antique auto shows, rice-cooking contests, street and square dances, and professional entertainment. (409) 296-2231 or 296-4404.

Texian Market Days. Reliving the early days of ranching, this late October weekend event has pioneer life demonstrations, arts and crafts booths, entertainment, and tours of two old homes at the George Ranch Historical Park. *Also here:* a reenactment of an 1860s Confederate military camp and the 1820s settlement of Stephen F. Austin's first colony, including a working farm. (281) 545-9212 or 343-0218.

Trinity Valley Exposition and Rodeo. Liberty gears up the third week of October with a variety of family activities, including a baby parade held annually since 1909. *Also here:* concerts, a barbecue cook-off, and a mule show. (409) 336-5736.

NOVEMBER

Why not an outing on Thanksgiving weekend to cut your own Christmas tree? There are more than five dozen commercial Christmas tree farms within the area covered by this book. For a list by county, contact the Texas Department of Agriculture, Box 12847, Austin 78711, (512) 463–7555; or the Texas Agricultural Extension Service, 4390 FM–1488, Conroe 77384, (409) 273–2120.

Annual Wooden Boat Festival. Watergate Marina in Clear Lake Shores hosts this outstanding show. (281) 334–3101.

Christmas Previews. You will find "welcome to the holidays" celebrations at various times and in a variety of styles at the following: Beaumont, (409) 835–7100 or (800) 392–4401; Bellville, (409) 865–3407; Brenham, (409) 830–8445; Bryan–College Station, (409) 260–9898 or (800) 777–8292; Columbus, (409) 732–8385; Crockett, (409) 544–2359; El Campo, (409) 543–2713; Groves, (409) 962–3631; Lake Jackson, (409) 265–2508 or 297–4533; Old Town Spring, (281) 353–9310 or (800) OLD TOWN; Port Arthur, (800) 235–7822; Tomball, (281) 351–7222; and Woodville, (409) 283–2632.

Fall Festival and Texas Heritage Days at Armand Bayou. All the old-time skills are demonstrated, including cane pressing and hay baling. Add a pie-eating contest, animal demos, and horseshoes for family fun. (281) 474–2551.

Fall Festival of Roses. Independence's Antique Rose Emporium hosts seminars, exhibits, demonstrations, shopping, and food the first weekend of the month. (409) 836–5548.

A Festival of Lights. Boys and Girls Country sponsors this festival late in the month. Events include holiday entertainment, an open house, choirs, and a holiday handcrafts sale. (281) 351–4976.

Fly Day at Lone Star Flight Museum in Galveston. The state's largest collection of old warbirds, including B-25 bombers, takes to the skies. Displays, exhibits, and speakers explain all. (409) 740–7722.

Great Texas Crackling Cookout. A full day of barbecue, live entertainment, tours, crafts, and so on, at Pelt Pond Rural Life Museum in Kountze. (409) 246–3056.

Home for the Holidays. Old Town Spring ushers in the holiday season the second and third weekends of the month with special events, evening programs, and beautiful decorations and lights. (800) OLD-TOWN.

Messina Hof Wine Cellars. Texas Country Christmas Tours and a Mulled Wine Weekend bring visitors to this Bryan-College Station attraction. Expect an international theme, food and wine tastings, elegant dinners and a jazz brunch, culinary seminars and demonstrations by noted chefs, children's activities, hayrides, and an art exhibit. Reservations and tickets required for most events. (409) 778-9463.

Pioneer Days at Jesse Jones Park & Nature Center, near Humble. All the homely arts that ultimately tamed the Texas frontier are demonstrated, and the park's reconstructed homestead is open to the public. (281) 446-8588.

Poinsettia Celebration. Ellison's Greenhouses on the outskirts of Brenham brim with 80,000 blooming plants for this special benefit weekend, usually after Thanksgiving. Booths feature plant care, holiday designs, food, and entertainment. (409) 836-0084.

Round Top Arts Festival. This juried art show on the first weekend of the month includes paintings, sculpture, carvings, and ceramics. (409) 249-3308.

DECEMBER

Beaumont's Symphony of Trees. Custom decorated trees as well as children's activities enliven the civic center. (409) 835-7100.

Bellville's Small Town Christmas & Holiday Home Tour. This also includes seasonal dramas in the Little Country Theater on the first weekend of the month. (409) 865-3407.

Brookshire Christmas Festival. Santa, caroling, dancing, and a carnival welcome the season on the first full weekend in December. (281) 375-8100.

Christmas Bird Count in Brazosport. Birders from all over the country gather here between Christmas and New Year's for this annual event. As many as 226 species have been sighted some years, 326 overall. Binoculars are essential. (409) 265-7661 or 297-2110.

Christmas in Calvert. Antiques sales and five old homes that are open for tours brighten the first weekend in December. (409) 364-2559 or 364-2020.

Christmas on the Colorado. Columbus puts on a three-day celebration in its historic downtown district early in the month. Expect guided walking tours, open houses in vintage homes, a market, "Messiah" in the old opera house, and cowboys serenading. (409) 732-8385.

Christmas at the Depot. Burton sponsors a holiday celebration at its restored historic train station. (409) 289-2863.

Christmas Holiday Festival and Homes Tour in Wharton. Call for specifics. (409) 532-1862.

Christmas Fantasy of Lights in Sealy. The entire town turns out for a Christmas market and lighted parade on the first Saturday of the month. (409) 885-3222.

Christmas in Navasota. December's first weekend brings historical homes tours, carriage rides, strolling carolers, breakfast with Santa, a parade, and copious amounts of homemade food. (409) 825-6600 or (800) 252-6642.

Christmas on the Neches. Port Neches celebrates early in the month with a night boat parade and fireworks. (409) 722-9154.

Christmas Open House at Winedale. All the old German Christmas traditions seem right at home for this one-night event. (409) 278-3530.

Christmas in Round Top. Sleigh rides, singing, shopping, and decorations liven up the town square early in the month. (409) 249-5294.

Clear Lake Area Christmas Boat Parade. Clear Lake, Seabrook, League City, and Kemah join floating forces on December's second weekend to celebrate the season in their own unique way. Clear Lake Park and the Kemah-Seabrook channel are the best public viewing sites. (281) 488-7676.

Clute's Christmas in the Park. Decorated trees, foods, and crafts of the season, and so forth, on the second weekend of the month. (409) 265-8392.

Country Christmas in Chappell Hill. Santa arrives via fire engine, choirs sing and ring hand bells, and teddy bears dressed for the occasion parade down Main Street. It's also open house at several historic homes. (409) 836-3695.

Country Christmas on the Square. Coldspring celebrates the holiday with East Texas spirit on the second Saturday of December. Expect folk-dancing exhibitions, a country market, a lighted Christmas parade, choirs, and scads of food. (409) 653-2184.

A Cowboy and Western Heritage Christmas. Varner-Hogg State Park in West Columbia celebrates the season with vittles, blacksmithing demonstrations, sing-alongs, and cowboy storytellers and musicians. (409) 345-4656.

Crystaland Christmas. Much of the Bolivar Peninsula gets involved in a boat parade down the Intracoastal Waterway and other events. (409) 684-5940.

Dickens-on-the-Strand. Galveston's famous Strand becomes a 4-block stage for Victorian Christmases past. Dress up in your best period duds and join the fun. There will be a mix of characters from Dickens: town criers, British bobbies, carolers, bell-ringing choirs, horse-drawn coaches, and more. (713) 280-3907 or (409) 765-7834.

Downtown Christmas Stroll. Special shopping and holiday events, including a 4-H Christmas tree auction, fill historic downtown Brenham. (409) 836-3695.

Griffin House Christmas Candlelight Tour in Tomball. The traditional songs and wassail of Christmas on the second weekend of the month. (281) 255-2148.

Holly Days. This fundraiser for the Heritage Museum of Montgomery County is always held on the first Wednesday of December in Conroe. (409) 539-6873.

International Holiday & Candlelight Promenade. Port Arthur glows all month with more than 700,000 lights depicting biblical scenes. Eleven different ethnic groups display holiday trees and traditions, including Las Posadas, on December's first weekend. Call for details. (409) 985-8838 or (800) 235-7822.

Kreische House Christmas Tours. Visitors to Monument Hill in La Grange experience the holiday in an early German atmosphere. (800) LA GRANGE.

Light Up The First Capitol. West Columbia celebrates on December's first weekend with a night parade, caroling, story time with Mrs. Claus, Santa Claus visits, and holiday home tour. (409) 345-3921.

Montgomery Candlelight Tours. Lovely homes dressed for the season, as well as a cookie walk and community dinner. (409) 597-4155 or 597-4899.

A Nineteenth Century Christmas. Washington-on-the-Brazos State Park demonstrates how the citizens of the Texas Republic celebrated the holiday more than 150 years ago. Children get to make ornaments and rag dolls, and candlelight living history tours light up Independence Hall and the Anson Jones Home. (409) 878-2214.

One Hundred Years of Christmas, 1845–1945. Two of Beaumont's historic jewels, the McFaddin-Ward House and the John Jay French Museum, glow with a joint celebration on the second Sunday of the month. You may get to help costumed French characters decorate an old-time tree. (409) 898-3267, 898-0348, or 832-1906.

Ranch Holidays. The George Ranch in Richmond lights up with campfires, a holiday feast, wagon rides, and so on. (281) 545-9212 or 343-0218.

Santa's Lane of Lights. Ledbetter returns to its 1800s roots with hayrides through the woods, chuckwagon campfires, and more. (409) 249-3066.

Spirit of Christmas in Galveston. Several of Galveston's grandest homes are at their best during this annual event. (713) 280-3907 or (409) 765-7834.

Woodville's Christmas Extravaganza. A twilight tour of Heritage Village along with a craft fair and bluegrass fiddling highlight this event on the first Saturday of the month. (409) 283-2272.